D1095255

provigo

ISBN 0-13-731613-5

provigo

The Story Behind 20 Years of Entrepreneurial Success

by René Provost and Maurice Chartrand

Prentice-Hall Canada, Inc., Scarborough, Ontario

Canadian Cataloguing in Publication Data

Provost, René
Provigo : the story behind 20 years of
entrepreneurial success

Translation of: Provigo : le plus grand succès de
l'entrepreneurship québécois.
Includes bibliographical references.
ISBN 0-13-731613-5

1. Provigo (Firm) - History. 2. Supermarkets -
Quebec (Province) - History. 3. Grocery trade -
Quebec (Province) - History. 4. Food industry and
trade - Quebec (Province) - History. I. Chartrand,
Maurice. II. Title.

HF5469.23.C24P7613 1989 381'.456413'0060714
C89-094895-X

Originally published by Les Editions de l'Homme under the title
Provigo : Le plus grand succès de l'entrepreneurship québécois.

First English edition published by Prentice-Hall Canada, Inc.

Prentice-Hall Inc., Englewood Cliffs, New Jersey
Prentice-Hall International, Inc., London
Prentice-Hall of Australia, Pty., Sydney
Prentice-Hall of India Pvt., Ltd., New Dehli
Prentice-Hall of Japan, Inc., Tokyo
Prentice-Hall of Southeast Asia (Pte.) Ltd., Singapore
Editora Prentice-Hall do Brasil Ltd., Rio de Janeiro
Prentice-Hall Hispanoamericana, S.A., Mexico

Cover Design: Davidson and DiMaulo Inc.
Interior Design: Anita Macklin
Manufacturing Buyer: Luke Di Nicola
Composition: Typografix Inc.
ISBN: 0-13-731613-5
Printed and bound in Canada by Gagne Printing

1 2 3 4 5 GP 93 92 91 90 89

Table of Contents

This book is dedicated to all the men and women who over the years have worked at Provigo and its constituent companies. They are the builders of Provigo's success.

provigo

Foreword

Albert Einstein used to say that splitting the atom was easier than erasing a prejudice. Yet the Provigo builders managed to do just that. They created a company that has become a source of pride among Quebeckers and a model for business people across the nation, a company whose performance elicits feelings of admiration, respect and, at times, awe throughout Canada.

René Provost, in collaboration with Maurice Chartrand, has rendered Canadians a great service by writing the history of Provigo. "Provigo — The Story Behind 20 Years of Entrepreneurial Success" clearly shows that the development and emergence of Quebec entrepreneurship is not a recent phenomenon. On the contrary, it can be traced back to the powerful social movements of the sixties and seventies that forever changed the face of Quebec society. This book underscores an important social truth: significant organizations do not spring up overnight. They must be built piece by piece, through hard work, determination and boldness.

Paradoxically, the companies that are the most cognizant of their history are precisely those that can best address the future with confidence and undertake necessary changes without hesitation. It is the responsibility of those who shape corporate destinies to leave a record of their achievements. Not surprisingly it was one of the co-founders of Provigo, a man who has often been considered the embodiment of the company's culture, a prime catalyst of its success, who took it upon himself to write the story of this incredible human and corporate adventure. We are fortunate to have in our midst a businessman of René Provost's calibre, a captain of industry who sees his role as transcending the bottom line to include an important social responsibility.

Provigo is the work of inspired, ambitious people who combined an uncommon sense of business with the goal of building a major Canadian company with its roots in Quebec. While the Provigo pioneers were establishing a powerful presence throughout the province, other talented entrepreneurs in Canada and the U.S. were pursuing their own dreams and creating companies which are now part of Provigo. Loeb in Ontario, Horne & Pitfield in the West, National Drug (now Medis) across Canada, and Market Wholesale in California gave Provigo the Canadian and North American dimension pursued by the Provigo builders. The development of these companies is an integral part of the history René Provost and Maurice Chartrand skilfully recount.

De Gaulle once said that a lasting achievement is the mark of a great man. There is no doubt that the Provigo builders have achieved much. However, in the business world, the only constant is change; we are always rebuilding and moving in new directions. René Provost's story focuses our attention on the enduring legacy of the Provigo builders. Not only did they give their fellow Quebeckers a new sense of what was possible in the world of commerce, they demonstrated to Canadian entrepreneurs that single-mindedness of purpose and clarity of vision are needed to become a genuine industry leader and innovator. It is this legacy that the current team must carry forward in order to cross new frontiers and conquer new markets.

In this book, René Provost gives us much more than a prototype for entrepreneurial success. A man of vision, René Provost has written a prologue to the future of Provigo. On behalf of every member of the Provigo team, bravo and merci, René!

Pierre Lortie

Preface

Until the very end, it looked as if I would not be part of Provigo. The die was cast between Couvrette & Provost and Denault and they were not keen on a three-sided partnership. Fortunately, sheer tenacity on my part won the day and Lamontagne was part of the 1969 merger.

Since then, I have been intimately associated with Provigo's development. Even so, this book has taught me a great deal, particularly about the other actors who have played a key role in making Provigo the number one company in Quebec, based on sales, and among the ten largest in Canada.

The authors have left no stone unturned in their research. They learned much more from the pioneers and builders themselves than they could ever have from the company archives. We were all too busy trying to make a go of the business to record every detail of its history.

Luckily, on this twentieth anniversary of Provigo, the story of the company has been committed to paper. The reader will find in these pages incontrovertible proof that Quebec is a most fertile ground for cultivating a talent for business.

Jean-Louis Lamontagne

INTRODUCTION

Provigo is undoubtedly one of the great entrepreneurial successes achieved by Quebeckers. The story begins in 1969 when three modest but ambitious food wholesalers in Montreal, Sherbrooke and the Saguenay/Lac-Saint-Jean area decided to join forces and create a new company. Today, two decades later, Provigo has over $7 billion in sales, making it the largest company in Quebec and the tenth in Canada.

Various acquisitions have enabled the company to expand to all of Canada and to parts of the United States. And no longer is Provigo solely a distributor of food products. It has branched out into the distribution of pharmaceutical products, sporting goods, semi-durable goods and gasoline products. Provigo also offers a multitude of marketing and warehousing services.

All this is known to some extent. Perhaps it is time to take stock of Provigo's accomplishments and to look behind the evident facts and figures to see the considerable human effort that went into building this Canadian company over the past thirty years.

Certainly, the generation of the original Provigo pioneers has come to an end. The events that even today I recall so vividly — deliveries with my two brothers Roland and Ernest; first meetings with Antoine Turmel, Jean-Louis Lamontagne and J.A. Tremblay; manoeuverings during the Loeb acquisitions — are receding all too quickly into history and have become part of the company's folklore. We thought that it would be worth the effort to organize all the corporate episodes that mark Provigo's rapid development into a coherent story accessible to a wide audience.

Our first priority was to write a history of Provigo as interesting as the company itself. Above all, Maurice Chartrand and I didn't want the Provigo history to become a mere catalogue of acquisitions with supporting financial statements. We wanted to capture the spirit as well as the context of Provigo's emergence as a distribution and retailing force across Canada. To this end, we reviewed official and unofficial corporate documents, and the financial press; we interviewed the major actors in the company's history, from the founding directors to the current senior executives. Maurice Chartrand and I are grateful to those who granted us interviews, since the official and public record was too often inadequate for our purposes.

Provigo's history would hardly be complete without a careful look at the origins and development of its various components. This commitment has led us through interesting corporate terrain marked by significant entrepreneurial achievement. Indeed, the successes of Kenneth W. Quinn with Horne & Pitfield in Western Canada, Carl R. Goslovich with Market Wholesale in California, Gordon J. Odell with National Drug across Canada and, certainly, the efforts of Bertram Loeb in building his dynamic company are today important components of Provigo's history. In Quebec we should certainly add the names of Jean Boiteau with Jato and Claude Beaulieu with Sports Experts. We hope the book does justice to all their accomplishments.

It has been our policy to avoid romanticizing situations and personalities. We have tried to deal in verifiable facts. However, we could not resist introducing a sprinkling of behind-the-scenes glimpses. Our intention was to lend some personality to the portrait of a company on the move.

It should be noted that the information contained in these pages does not extend beyond August 1988, except the preliminary overview in Chapter 1, which has updated the company's financial performance in January, 1989.

The text is an English version of the French text which appeared in 1988. Daniel H. Fritschi of Multiscript/La Langagerie did the translation and Bryan Campbell the revision; their diligence, attention to detail and pertinent observations were much appreciated. Special thanks go to Kathy Megyery, who co-ordinated the project with her customary competence and style, and to Madeleine Bélanger, France Durand, Alison Fowles and Hélène Thomas for countless services and support.

I would like to offer a final word of thanks to Maurice Chartrand. Without his considerable efforts the Provigo story would not have been written. At least not by me.

René Provost

P.S. This book, published in English and French, is the result of three years of research and compilation. I wish to thank the executive of Provigo for having put at my disposal the budget and facilities required to bring this project to a timely conclusion. Most particularly, I would like to thank Pierre Lortie who gave me not only the challenge, but also the encouragement.

CHAPTER ONE

NUMBER ONE IN QUEBEC

Provigo's history is striking proof that many things have changed in Quebec since the 1960s. It begins in the early days of the Quiet Revolution, the story of ordinary businessmen who had the vision and determination to become more than small-scale regional merchants and enter the major leagues of North American business.

The story shows that Quebeckers who dare to take chances, venture beyond their own territory, share ownership of their businesses through stock issues and, above all, work together as a team, can overcome any obstacle.

In the same way that the Quiet Revolution, which broke out in the 1960s, had been simmering for a few years, the arrival on the Quebec market of the Provigo pioneers dates back to well before the Company's official debut. From Montreal, Sherbrooke, Jonquière, Chicoutimi and St-Félicien, the Provigo founders pooled their resources and talents, eventually joining the ranks of the leading Canadian companies.

Together they built a company whose revenues have made it the largest in Quebec.

Weeks before January 28, 1989, the end of Provigo's fiscal year, its directors and officers knew that 1988 had been satisfactory and that, for the first time, the company's sales would exceed $7 billion.[1] When all the figures were in and duly audited, the total reached $7.4 billion, up 17 percent from the previous year. Net income amounted to $51.5 million.

In less than twenty years, Provigo has become one of North America's leaders in the wholesale and retail distribution of consumer goods, the largest food distributor in Quebec, second largest in Canada, and among the ten largest in North America. Provigo is also the leading distributor of pharmaceutical and health and beauty products in Canada, the top national sporting goods chain and one of the largest independent distributors of gasoline and petroleum products in Canada.

Provigo owns the leading chain store specializing in catalogue and over-the-counter sales; it is also one of the largest in North America. In addition, it is among the most important retailers of jewelry, small household appliances and toys in Canada.

In all, the company comprises 69 distribution centres, 67 cash-and-carry warehouses, 2,710 affiliated or franchised stores, 446 corporate stores and several thousand independent clients. Provigo supplies over 10,000 businesses as diverse as supermarkets, pharmacies, convenience stores, gas stations, sports stores, restaurants, hotels, institutions and cafeterias.

Today, Provigo directly employs some 22,000 people and is responsible for over 50,000 jobs, if we include employees in stores under the various Provigo banners.

Success Built on Food

Provigo's success story began in the food sector. In 1969, three companies, Couvrette & Provost Ltée, Denault Limitée and Lamontagne Limitée, merged and adopted the name Provigo Inc. in 1970. Within a few years, the new company was to become the largest business incorporated in Quebec.

Food distribution is still at the heart of Provigo's activities. The food sector represents 70 percent of the company's total sales. In Quebec, with a 30 percent share, Provigo Distribution Inc. dominates the market with the retail banners Provigo, Axep, Jovi, Proprio, Intermarché, Octofruit, Héritage and Maxi. If we include the sales of Loeb in Quebec and Provi-Soir, this market share rises to 35 percent.

Loeb Inc., responsible for operations in Ontario and western Quebec, supplies the IGA, Loeb, Loeb IGA, M/M, Héritage and Orange Store retail outlets. In the Ottawa region its market share exceeds 40 percent. In Alberta, another subsidiary, Horne & Pitfield Foods Limited, oversees the operations of IGA, M/M, Mayfair, Triple S, Food Giant and Garden Market and Reddi Mart stores. This network serves about 12 percent of the market. In all, the vast Provigo family comprises 16 food store chains, catering to all tastes and needs. The ability to serve various segments of the population and diverse consumer groups is a chief characteristic of the company. Versatile merchandising techniques have become the firm's hallmark, enabling it to occupy several food distribution market segments successfully. In addition to supplying grocery stores, Provigo is highly active in institutional food services through its subsidiary Dellixo.

Provigo is also active in the United States food sector under the name Provigo Corp.[2], which has two divisions, Market Wholesale Grocery in California and Tidewater Wholesale in Virginia.

Within Provigo the Food Group accounts for sales of $5 billion and income of $68.2 million.

Open 24 Hours

Through food retailing Provigo eventually introduced the concept of the *dépanneur*, a contemporary version of the neighbourhood corner store. Food merchandising no longer dominates in this type of business, as the revenue from all types of non-food services has become increasingly important. Provi-Soir is the number one convenience store chain in Quebec. The majority of Provi-Soir outlets are twinned with a gasoline station, an advantage which is reflected in the company's success, and it is through Provi-Soir that Provigo has become the undisputed leader in the fast-growing convenience store sector. Provi-Soir is the model for the C Corp. network of convenience stores. As well as Provi-Soir, C Corp. now manages the Pinto, Top Valu and Winks outlets in Ontario, and the Red Rooster stores in western Canada. In all there are 485 outlets in the C Corp. network.

In this convenience sector, sales total $373 million with income of $10.8 million.

The Health and Pharmacy Sector

In 1977, Provigo purchased M. Loeb, Limited. With this acquisition, Provigo significantly extended the reach of its activities, which had been previously confined to Quebec, while at the same time expanding its scope beyond the food sector to carve out a major share of the pharmaceutical, health care and beauty aids market.

Since 1987, Provigo has combined within a single subsidiary (MEDIS) all the operations of its Health and Pharmaceutical Group. Sales for this sector exceeded one billion dollars in 1988–1989, and its distribution network supplies over 4,300 pharmacies and retail stores throughout Canada.

Specialty Retailing

Provigo is open to every opportunity which will further its avowed objective to "become a North American leader in the wholesale and retail distribution of consumer goods." Nonetheless a single thread runs through all its diverse operations: the efficient, integrated management of the entire supply chain.

In the specialty retailing sector Provigo owns Sports Experts Inc., the network which, in addition to the Sports Experts stores, includes the Collegiate and Intersport outlets, and forms the first national chain in the sporting goods sector. It showed sales of $164 million and income of $2.1 million in 1987–1988.

Provigo also owns Consumers Distributing, which reported sales of $1 billion and income of $11.4 million in 1987–1988. Until November 1987, Provigo owned no more than 23.5 percent of Consumers Distributing, which it accounted in the company's earnings using the equity method. Since then, Consumers Distributing has become a wholly-owned subsidiary of Provigo.

The network of stores within the specialty retailing group now comprises some 420 outlets.

Provigo among the Giants

Provigo's 1987-1988 sales ranked 10th among the largest 500 Canadian companies.[3]

Only General Motors, Bell Canada, Ford, Canadian Pacific, George Weston, Alcan, Imperial Oil, Noranda, and Chrysler amassed greater revenue than Provigo. It comes as a surprise to many that Provigo is now among such an elite group.

It is difficult to imagine that selling flour, green peas and other day-to-day items could have led to such a spectacular destiny. The list of companies outranked by Provigo is surprising too: Petro-Canada, Canadian National, Ontario Hydro, Shell Canada, Hydro-Québec, Brascan, Imasco, Sears,

Seagram, Air Canada, Canadian Tire, Woolworth, Molson, Teleglobe, Agropur… the list goes on. In only one month, Provigo's revenues match the annual revenues of the company in 173rd place; Provigo's revenues in a week match the annual revenues of the 482nd company!

But the scope and success of Provigo cannot be measured solely by its sales; a company's sales can be high without its earnings following suit, and profit margins vary with the type of business. Other criteria, such as return on shareholders' equity, must be used. Provigo has set itself an annual objective of an 18 percent return and attained 19.8 percent in 1987–1988. The same year, only 14 percent of the largest Canadian companies attained or exceeded this rate of return.[4] Earnings per share, for their part, have been growing at an average annual rate of 19.28 percent for the past twenty years. Total assets exceed $1.5 billion, while the debt is only $465.3 million, another indication of Provigo's financial vitality and, in 1987–1988, the company invested over $300 million to generate further growth.

On the Montreal and Toronto stock exchanges, Provigo's 84,844,061 outstanding shares had a book value of over $365 million as of June 1988 and a market value of nearly $1 billion reflecting its high performance.

Exceptional Performance over the Years

An investment in Couvrette & Provost in 1961 has since grown 157 fold, for an average annual return of 78 percent.[5] According to analysts, this exceptional return has made Provigo one of the best investments in Canada over the past twenty-five years.[6] If we compare the current results with those achieved by the original companies in 1966, we can see that Provigo multiplied its net sales by 53.3, net earnings by 84.7, total assets by 67 and shareholders' equity by 50.5.[7]

How did the company rise to the top ranks of Canadian businesses so quickly? To find out, we must return to the days of the Quiet Revolution and those tradesmen who dared to take chances, break new ground and confront formidable challenges. Their efforts built the largest company in Quebec — number one!

Notes

1. The financial results reported in this chapter reflect Provigo's situation for the year ended January 28, 1989 unless otherwise indicated. The figures quoted in the remainder of the book generally indicate results as of January 30, 1988.
2. Taking its cue from Provigo in Canada, Provigo Corp. expanded its traditional

role of wholesaler in 1987 and started to provide its retailers with support services. The following year, Provigo Corp., acquired the 11 Petrini supermarkets, as well as the 15 Lucky Store and Alpha Beta supermarkets located in the San Francisco area, which represent annual cumulative sales of some $260 million US.
3. The Financial Post 500, 1988 edition.
4. During the past 20 years, Provigo's annual average return has been over 20%.
5. An investor with 100 Couvrette & Provost Class A shares worth $5.50 each in 1961 — a total investment of $550 — would have had 8,000 Provigo Inc. shares in June 1988, taking into account successive stock splits. His investment would be worth $86,000, with an additional $11,400 in dividends for the period in question. See Appendix IV for details.
6. The increase in value of Provigo shares was far superior to that of the TSE during that period. For example, an article by Michel Girard published in La Presse (June 13, 1988) stated that a $1,000 investment in a portfolio reflecting the Canadian market, i.e., the TSE 300, was worth a "mere" $7,640 by the end of 1986.
7. Further details can be found in Appendix II.

PROVIGO

CHAPTER TWO

FROM THE GENERAL STORE TO THE SUPERSTORE

The retail business we know today is merely a development of the old general store. A 60,000-square foot superstore with wall-to-wall merchandise is simply the traditional general store on a grander scale. Rapid technological changes such as refrigeration, the automobile, credit cards, electronic cash registers with optical scanners and phenomenal memories, and computers of every description, as well as accelerated social changes resulting from automation and the influx of women into the labour force seem to have changed everything about retailing, except perhaps the basics.

In the old days, the general store in the Quebec village carried everything, or just about. It stocked all the food staples, that is to say goods that could not be produced in one's own kitchen.[1]

Merchants also had a hardware department stocked with materials and tools,[2] and a dry goods counter tended by the women of the house.

In addition, the village storekeeper sold strong liquor, mainly gin and grain alcohol. He also ordered eyeglasses, coffins, farm equipment, and much more. The best day of the week for business was Sunday, after mass. Any items that couldn't be bought at the general store, people would order by catalogue from Dupuis, Eaton's or Simpson's. Today, Sears and Consumers Distributing have catalogues but fewer and fewer people shop by mail.

A typical general store in the country with a full selection of goods. (Private collection: Germain Beauchamp and daughter, Saint-Eustache.)

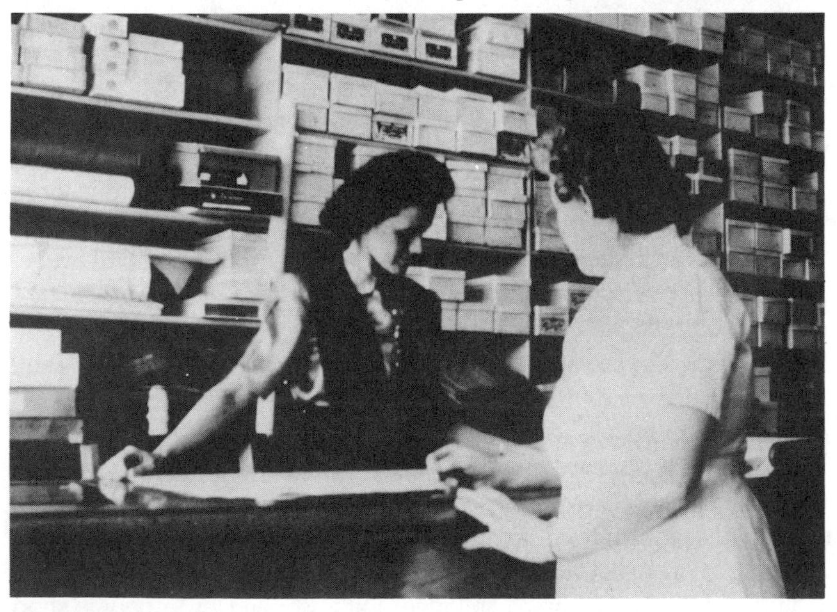

Women tend the dry goods counter.

In the City

Things were different in the city, where the general store did not have a monopoly. Shops were more specialized and the sale of food products more segmented. At dawn, the milkman would deliver his products by horse-drawn wagon. He would be followed by the baker with his bread, cakes, pies and famous baked beans in earthenware jars. Many peddlers plied their trades through the streets, among them produce sellers, ice men, rag pickers and the men who sharpened knives and scissors.

The milkman making his rounds in the country, ... and in the city, circa 1930.

Each neighbourhood, and each parish had its specialized food stores: grocery stores, butcher shops, fruit and vegetable stores, dairies, pastry shops, corner lunch counters and handy stores. They were the equivalent of today's boutiques and convenience stores.

The Corner Grocer

The grocer sold mostly dry groceries: canned food, cereals, flour, dried peas, beans, biscuits, tea, coffee, spices, etc. In summer he would also offer fresh fruit and vegetables and, in winter, a few vegetables that kept well. He also offered various odds and ends such as thread, shoelaces, work gloves, and heating oil. Licensed grocers were allowed to sell "booze," often a short-lived privilege subject to the discretion and, at times, the whims of the political party in power.

The neighbourhood convenience store, forerunner of the *dépanneur.* (ADA collection)

After the creation of the Quebec Liquor Board in 1921, liquor could no longer be sold anywhere but in the Board's outlets and the licensed grocer's privilege was restricted to selling beer. In addition, to comply with the law governing business hours, grocers were required to partition their stores to forbid access to the grocery section in the evening. Beer, apparently, was a greater necessity than groceries!

In the summertime grocers made deliveries by bicycle or horse drawn cart and in the winter by sleigh, complete with bells.

Like the country shopkeeper, the grocer was a veritable repository of information. He was on top of current events, knew how to read, write and count, skills which were essential when it came to taking orders, checking the accounts and keeping track of the credit granted to his customers on a weekly or monthly basis. As was the custom in those days, wholesalers and retailers alike gave credit.

Some grocers introduced a give-away system, in the form of punch cards, a precursor of the trading stamps that were so popular in the 1960s.[3]

A typical corner grocery store.

In those days, most products were sold in bulk, a practice which is coming back into use. Pre-packaged products were known as fancy goods.

The Butcher

The butcher's counter only made a later appearance in grocery stores. In his shop the butcher sold primarily fresh meat that he had cut himself, some pickled or smoked products, and locally made sausage and other meat specialties. Each piece was cut in front of the customer. This type of personal service became more and more widespread. The range of meats available depended on the season and even on the day of the week. For example, Thursdays and Fridays (and Wednesdays during Lent) fresh fish was available. In winter, one could purchase smelts, hare and rabbit, frozen by Nature herself, right on the grocer's doorstep.

Specialty Shops

In Montreal, each neighbourhood had its grocery stores and butcher

The itinerant butcher, carefully weighing his merchandise. (ADA collection)

A grocery store/butcher shop in the city. Note the prices. (ADA collection).

shops. Greengrocers specialized in fresh fruit and vegetables, as well as dried fruit. Some of them were famous for their imported produce. They were often located in the vicinity of churches, and they were open on Sunday. Pastry shops, full of tempting treats made on the premises, were also open on Sunday. Today, the same aroma of freshly baked bread is often found in supermarkets. Pastry shops also sold fancy chocolate, fine cheeses and delicatessen items.

The Markets

Public markets are certainly not new. In the old days, each town, no matter how small, had its market place. Market day was a special day, attracting both suppliers and consumers. In Montreal, public markets were very popular during the 1930s and 1940s. Owned by the City, they covered an area of some 10,000 to 15,000 square feet[4], and contained row upon row of stalls and display counters. The open air spaces were rented to farmers selling their produce or livestock. Above the ground floor of the market building there was usually a large hall that people could rent for parties, political rallies, and other important events. Among today's public markets in Montreal, Atwater and Jean-Talon are still popular. Several new privately owned markets can also be found on the outskirts of the city.

Chain Stores

The so called chain store first appeared in Quebec around the 1920s and completely revolutionized the food business. In Montreal, chains like Steinberg (long the model in Quebec), Tousignant & Frères, Dominion, A&P, Stop & Shop, Thrift Stores, Dionne, and many others developed rapidly. Dominion, Dionne and A&P have since been absorbed by Provigo, which also integrated four other chains: JAT (founded by Joseph-Arthur Tremblay, in Chicoutimi), Lamontagne (founded by Jean-Louis Lamontagne, in Saint-Félicien), Jato (founded in Quebec City by Jean Boiteau) and Aubaines Alimentaires in Trois-Rivières (long under the direction of Gérard Bourget and Gérard Charrette).

Four times the average size of traditional grocery stores, the chain store combined the grocery store, butcher shop and greengrocer's under one roof. The era of 'one stop shopping' had begun. Each department was expected to show a profit and each had its own manager. Stores were not run by and under the direction of a merchant or retailer but rather operated by a store manager.

Chains did not give credit, nor did they deliver or take orders. They promoted private brands, packaged products bought in bulk and operated on a self-serve basis. In return, they offered prices that were lower than elsewhere.

With their considerable purchasing power and centralized purchasing methods, chains were in a position to buy directly from the manufacturer or supplier and thus avoided paying a percentage to the wholesale grocer. They obtained allowances for advertising, displays and specials, not to mention cash discounts for rapid payment. Indeed, chain stores were able to sell their merchandise at a lower price while earning a good profit.

At the time, some independent grocers doubted whether these new retailers would succeed in Quebec. In fact, the majority of wholesalers and retailers remained indifferent to this new phenomenon, if not downright apathetic. It took them years to get together and adopt the administrative structures needed to compete with the chains.

In 1942, a committee of the Chambre de Commerce de Montréal[5] called for a meeting of Quebec wholesale grocers who were finally feeling threatened by chains and cooperatives. They had to unite to promote and defend their interests. They felt, moreover, the need to improve their management and their relations with manufacturers and retailers. But, it was not until 1953 that the Association des Épiciers en Gros de la Province de Québec (AEG) was incorporated. Individualism was so strong that those involved seemed to mistrust working together for a common cause more than they feared the food chains themselves.

For their part, the retailers had associations such as "Les Marchands Détaillants" for grocers, butchers and other merchants, but it was not until 1955 that the Association des Détaillants en Alimentation du Québec (ADA) was formed. ADA was a well organized group, capable of defending the interests of its members, promoting more professional business methods and working towards better relations with the other players in the food sector. The combined efforts of the AEG and ADA can be credited with shaking wholesalers and retailers alike out of their apathy and reversing the trend which had been threatening them in Quebec. In time they became leaders capable of outperforming the chains themselves. The Provigo story begins with the acceptance of this new challenge.

Notes

1. People used to make their own bread, pies and cakes, and a variety of prepared meats. Milk, cream, butter, eggs and meat would come directly from the farm. Fresh fruit and vegetables were grown in the garden. Hunting and fishing added variety to the menu.
2. But not lumber, which came from the sawmill and was often harvested on land owned by certain townspeople.
3. Today, in addition to saving cash slips for prizes, there are all kinds of contests and draws, as well as discount coupons (and the tedious bookkeeping they entail).
4. The largest of these, the Bonsecours Market, was located in the heart of Old Montreal. It was the supply centre for retailers and storekeepers. Bonsecours Market was later replaced by the Marché Central Métropolitain in north-east Montreal as a major wholesale centre for produce.
5. Jacques Melançon, who later became a consultant and a director of Couvrette & Provost, was then secretary of the Chambre.

CHAPTER THREE

THE PIONEERS

While Provigo does not go back quite as far as the days of the Hudson's Bay Company or the Company of One Hundred Associates, few people realize that the food distribution business has deep roots in the province's business history. Indeed, as Mr. Couvrette, now in his eighties, often points out, this particular industry has been controlled by francophones since the 19th century. A look at the career of Bernard Couvrette, one of the leading figures in the Provigo saga, will help bring into focus the development of Quebec's wholesale food business.

According to a study conducted by economist Gérard Bélair,[1] the first wholesale grocers were established in Montreal around 1825. Between 1835 and 1900, 45 wholesale grocers started their own businesses. Between 1900 and 1982, another 121 were set up. The transportation and communication problems that prevailed in Quebec a century ago forced retailers to obtain their supplies from a wholesaler in their own regions; this resulted in an exceedingly large number of different enterprises. Very few, however, survived into the second half of the century. The Liquor Act effectively abolished the unregulated sale of alcohol and the Great Depression had devastating effects on wholesalers. With bankruptcies and mergers, there were only 35 wholesale businesses left in Quebec by 1982. It should be added that companies such as Couvrette & Provost, Lamontagne, and Denault greatly contributed to the overall reduction and

The dean: Bernard Couvrette.

consolidation of the market by absorbing and combining the operations of some 40 wholesale grocers in Quebec between 1961 and 1969. Thus the way was paved for Provigo's future outstanding success.

In 1921, the Quebec government secured a monopoly over the importation and sale of alcohol[2] with the creation of the Liquor Board, and provoked a crisis that shook the food sector. Without the profitable business of wine, liqueurs and spirits imported from Europe, many companies were forced to reorganize. Several went bankrupt. The three largest wholesalers in Quebec, L. Chaput & Cie (founded in 1842), Laporte and Martin (founded in 1875), and Hudon, Hébert & Cie ltée[3] merged to form Laporte, Hudon, Hébert, which existed until 1947. Couvrette & Sauriol Limitée, for its part, weathered the crisis without too much difficulty. Founded by Bernard Couvrette's father in 1901, the business was too small to be granted a licence to sell alcohol and was little affected by the government's intrusion into the market.

Couvrette & Sauriol Limitée

Founded by Eugène Couvrette and J. Féréol Sauriol, Couvrette & Sauriol[4] started as a modest business supplying storekeepers with paper bags and wrapping supplies. The concern grew slowly but steadily, never perceived as a threat by larger companies. It eventually benefited from the difficulties experienced by those wholesalers affected by the Liquor Act. In 1922 it acquired Patenaude & Carignan, a major company. Without too much damage, Couvrette & Sauriol was also able to withstand the emergence of such food chains as Steinberg (1917), Dominion stores (1921), Stop and Shop (1925) and A&P (1926). The chains first appeared in Montreal. In their heyday they numbered several hundred food outlets and made life difficult not only for wholesale grocers, for which they had no need, but also for the corner grocery stores and general stores. Already badly shaken by the loss of the liquor market, the local stores were badly threatened by this new tidal wave. Adapting an American method to the Quebec situation, Couvrette & Sauriol grouped its clients to form a type of chain under the name Magasins Frontenac. This was the very first association of independent grocers, known then as voluntary groups. The Magasins Victoria, affiliated with Laporte, Hudon, Hébert, and the Épiciers Modernes, headed by Paul-Émile Guilbault, also made their business debut around this time. These were the forerunners of affiliated and franchised merchant conglomerates.

The creation of the Magasins Frontenac chain enabled Couvrette & Sauriol to weather the Great Depression. Under their agreement, each of its 800 members paid an annual fee of $25, and thereby ensured that the chain could count on an annual income of $20,000 in franchising fees — a sizeable amount at the time. In addition, the stores agreed to purchase their supplies from Couvrette & Sauriol, where they benefited from attractive purchasing conditions, promotions, and group advertising. As early as the 1920s and 30s, this formula heralded the groupings of retail grocers into the more complex forms of affiliations or franchises that we know today. In the 1950s, Antoine Turmel adopted a similar strategy in Sherbrooke.

It was in 1936, during the worst days of the Depression, that Bernard Couvrette, along with his brothers Gilles and Jacques and their sister Claire, took over the family business after the death of their father. Bernard had already been sitting on the Board of Directors for a few years and practising law for seven years when he was appointed President of the company. In 1937, Couvrette & Sauriol moved into the vast premises vacated by L. Chaput Fils & Cie and Hudon, Hébert & Cie on de Bresoles Street in Old Montreal. To round out his knowledge of the business world, Bernard Couvrette participated in the activities of the Chambre de Commerce de Montréal (he would later become its president), attended special seminars and conventions in the United States, visited numerous facilities and read everything published on the food distribution business. He became President of the Canadian Wholesale Grocers Association and, in 1942, founded the Association des Épiciers en Gros de la Province de Québec (AEG), of which he was President until 1945. In fact, the AEG was an initiative of a committee of the Chambre de Commerce de Montréal.

Its first secretary was Jacques Melançon, who belonged to the organization, as did five of his successors.[5] Next in line was Aimé Boivert, the first full-time secretary of the AEG, who played a key role for twelve years.[6] Bernard Couvrette's interest in research, progress, management techniques and cooperation stemmed from his association with the Chambre de Commerce de Montréal and the influence of its Director General, Gilbert A. Latour, who guided his early business career.

An efficient distribution service was an important asset of Couvrette & Sauriol. Customers could have orders delivered several times a week whereas other wholesalers would only deliver once or twice a week. With deliveries in the Metropolitan area, as well as to the North Shore and Lower St. Lawrence, the sales of Couvrette & Sauriol quintupled between 1937 and 1950. The company had a merchandise catalogue, price lists, and travelling salesmen. It even took phone orders and gave credit. *Notre Vendeur,* the catalogue published by Couvrette & Sauriol was the grocer's number one guide, often referred to as the Bible of the trade. Four thousand copies were distributed every month; even retailers who were not Couvrette & Sauriol customers received it.

The Presto self-service (cash-and-carry) warehouses were another innovation introduced in 1961 and headed by Jacques Couvrette. Acting as a sort of branch or satellite of the main distribution centre, these mini-centres operated on the cash-and-carry principle. Storekeepers would shop in person, choosing from a variety of products available in small quantities. The system enabled storekeepers with limited resources to purchase a wider variety of goods.

These innovations demonstrated how Couvrette & Sauriol was a pioneer on its way to becoming a leader in the wholesale grocery business.

Couvrette & Sauriol's new methods soon put them in the forefront of Canadian grocery wholesalers. Before long, the 100,000 square foot, six storey warehouse was no longer adequate. Modern business required facilities confined to a single floor, with high ceilings, where forklift trucks could circulate freely and merchandise be stored according to more logical methods based on the type of products and order-form sequence.

Bernard Couvrette may have had the confidence of his family, but he felt that they might not be ready to invest the available resources in the construction of a modern warehouse. It struck him that the solution might be to join forces with other interested parties.

Distribué exclusivement à nos clients...

PAIN CHAMPION

COUTANT 17¢ VENDANT 20¢

• Demandez plus de détails à nos représentants ou à notre bureau . . .

Blé-d'Inde épis — Corn on cob

Blé d'Inde Lessivé — Hominy

Maheu	24 x 20 on	cse	4.20

Carottes — Carrots

Aylmer Shoestring choice	24 x 15 on.	cse	3.15
diced choice	24 x 20 on.	cse	3.60
Bedford cubes	24 x 20 on.	cse	2.05
Denis cubes choix	24 x 20 on.	cse	2.30
Ferlandière cubes	24 x 20 on.	cse	2.25
Ideal cubes	24 x 20 on.	cse	2.30

Champignons — Mushrooms

Leaver			
Button choice	24 x 10 on.	cse	7.85
Cocktail	24 x 3 on.	cse	6.80
Pieces and stems	24 x 10 on.	cse	6.85
Whole choice	24 x 10 on.	cse	7.90
Slack's choix	24 x 10 on.	cse	7.90
Slack's Hotel	24 x 10 on.	cse	6.95
Slack in brown gravy	24 x 10 on.	cse	4.50
Slack creamed	24 x 10 on.	cse	6.95
Waterloo sliced	24 x 5 on.	cse	4.90

Citrouilles — Pumpkin

● Aylmer fcy	24 x 28 on.	cse	4.50
Libby	24 x 15 on.	cse	2.75

Epinards — Spinach

★ Aylmer fcy	24 x 20 on.	cse	5.00
Del Monte	24 x 20 on.	cse	5.85

Fèves Jaunes — Wax Beans

Coupées choix — Choice cut			
Bedford choix	24 x 15 on.	cse	3.55
■ Gazelle	24 x 20 on.	cse	2.95
Green Giant	24 x 15 on.	cse	4.05
Ideal	24 x 20 on.	cse	3.15
	6 x 105 on.	cse	3.70
■ Raymond	24 x 20 on.	cse	3.35
Rougemont	24 x 20 on.	cse	4.05
Longues choix — Whole choice			
Ideal ·	24 x 20 on.	cse	3.95
■ Raymond	24 x 20 on.	cse	4.15

Vertes Refugee Beans

Coupées choix - Choice cut			
Green Giant	24 x 15 on.	cse	4.05
Ideal	24 x 10 on.	cse	2.70
Ideal	24 x 20 on.	cse	3.05
Royal Rose	24 x 10 on.	cse	2.70
Longues choix — Whole choice			
Ideal	24 x 20 on.	cse	3.95

Macedoine

Denis	24 x 20 on.	cse	3.00
Ferlandière	24 x 20 on.	cse	3.45
Ideal	24 x 20 on.	cse	3.20
	6 x 105 on.	cse	3.45
Libby	24 x 15 on.	cse	4.00
Mad. de Verchères	24 x 20 on.	cse	3.20
	6 x 105 on.	cse	3.35

Pois & carottes — Peas & carrots

Aylmer choix	24 x 20 on.	cse	4.70
Ideal	24 x 20 on.	cse	3.50

Pois — Peas

Choix — Choice			
Aylmer "Salt free" assorted	12 x 10 on.	cse	2.15
Aylmer assorted	24 x 20 on.	cse	4.05
Del Monte	24 x 10 on.	cse	3.20
	24 x 15 on.	cse	4.15
Ideal No 1	24 x 20 on.	cse	6.95
No 2	24 x 20 on.	cse	5.95
No 3	24 x 20 on.	cse	4.30
No 4	24 x 20 on.	cse	3.70
Non classés	24 x 10 on.	cse	2.65
No 3	6 x 105 on.	cse	4.50
No 4	6 x 105 on.	cse	4.00
■ Legion	24 x 20 on.	cse	3.10
President No 4	24 x 20 on.	cse	4.25
Royal Rose			
No 1	24 x 20 on.	cse	7.10
No 2	24 x 20 on.	cse	6.10
No 3	24 x 20 on.	cse	4.50
No 4	24 x 20 on.	cse	3.90
Non classés	24 x 10 on.	cse	2.65
Teenie Weenie No 2	24 x 20 on.	cse	6.25
De luxe — Fancy			
Blue & Gold	24 x 15 on.	cse	4.15
	24 x 10 on.	cse	3.20
Green Giant	24 x 15 on.	cse	4.15
	24 x 10 on.	cse	3.20
Royal Rose Non classés	24 x 10 on.	cse	2.65

Salade légumes — Vegetable salad

Heinz	24 x 8 on.	cse	5.05

Tomates — Tomatoes

Aylmer "Salt free"	12 x 10 on.	cse	2.00
Aylmer choix	24 x 20 on.	cse	4.70
	24 x 28 on.	cse	5.80
Aylmer stewed choice	24 x 20 on.	cse	5.70
Del Monte Stewed	24 x 20 on.	cse	5.85
Gattuso peeled	24 x 15 on.	cse	3.75
Ideal choix	24 x 20 on.	cse	3.75
	24 x 28 on.	cse	4.65
	6 x 105 on.	cse	4.55
Libby choix	24 x 20 on.	cse	4.55
	24 x 28 on.	cse	5.70
■ Lotus	24 x 28 on.	cse	4.20

LESSIVE — LYE

Gillet	24 x 9½ on.	cse	4.55
	6 x 5 lbs	cse	9.00

LEVURE — YEAST

Fleischmann Royal Dry Fast	48 enveloppes	carton	2.30

Notre vendeur, the grocer's Bible.

The Provost Brothers

The Provost brothers had been exposed to the food business all their lives.[7] In 1932, with their studies completed and few prospects of employment during those Depression days, they decided to create their own jobs. Roland, then 21, suggested to Ernest, two years his junior, that they go into the flour business. Having worked in the grain and flour trade (at Gee & Mahaffey), he had noticed that there were no French-Canadian packers in that field. With his brother, he began to buy flour wholesale which they would then pack and resell in 7 lb bags. Their father, J. Omer Provost, who had operated a grocery store on Hôtel-de-Ville Avenue in Montreal since 1907, came up with the name *La Cuisinière* for their new business, gave them space for their merchandise and even lent them the family car to make deliveries.

The Provost brothers: Roland, René and Ernest.

The two brothers got down to work without any start up money. Their flour supplier had thousands of bags, bearing their label, printed for them. By buying on credit and using the proceeds from sales to pay their suppliers for the previous order, their working capital increased steadily from one transaction to the next. Eventually they started selling sugar, salt, baking powder, oat meal and a few other dry staples such as peas, navy beans and rice. Their business was small but prosperous. At one point, they managed to move all their merchandise and pocket the money before having to pay the supplier's bill, thanks to their efficient application of the rapid turnover system.

Roland Provost, standing proudly by his new truck.

The first product bearing the label of Provost & Provost.

Their profit margin was so small that the competition thought the company was just a step away from bankruptcy. Little by little, however, their operations extended to all of Montreal and the surrounding areas. They hired Lucien Gratton, an experienced sales representative. Roland Provost, who had until then been working as an insurance agent, started devoting all his time to the business, which was then known as Provost & Provost. He had but one goal: to improve the company's profitability. For example, he would return from deliveries outside Montreal with farm produce in his truck. Ernest was more of an administrator. Roland would come up with initiatives while Ernest looked after home-base operations, administered the company's finances and managed personnel. In 1945, after completing his studies at Collège Mont St. Louis, René joined the firm as a sales representative and later assumed responsibility for purchasing and sales. Ironically, in 1947 the demise of Laporte, Hudon, Hébert — a major wholesaler — forced suppliers to do business with the Provost brothers, whom they had all but ignored. Provost & Provost had become a true wholesale grocer.

Towards the end of the 1940s, a wholesale grocer stocked what was known in the trade as ''dry grocery.'' Provost & Provost sold some 1,500 items whereas a good-sized grocer/butcher kept anywhere between 2,500 and 3,000 items in his store. In the early 1950s, a few wholesalers adopted the cash-and-carry method popular in the United States. The new method enabled them to eliminate expenses related to sales representation, credit and delivery.

Born during the Depression and nurtured during the War, the young company of Provost & Provost became more and more aggressive. It set up the '''Metropole Cash System'' and managed to reduce its operating expenses even further. While the traditional wholesale grocer needed a profit margin of 8 to 11 percent, the new system proved profitable with a margin of 4 percent. Savings were passed on to appreciative retailers and the new cash system provided Provost & Provost with cash in hand from sales before bills were due; the formula became popular and ensured rapid, steady growth.

Antoine Turmel successfully established a similar system for the shareholding customers of Denault in Sherbrooke. At the time, Provost & Provost did not yet distribute the usual tobacco, cigarettes or candy products now found in all grocery stores.

Difficulties among members and management of Les Épiciers Modernes Ltée provided Provost & Provost with the opportunity to acquire the complete wholesale division of this voluntary group in 1955. With this move, they had acquired a high profile, increased sales and a new set of suppliers, as well as a permit to sell tobacco and cigarettes.

Needing larger premises, the company moved to St. Denis Street, to the former warehouse of Lake of the Woods (millers of Five Roses Flour) which had been bought by Ogilvie Flour Mills, a company Roland Provost knew well. Provost & Provost was now located in a modern warehouse with all the merchandise on one floor. Orders could be assembled according to product category, customer order and delivery route. Here Ernest Provost developed the ''assembly line'' system. The Provost brothers recognized that careful control of incoming merchandise, storage and shipping was the key to efficiency, productivity and profitability.

During the same period, Provost & Provost went after the institutional market, supplying hotels, hospitals and the like. This special sector calls for a different inventory and delivery system, as well as special price structures and payment conditions. The institutional division would become increasingly successful.

Provost & Provost contributed to the revitalization of the voluntary group movement through Métropole, EM (Épiciers Modernes) and F.D.L banners.

Wholesalers soon realized that, like retailers, they would benefit from joining forces to face the competition from food chains.

By the end of the 1950s, at the initiative of Léopold Pigeon, who was then general manager for the Métro merchants, a number of wholesalers closed ranks. Léopold Pigeon suspected that their competitors benefited from advantages that the independent grocers did not have access to. With the collaboration of Roger Messier of Épiciers Richelieu, and René Provost, they created the Montreal Grocery Buying Group.[8]

The original three wholesalers — Métro, Richelieu and Provost & Provost — were eventually joined by E. Deaudelin & Fils. Their objective was to pool their sales to maximize supplier discounts and obtain rebates. Until then, only major distributors — including chain stores — had access to these advantages.

Couvrette & Sauriol joined the buying group in 1962, followed by Denault,[9] in Sherbrooke, during the mid-60s.

Provost & Provost continued to expand. It became a partner in Conserverie Saint-Denis, one of the largest canneries in Quebec, and formed a subsidiary, P. & P. Packaging, headed by René Provost and Gérard Miron.

P. & P. Packaging packaged a variety of products in cellophane bags, among them unshelled nuts, peanuts, pasta, soup mixes, dried peas, kidney beans, lima beans, barley and rice, to name but a few. Already, in the mid-50s, this innovation amounted to a breakthrough for private brands.

In addition to sales to the parent company, P. & P. Packaging had major dealings with several wholesalers outside the Montreal area, particularly in Quebec City, the Saguenay/Lac-Saint-Jean region, along the North Shore, in the Lower St-Lawrence and as far as Gaspé.[10]

The tobacco wholesaler permit, a highly desired privilege in those days, had been obtained at the time of the acquisition of Magasins EM. Provost & Provost paired this type of business with that of P. & P. Packaging and created a separate division.

For the tobacco business, they adopted the Métropole Cash System, a departure from the traditional method used by tobacco and confectionery distributors.

This approach caused a scandal. Whereas other wholesalers sold a carton of cigarettes to retailers for $3.31, Provost & Provost sold it for $3.11. The new division was practically an overnight success. The same approach would make the Cash & Carry Presto outlets famous. Cigarette manufacturers gave Provost & Provost a hard time for a while, but they soon realized that this was the way of the future and decided to cooperate.

The growth of Provost & Provost was such that, in 1960, the company had sales of approximately $9,000,000, with a profit of $100,000. But since earnings had been reinvested, the company found itself without sufficient working capital to implement all its expansion projects.

At a meeting of the Wholesale Grocers Association in Toronto, Roland Provost met Bernard Couvrette. Over a cup of coffee, the two began discussing the possibility of a merger.

At first, they wanted to unite the four Montreal companies: J.H. Lamarche, Laviolette & Brosseau, Couvrette & Sauriol and Provost & Provost. Discussions were initiated and they consulted Jacques Melançon, now a financial advisor, who suggested creating a public company with shares listed on the Exchange. The management of J.H. Lamarche and of Laviolette & Brosseau decided early on not to go ahead with the merger project. Couvrette & Sauriol and Provost & Provost, however, continued to discuss a future together.[11]

Couvrette & Provost: A Merging of Interests

On November 14, 1961, Couvrette & Sauriol, a Montreal company established in 1901, and the more aggressive Provost & Provost, operating in Montreal since 1932, merged to form a corporation under the name Couvrette & Provost Ltée, which soon after went public with shares listed on the Canadian Stock Exchange.[12] Together they valued their joint assets and rationalized inventories. The capital stock of the new company was distributed in accordance with the pro forma balance sheet, and everyone involved was given shares in the new company. The operating results of the two companies for the previous year had been quite similar: Couvrette & Sauriol had sales of $9.7 million; Provost & Provost, $9 million (plus some $180,000 for P. & P. Packaging). Net income for Couvrette & Sauriol was $20,684; for Provost & Provost it was $45,611 (plus $3,280 for

P. & P. Packaging). While profits at Couvrette & Sauriol were dropping, those of Provost & Provost were rising steadily. The former had reserve capital, while the latter had been reinvesting as it expanded. It was the perfect match.

Two families successfully working together was a rare occurrence in those days. Together they laid part of the foundation for what would become Provigo a few years later.

On November 20, 1961, Couvrette & Provost, through a legal agreement, became the owner of Entreprises Couvrette; it also acquired the shares of Provost & Provost (1961), Provost & Provost Packaging, and Épiceries Presto.[13] Bernard Couvrette was appointed President of the new company and René Provost became its Executive Vice-President and General Manager. For René Provost, the challenge was to take two entities with very different corporate cultures and methods, and mold them into an efficient unit. His mandate was to adapt the Provost & Provost methods to Couvrette & Sauriol, while respecting the personnel and background of each company. It was a heavy responsibility where success ultimately depended on the dedication and competence of his colleagues. Meanwhile, management restricted its objective to the wholesale distribution of grocery, tobacco and confectionery products. The other businesses were sold. Provigo's mission, established in 1970 and reaffirmed in 1986, was beginning to take shape.

The new company adopted and pursued three strategies: to supply retailers from a modern, efficient, central warehouse; to serve smaller merchants through a network of satellite Cash & Carry Presto warehouses; and to supply the institutional sector — hospitals, schools, homes for the elderly, cafeterias, etc. — from a specialized department, using the Provost & Provost warehouse on Saint-Denis street. The results were remarkable.

The First Large-Scale Project

A sizeable portion of the proceeds from the sale of Couvrette & Provost shares was earmarked for the construction of the warehouse both companies had long been dreaming about. The company issued $600,000 worth of first mortgage bonds and 50,000 Class A shares with a par value of $5. Out of the net proceeds from these offerings — some $784,000 — a sum of $470,000 would be allocated to the construction of the warehouse.

It would be the most modern and best equipped warehouse. Located on the Marché Central Métropolitain property in Montreal, it would cover 100,000 square feet with a clearance of up to 30 feet for storage purposes.

Moreover, it would have a special siding for receiving by rail, separate bays for shipping and receiving, mechanized equipment, and so on. Inventory and purchases would soon be controlled by computer — in short, the most up-to-date facilities.

The warehouse built by Couvrette & Provost on rented land cost a little over $500,000. Immediately after construction, it was sold to the Compagnie du Marché Central Métropolitain and the property, including the building, was leased for twenty five years at an annual rent of $48,250. In this way, the net proceeds from the issue of shares and bonds could be used to develop and expand the company.

The warehouse was large enough to accommodate a doubling of the company's sales. Later, and for quite some time, it would be the site of all Provigo operations in the Montreal area.

Ernest Provost devoted his time to getting the best possible performance out of the new facilities. His innovations considerably improved the productivity of both physical and human operations.

Everything was new at Marché Métropolitain, even the inventory. The Saint-Denis street warehouse continued under the name Provost & Provost (1961) to serve the institutional sector for another two years. Roland Provost was its President.

The First Annual Reports

The new company started operations in the fall of 1961. On March 31, 1963, it published the annual report for its first complete fiscal year. The merger was an unqualified success. Over the years, many retailers joined the voluntary groups affiliated with Couvrette & Provost; Épiceries Presto, for instance, opened several branches. The company acquired in succession Laviolette & Brosseau Inc. of Montreal, Magasins Régal Inc. of Trois-Rivières, H. Dubois & Cie, Provisions Dubois of Montreal, and Conrad Lajoie Inc. of Shawinigan.

In order to offer customers the then highly popular trading-stamp system without relying on an outside supplier, Couvrette & Provost set up Primes Régal Inc. The new company issued its own trading stamps and published a catalogue of the prizes offered to consumers when they redeemed their stamps.

Within five years, Couvrette & Provost sales soared from $21.1 million to $53.6 million and net income rose from $104,093 to $405,600. It was a remarkable feat. In today's dollars, one would have to multiply these figures by four or five to describe accurately the company's performance during these early years.

The trading-stamp craze.

With average annual growth of 25 percent in sales and 44 percent in earnings, satisfaction was more than justified. Shareholders — individual and institutional alike — were extremely pleased.

In January 1965, Couvrette & Provost offered $1,000,000 in 6 percent debentures with subscription rights to Class A shares. The issue sold out in no time. It enabled the company to finance its program of expansion and acquisitions.

On May 13, 1965, Couvrette & Provost was granted Supplementary Letters Patent authorizing it to increase its capital stock; a five-for-one share split was undertaken.

The Company Goes Entirely Public

Business was humming when Bernard Couvrette, a sixty year old veteran in the food business and mayor of Outremont, decided to reduce his professional activities after thirty-five years in the field.

But it wasn't that simple. Bernard, Jacques and Claire Couvrette controlled 78 percent of Couvrette & Provost's voting shares. There was no shortage of candidates for control of the company. These included Jean-Louis Lamontagne,[14] Loeb[15] and Deaudelin. In the end, Bernard Couvrette offered control of the business to the Provost brothers. The transaction was made possible by a $2.7 million loan from the Bank Canadian National[16] and a commitment on the part of Nesbitt Thompson to proceed with a secondary distribution of shares.[17] This move made Couvrette & Provost a truly public company with its capital stock made up solely of common shares.[18] In September 1967, a prospectus announced the sale of 400,000 common shares without par value at a price of $5.85 per share.[19] This successful transaction enabled the company to become entirely public without incurring significant costs, a transition many thought impossible.

The share market price rose, much to the obvious satisfaction of investors and shareholders.

Bernard Couvrette became Chairman of the Board of Couvrette & Provost ltée, and René Provost was appointed President and General Manager.[20]

René Provost had worked under the discreet direction of Bernard Couvrette from 1961 to 1967. With sound judgment and an open, inquisitive mind, Bernard Couvrette was well versed in many fields other than the food business. He was a cautious, level-headed man who, even though he had control of the company, never exercised his absolute power. Rather he gave René Provost the latitude he needed to manage the company's affairs efficiently.

The business continued to grow. From 1967 to 1969, sales went from $53.6 million to $72 million, and net income from $400,000 to $572,000. After 1969 the rate of acquisitions intensified.[21]

With 25 percent of the outstanding shares, the Caisse de dépôt et placement du Québec had become the principal shareholder of Couvrette & Provost. The directors and officers of the company were next, with 20.5 percent, followed by institutions such as La Sauvegarde, the Bank Canadian National, Corporation Prêt et Revenu, Imperial Life, Empire Life, Sun Life, Les Prévoyants, Alliance and La Laurentienne.

About this time, two Ontario companies with designs on the Quebec market approached in turn Lamontagne, Denault and Couvrette & Provost. Each was a giant in its own right. One was Loeb, from Ottawa, which had already bought out Painchaud in Montreal; Armstrong, in Sherbrooke and Drouin in Amos. The other was the Oshawa Group from Toronto, which had acquired Shop and Save (IGA), later to become Hudon & Deaudelin, in Montreal. But Antoine Turmel, President of Denault of Sherbrooke, had other plans. He envisaged a group of strictly Quebec owned companies. In the fall of 1968, he began the negotiations that would lead to the creation of Provigo.

The JAT Stores

It was in the Saguenay/Lac-Saint-Jean area, with the initiatives of Joseph-Arthur Tremblay and Jean-Louis Lamontagne, that the Provigo pioneers had acquired their knowledge and expertise in the retail food business.

In 1933, Joseph-Arthur Tremblay opened his first grocery store in Jonquière. His father, a grocer himself, had been forced to close his business in 1929 because of the Crash.

Borrowing 500 dollars with the endorsement of five backers, Joseph-Arthur Tremblay started Le Vieux Poste directly across from a Dominion store, which ruled the roost in the area. Even today, Joseph-Arthur Tremblay recalls vividly the opening of his first store. He was twenty years old and going into business for himself.

To establish a clientele, he went to the fussiest and most prominent people in town. Each morning, he would set off on his bike at eight o'clock to take their orders, which he would deliver well before noon.

J.-A. Tremblay had a plan. If these families shopped at his store, the whole town would soon hear of it and he would become more popular than Dominion. A few years later, his plan had been so successful that he bought two Dominion stores, one in Kénogami, the other in Chicoutimi. In those end-of-Depression days, J.-A. Tremblay worked hard to make ends meet, all the more since his customers often had nothing but tokens to pay with. Commonly referred to as *pitons*, these tokens were distributed to the unemployed so they could at least buy the essentials. They could not be deposited in the bank; what's more, merchants who accepted them could use them only to pay their municipal taxes. Luckily, if he had a surplus, he could resell them at a ten percent loss to people who would then use them to pay their own taxes and gain the discount.

In 1945, fire swept through part of Jonquière, including Joseph-Arthur Tremblay's store. Miraculously, the cellar and cold room, which contained much merchandise, were spared any damage. J.-A. Tremblay credits

Saint Joseph, to whom he was always greatly devoted, with the miracle. The store was rebuilt, greatly expanded and modernized.

In 1943, J.-A. Tremblay had started to open new grocery stores. The second of these was named Marché St-Hubert and the third, Marché Ste-Famille. When he opened his fourth business, J.-A. Tremblay, at the suggestion of a relative, decided to group them under a single banner with his initials, JAT, serving as the new name.

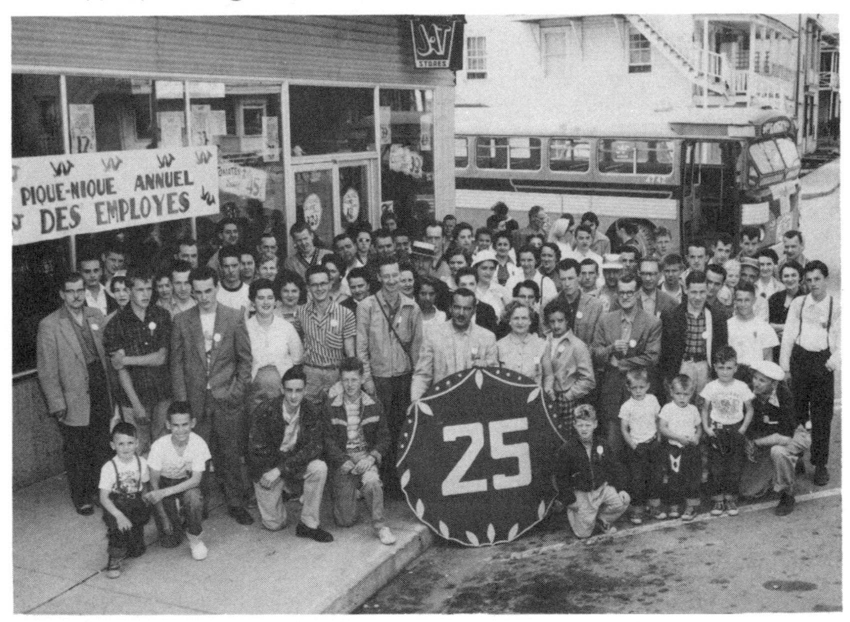

JAT employees off to the annual company picnic.

In 1964, the JAT chain of stores operated 27 establishments in Jonquière, Kénogami, Chicoutimi, Bagotville, Grande-Baie, Dolbeau, Alma and the surrounding areas. By today's standards the outlets were certainly small, but they were well laid out by a man who had selected competent, responsible associates.[22] Best of all, the stores were profitable.

From the outset, J.-A. Tremblay was enthusiastic about marketing; he was very strict about anything concerning the operation and management of his stores. He was demanding with his staff and delegated responsibilities widely. Frequent meetings enabled him to keep an eye on the performance of each independently managed store and determine whether it had attained its objectives.

JAT also engaged in wholesale operations. In 1951, along with some other merchants, J.-A. Tremblay had founded Grosserie Centrale Inc. to serve his own and other stores in the region. Later came the opening of Jonquière Fruits. Both these businesses officially became subsidiaries when the company was incorporated in 1964.

From 1955 to 1964, the combined sales of JAT and its subsidiaries rose from $1.4 million to nearly $8.8 million, while income climbed from $18,673 to $145,286. It was at that point that J.-A. Tremblay started discussing a possible merger with Jean-Louis Lamontagne.

Jean-Louis Lamontagne

Joseph-Arthur Tremblay's business had been in operation for nearly twenty years when Jean-Louis Lamontagne opened his first grocery store in Saint-Félicien. The year was 1951. The new store was located right across from his parents' home.

Money was no problem; he had spent five years working in the demolition of military camps in Newfoundland and in the Maritimes. Although he knew nothing about the grocery business, Jean-Louis Lamontagne had a great entrepreneurial sense. In the demolition industry, he had quickly risen from employee to foreman and, eventually, partner.

No sooner had he bought his first grocery store than a nearby competitor offered him his. Jean-Louis accepted without hesitation. He was now the proud owner of two stores. To learn about the business, he visited several grocery stores, including some Steinberg outlets in Montreal. In premises no bigger than 1,000 square feet, he decided to set up a self-service system with separate departments for groceries, produce and meat.

During renovations to his first store, J.-L. Lamontagne continued to operate temporarily from the other, which he planned to close as soon as he was ready to venture forth in a big way. The first week, his sales came to $900; the first year brought in scarcely more than $125,000. But he had learned, along with his sister Germaine, how to operate his store, carry out purchasing, put out posters and circulars and, above all, respond to his customers' needs. Customer satisfaction would remain his primary goal throughout a long and productive career.

To satisfy a small number of customers, J.-L. Lamontagne would not hesitate to split a case of spinach, mushrooms or exotic products between his stores, or even to buy fancy fruit and vegetables from Steinberg stores at retail prices to satisfy his clientele. These visits would give him the opportunity to pick up new ideas as well.

At first he gave credit but once he discovered that people were abusing this privilege, he stopped the practice. As a result, he was able to offer his customers better prices, particularly on specials.

Jean-Louis Lamontagne was a born entrepreneur. In 1952, he built a store in Chibougamau before anyone had taken up permanent residence. The building provided living quarters for his manager, in addition to being used for community activities, meetings and even church services. His customers consisted of engineers, prospectors, drillers, lumberjacks and labourers who literally came out of the surrounding woods. Instead of having to rely on a limited selection of food supplies flown in by plane irregularly, these people could now stock up on food at their convenience. Business was so immediate and brisk that two weeks after opening, the store required four additional employees.

Soon a new store had to be built. This one had two storeys and a cellar with a total area of 6,000 square feet. Built 150 miles from the nearest town, the store took in $46,000 a week in 1956, the equivalent of some $365,000 in 1988. For a single store, even in Quebec City or Montreal, these sales figures were extraordinary.

After Chibougamau came Chapais, followed by Dolbeau, then a second store in Saint-Félicien where he also operated a small modern warehouse. Jean-Louis Lamontagne was not deterred by distances. He set up stores in Sept-Iles, Gagnon and Schefferville, which seemed like the ends of the earth in those days.

In 1959, through his affiliation with Quebec Catering Ltd., he held a minority interest in Lamontagne Co., which had been created specifically to serve the vast mining and hydroelectric development sites in Quebec. J.-L. Lamontagne Ltd., incorporated in 1955, operated and managed this company, which would become a wholly owned subsidiary in 1961.

Given the company's growth, it was imperative to organize the wholesale business along professional lines. In 1956, J.-L. Lamontagne formed a partnership with Gérard Dumais (who had been J.-A. Tremblay's partner in Grosserie Centrale) to create Gérard Dumais Ltée, a food wholesaler. Although he controlled the company, he settled for a minority interest to keep separate, in the eyes of the independent grocers he was serving in the region, the wholesale business from the Lamontagne grocery stores. Gérard Dumais then organized a group of independent grocers known under the name Magasins Idéals.

The traditional blessing of a new Lamontagne store.

Jean-Louis Lamontagne was not only an entrepreneur, he was also an innovator. He achieved his success in remote centres by being able to sell perishable foodstuffs such as fresh fruit and vegetables, and fresh meat, a first for those distant regions.

Nothing could daunt Jean-Louis Lamontagne. He would go all the way to Quebec City or Montreal to obtain fresh products, sleeping in his truck if he had to. Before there was a direct route to Sept-Iles, he had a special trailer outfitted with separate compartments for frozen products, meat, produce, canned goods and dried food. Each compartment was kept at the required temperature, summer and winter; the one that kept things cool in summer protected them from freezing in winter. The trailer had to travel by road, railway and ship to reach its destination. Sept-Iles could enjoy the same food products as did Saint-Félicien or Montreal.

In Chicoutimi-Nord, J.-L. Lamontagne built a supermarket which, in 1962, was said to be the most modern in Quebec. It had skylights, product islands, and featured many marketing innovations. There he implemented ideas he had gathered from the Supermarket Institute of America or from competitors, not only in the region but also in Montreal and the United States.[23]

In 1961, needing money to finance expansion, he was persuaded by Jacques Melançon, as others had been before him, to become a public company. To that end, Jean-Paul W. Ostiguy and Guy L. Hudon, of Morgan, Ostiguy & Hudon, a Montreal brokerage firm, issued $640,000 worth of Series A first-mortgage bonds with subscription rights to Class A shares. The successor to existing companies, Lamontagne Limitée was incorporated on July 20, 1961.

At the time, Jean-Louis Lamontagne owned or controlled the company's 35,000 Class B shares. As of November 1961, Lamontagne's Class A shares were listed on the Canadian Stock Exchange.

Through its subsidiary, Gérard Dumais, Lamontagne did some wholesale business. But the wholesale aspect of the company assumed greater importance with the acquisition of Côté & Boivin & Co. of Chicoutimi.

Côté & Boivin, in which the prominent Murdoch family held 49 percent of the shares, dealt in both hardware and food. The Giroux estate, which controlled the company, put up its 51 percent of the shares for auction to liquidate its interest.

Jean-Louis Lamontagne studied the balance sheets, and the financial and operating statements of Côté & Boivin. Although the company was not very profitable, he quickly realized that it had considerable liquidity. Jean-Louis Lamontagne offered $985,000 for the shares; as the only bidder he became partners with the Murdochs.

Soon after, they split the business in two. Lamontagne let the Murdochs have the hardware side, which held little interest for him, and kept the food sector that he now fully owned.[24]

By selling bonds from the Côté & Boivin portfolio, Jean-Louis Lamontagne raised the money needed to build a modern warehouse in Chicoutimi; this enabled his company to consolidate its wholesale operations.

However, Jean-Louis Lamontagne had overreached himself; the warehouse was far too big for his needs. In addition to his own wholesale operations, there was more than enough space to accommodate those of J.-A. Tremblay. The subsequent negotiations between Lamontagne and Tremblay would eventually lead to the creation of the second company in the group of Provigo pioneers.

A Marriage of Interests

Even the combined size of the Saguenay and Lac-Saint-Jean regions was not big enough for two food kings.

When Jean-Louis Lamontagne set up his large modern warehouse in Chicoutimi, after he had opened his style-setting supermarket in Chicoutimi-Nord, he was encroaching on Joseph-Arthur Tremblay's territory. A far-sighted man, Lamontagne realized that he needed the JAT stores if his wholesale operations were soon to become profitable.

Well aware of these complications, J.-A. Tremblay could afford to be demanding during the negotiations that preceded the merger of the two companies. When, for instance, the shares of Lamontagne Limitée and those of JAT (1964) Limitée were exchanged to divide control of Lamontagne Limitée down the middle, Tremblay demanded an extra $500,000 in cash for the JAT stores' goodwill.

The two men were poles apart in their attitudes and behaviour as well as in the way they conducted their businesses. But together they managed to build a thriving new enterprise.

Finalized in the fall of 1964, the merger provided the opportunity to tie up loose ends. The operations of L.B. Gagnon & Cie of Chicoutimi, a competing wholesaler that had just been bought out, were integrated into the new company. Within a year, Lamontagne Limitée sales shot up from $13.8 million to $33.3 million. Now the company was poised to expand.

Expansion to Quebec City

In 1963, Lamontagne Limitée had acquired J.B.E. Letellier Inc., a Quebec City food wholesaler. For Lamontagne this was a first step towards becoming the largest wholesaler in the Capital. Soon after, Lamontagne bought out Rioux & Pettigrew Limitée, another Quebec City wholesaler.

In 1965, the construction of a new warehouse was begun in Quebec City to accommodate the combined operations of the two acquired companies, which had been merged under the name Pettigrew & Letellier Ltée.[25]

There were more acquisitions to come. In 1967, Lamontagne acquired Wilfrid Proulx Inc., a Montmagny wholesaler, followed by Alimentation Centrale Ltée, a Jonquière wholesaler, and, in 1968, Société Provinciale des Épiciers, a cooperative of grocers in Quebec City.

In its last annual report published August 22, 1969, Lamontagne reported sales of $58.2 million for the year ended April 26. Net income for the year stood at $505,772. Quite a feat for a company that had managed only $7.6 million eight years earlier!

So when Jean-Louis Lamontagne met with Antoine Turmel and

René Provost, who advocated the merger which is the basis of Provigo, he could boast a well established, solid company. Lamontagne had previously convinced his partner, Joseph-Arthur Tremblay, of the good sense of the merger. The two associates and collaborators had very different personalities and did not always see things the same way. But they understood and complemented each other. Judging by the results, they certainly knew how to get ahead in business.

Denault Limitée

The story of Denault Limitée, the Sherbrooke-based partner in what was to become Provigo, is somewhat different from that of the first two companies. Antoine Turmel did not found his own company. Rather he bought a small concern on October 2, 1945, at the age of twenty seven, with two associates, Jacques Lagassé, a notary, and Ovila Pinard, a grocer. All were Sherbrooke residents. Among them, they raised the $18,000 needed to acquire the food wholesale business of Denault Limitée owned by Sinaï Perras, a former tobacco and confectionery distributor. The business was neither very large nor very prosperous; annual sales were in the vicinity of $400,000. By the time of the 1969 merger, they would reach $52 million.

Antoine Turmel had first become acquainted with the food business during his bookkeeping days with Genest, Nadeau Co. Ltd., a Sherbrooke wholesaler where he had started working at the age of sixteen as a $5-a-week clerk.

Despite the Depression and financial contributions to his family, Antoine Turmel managed to save three or four thousand dollars which he invested in a shop that made wooden toys. Unfortunately, the books were not kept up to date, the shop was poorly organized, production inadequate and the operating costs underestimated. Turmel tried to save the situation but in the end he had to give up the business. His fortune had vanished.

From this setback, Antoine Turmel learned that balance sheets and financial statements should always be carefully examined, as well as kept up to date and audited. From then on, he would test the ground before investing in a company. He had learned his lesson. It must have been at that time that he developed his bottom-line mania, focusing on clear and accurate results. These would remain his guiding principles.

At Denault, Antoine Turmel focused on productivity. Salesmen received a commission rather than a salary. Order assemblers and delivery drivers were paid by the piece. This was a clever, unusual system in the food distribution business. Each unit and department was expected to turn a profit.

To foster team spirit, he sold a number of Denault shares to the retail grocers who bought from him. To these shareholders, he proposed an advantageous supply formula. For their benefit he introduced the "cost plus" formula; that is, he sold them goods at cost plus 3 percent. Those grocers who were not shareholders paid between 7 and 11 percent, the usual going rate.

Antoine Turmel had principles but he knew how to adapt to change. In later years, he had to reassess this pricing formula to counter the competition from G.T. Armstrong & Sons Ltd., a Sherbrooke wholesaler who had the IGA franchise in that region. Ironically, this competitor, who had been bought out by M. Loeb, Limited in 1964, would later become part of Provigo.

In the early 50s, Antoine Turmel lost no time in recruiting such competent men as Gaston Roy who was in charge of developing voluntary groups. After studying the franchise formulas used by IGA, Red and White, Clover Farm and others, Gaston Roy adaptated them to the conditions specific to Denault. The result was a more flexible system, such as that used by the Marchés Suprême outlets, which obviated the need to pay royalty fees continually to foreign franchisers. Later came the Alouette group, among others.

For the sake of efficiency, Antoine Turmel was once again among the first in Quebec to have a one-storey warehouse with a continuous chain conveyor and to acquire an IBM computer. In 1959, he entrusted Jean Jutras, the first university graduate to work for Denault, with designing the integrated system required by the company.[26]

An ambitious man, Antoine Turmel set out to prove that francophone entrepreneurs were not restricted to small businesses. In 1960, when the brokerage firm of Morgan, Ostiguy & Hudon approached him to organize the financing of a future development, he consulted financial advisor Jacques Melançon, who had also collaborated with Couvrette & Provost and with Lamontagne. It was with Denault in 1961 that the impetus for the three companies (Denault, Lamontagne and Couvrette & Provost) to go public originated.

Before committing himself, however, Antoine Turmel took a course in finance and securities at Université Laval to learn the financial world's language and how to choose the method of financing best suited to his company.

Denault limitée in action, showing the Suprême sign and logo adopted by one of the first Quebec group of grocers, established by Denault.

Once the analysis was completed and after several months of negotiations, plans were made for a $500,000 bond issue with share rights. At the same time, the shares owned by client retail grocers were split and traded for shares identical to those offered to subscribers. As a result, those merchants who had put their trust in Antoine Turmel found themselves with shares listed on the Canadian Stock Exchange and the opportunity to make substantial capital gains.

Antoine Turmel was dedicated to sound management, good return on invested capital and judicious use of earnings. What interested him most was the bottom line.[27] Above all, he valued his credibility. He wanted shareholders to make a decent profit and enjoy fair dividends based on income earned.

The Acquisitions

When Denault went public in 1961, its sales had climbed to $9 million. Although it had been nurtured along rather conservative lines, the company's growth had been steady. It had developed its banner program carefully and had established an interesting clientele. It had also created Les Placements Denault, a subsidiary in charge of financing affiliated retailers who needed assistance to pursue their business development.

In May 1964, Denault bought all the shares of Maurice Chevalier Inc. of Trois-Rivières, the largest food wholesaler in the St-Maurice region. The territory served by Maurice Chevalier was just north of the area supplied by Denault from its Sherbrooke facilities.

Despite the eighty miles distance between the two centres of operations, the administrative work was done in Sherbrooke via computer relayed data. An innovation in every sense, the system was used as a model by Bell Canada; it was the pride of Antoine Turmel and Jean Jutras. Denault was one of the first companies bold enough to venture into advanced telecommunications.

To Antoine Turmel, the challenge was clear: "The wholesale grocery business will be dominated, in the future, by a small number of large operators with ample financial resources. These wholesalers will be able to help the retailers compete and take business away from the corporate chains by offering them, with the help of highly qualified field staff, a full range of services along with specialized technical know-how."[28] The future would prove him right.

During 1965, Denault acquired in succession three food wholesalers: The Dealers' Supply Co. Ltd. of Granby, Sylvestre & Fils Inc. of Saint-Hyacinthe, and Rheault & Frères Cie Ltée of Victoriaville. Several operations were consolidated and obsolete warehouses closed.[29]

In 1966, Denault bought Jos. H. Giguère Reg'd of Louiseville; in 1967, E.U. Limitée of Quebec City and Denault (Thetford Mines) Limitée of Thetford Mines; in 1968, J.A. Giroux & Fils inc. of Scott Jonction and Nadeau & Frères Limitée of Dosquet.

With the acquisition of E.U. in Quebec City, Antoine Turmel was more or less entering Lamontagne territory. Apart from the Quebec City region, he also had the capacity to serve a part of the North Shore, including Sept-Iles and Chibougamau, and several sectors in the Saguenay and Lac-Saint-Jean area. As well, in Trois-Rivières and Saint-Hyacinthe, he had penetrated into Couvrette & Provost territory. At times, competition can bring people together.

During 1969, Denault sales topped the $51.9-million mark, or 130 times the level of the first year of operation in 1945. Net income for 1969 reached $559,701.

But Denault was not only a fast-growing company, it was also a testing ground for Antoine Turmel, who fine tuned the management methods he would later apply at Provigo. Not only was Turmel an innovator in applied business technologies, he also had the vision to recruit exceptional people.[30]

Appendix

Purpose of Issue

Mr. Bernard Couvrette, who has been the President of the Company since its inception, has decided to reduce his business activities after thirty five years in the food wholesale business. In order to avoid estate problems, Mr. Bernard Couvrette, together with his brother, Mr. Jacques Couvrette, a director of the Company, and his sister, Mrs. Claire Couvrette-Hardy, have decided to sell their holdings of Class "B" shares of the Company owned by their family company, Les Entreprises Couvrette Ltée.

This sale has provided the opportunity of converting Couvrette & Provost Ltée into a truly public company with only one class of shares; the following steps have been taken:

a) A new company called Couprov Inc. was established. Its sole purpose was to purchase all the outstanding 500,000 class "B" shares from the Couvrette and the Provost families, to convert these, on a share for share basis, into no par value common shares, and then to resell some to the investing public generally, Messrs. René, Ernest and Roland Provost acquiring, however, 100,000 of these 500,000 converted shares.

b) A general meeting of class "A" and class "B" shareholders was held on August 8, 1967 and the shareholders approved the change in the capitalization.

On conclusion of the sale, Couprov Inc. will be liquidated. As the shares offered are outstanding shares, Couvrette & Provost Ltée will not receive any part of the proceeds.

Notes

1. Author of *Chronologie des épiciers en gros et des détaillants au Québec*, (A history of wholesale and retail grocers in Quebec), published in 1982 by the Association des Épiciers en Gros du Québec.
2. Beer was exempted.
3. Successors in 1900 to Hudon and Hamelin whose origins go back to 1842.
4. Their extremely small premises were on Bonsecours Street in Old Montreal.
5. Robert Letendre, Robert Perron, Jean Lamothe, Jean-Louis Rameau and Yvon Meunier.
6. J. Melançon and A. Boisvert participated in organizing the future Couvrette and Provost, one of the Provigo founding companies.
7. Their paternal grandfather, Norbert Provost, ran a general store in Saint-Gabriel-de-Brandon, while their maternal grandfather, Janvier Jasmin, operated a grocery store in the Saint-Henri/Sainte-Cunégonde district of Montreal. The family lived above the store run by their father, J.O. Provost, in Montreal's Saint-Jacques parish.
8. René Provost was President of the group for several years. Jean-Guy Deaudelin was Secretary and Roger Messier, of Richelieu, Treasurer. Léopold Pigeon looked after negotiations and relations with suppliers.
9. On that occasion, René Provost became better acquainted with Antoine Turmel and Gaston Roy, two senior executives from Denault.
10. These territories were served by the well-respected brokerage firm of Émile Gauthier & Fils in Quebec City.
11. J.H. Lamarche ceased operations in 1971, while Laviolette & Brosseau was acquired by Couvrette & Provost in April 1964.
12. Marcel Caron, C.A., of Clarkson Gordon, was both accounting advisor and auditor for the future company. Notary Lionel Leroux and solicitors Antoine and Guillaume Geoffrion provided legal advice. The underwriters were L.G. Beaubien & Cie, Maison Bienvenu, and McDougall and Christmas.
13. The Presto outlets introduced by Jacques Couvrette in 1961 have proliferated. In 1988, the network of self-service warehouses operated by the Provigo group comprised 67 centres, 30 in Quebec alone.
14. Jean-Louis Lamontagne would later participate in the creation of Provigo.
15. Loeb would be acquired by Provigo in 1977.
16. Which later became the National Bank of Canada after a merger with the Provincial Bank of Canada.
17. This plan was developed by Dominik Dlouhy, a member of the Board of Couvrette & Provost and President of Maison Bienvenu.

18. This capital stock structure would later make it easier for the three original Provigo companies to merge by means of an exchange of shares.
19. Appendix to this chapter contains an excerpt of the offering's "Purpose of Issue."
20. He held this position until 1976.
21. Couvrette & Provost took over Marchands Loyal and A.R. Cadieux, two Hawkesbury area companies, as well as Joliette Wholesale inc. of Joliette, and P. D'Aoust Limited of Ottawa. Owned by the Cholette family and directed by Philippe Cholette, P. D'Aoust was a well-known wholesale grocer in the Quebec Ottawa Valley region. Next came the acquisition of Beau Fruit, of Montreal, specialists in fresh fruit and vegetables and particularly frozen products.
22. Joseph-Arthur Tremblay was always ably assisted in his business by his wife Laurette and later his sons, particularly Gaby. In addition, several of his collaborators, including Gérard Tremblay and Alfred Martel, would later play a key role with Provigo.
23. At the time, Jean-Louis Lamontagne recruited such collaborators as Guy Lessard and Roland Ouellet, who later were to hold key positions at Provigo.
24. On that occasion, Yvon Deschênes, who was working at Côté & Boivin, joined the Lamontagne team. He would eventually become an important figure at Provigo.
25. Lamontagne Limitée then consisted of the wholesale grocery distribution centres of Côté & Boivin & Cie of Chicoutimi, Lamontagne Co. of Sept-Iles, Pettigrew & Letellier of Quebec City, the Vito cash & carry warehouses (the equivalent of the Couvrette & Provost Presto outlets) of Chicoutimi, Jonquière and Roberval, Jonquière Fruits, a produce wholesaler in Jonquière, the JAT stores in the Saguenay/Lac-Saint-Jean area, the Lamontagne markets in the Abitibi and North Shore regions, as well as the affiliated Trans Kebec, Normandie, Laval and Idéal grocery stores.
26. Thirty years later, Jean Jutras was Corporate Director, Administration, for Provigo Inc. and is now General Manager of Provigo's International Finance B.V.
27. He frequently used the expression throughout his career.
28. Excerpt from the 1964 Denault Annual Report.
29. It was in Saint-Hyacinthe that Antoine Turmel discovered Raoul Courtois, one of his most esteemed collaborators, first at Denault then at Provigo.
30. Gaston Roy, his right arm, was later joined by other collaborators. In addition to Jean Jutras were Jacques Mercier, Jacques Charland, Claude Perreault and Pierre Lessard, all of whom would later work at Provigo.

CHAPTER FOUR

1961: THE TRUE BEGINNING

The influence of the Quiet Revolution is a vital element in the story of the men who built Provigo. It was this deep rooted desire for a different society which prompted them to realize that, together, Quebeckers were capable of great things. In many ways, the Quiet Revolution was the impetus toward a new destiny for Quebec.

With the Quiet Revolution, Quebec joined the twentieth century. During that period, everything was reexamined. Swift progress was made; reforms abounded. *La Belle Province* was shedding its inferiority complex.

Primarily political in nature, the changes that took place affected the complete spectrum of economic, social, cultural and even religious activities. An entire people was growing conscious of its vast potential and taking charge of its future. From that era emerged a new distribution of responsibilities among government, groups and individuals. Every segment of society felt the winds of change that would still be blowing long after the first five or six years of what has come to be known as the Quiet Revolution.

On the economic front, the most striking result of the Quiet Revolution was the nationalization of electric power in 1963; this permanently changed the mission of Hydro-Québec. The utility was embraced as a symbol of success and pride. In 1965 the Caisse de dépôt et placement du Québec was created and rapidly became an important source of funds for Quebec companies seeking capital to finance their expansion. Quebec's new political rallying cry, *Maître chez nous* (Masters in our own house), must have struck a chord in the Provigo pioneers in 1961, for that was the year they decided to close ranks against the invasion of the food sector by foreign chains.

Each acting on his own but virtually at the same time and essentially for the same reasons, the pioneers decided to turn their businesses into public companies. They had learned the necessity of broader ownership with its discipline of reporting company activities and financial results to shareholders.

This first step was essential to the 1969 merger which would give rise to the giant we know today as Provigo.

In 1961 the proceeds from the bonds and shares issued by the funding companies — Couvrette & Provost, Denault and Lamontagne — had raised the capital needed for expansion. The three companies had built modern warehouses, acquired several wholesale grocery businesses and enlarged their territories.

Financial analysts and brokers were quick to realize the advantages of an eventual merger involving the three companies. A number of them had seen it coming even before the heads of the three companies had begun discussing the possibility.

The stage was set and the story ready to unfold. All three players were dynamic, prosperous, and eager to break new ground. In any event, they had already started invading one another's territory.

In 1967, Jean-Louis Lamontagne had tried to acquire control of Couvrette & Provost, but it was René Provost who had bought out the shares held by the Couvrette family. Lamontagne had also declared his intention to buy Antoine Turmel's business, only to be told that it was not for sale. In fact, quite the opposite was true; Denault was ready and willing to buy Lamontagne, which was not for sale either.

Each of the three entrepreneurs was intent on keeping his own business and acquiring others. Antoine Turmel tried in vain to buy Shop & Save Limited, which in 1955 had acquired the interests of Hudon & Orsali Limitée as well as the IGA franchise for nearly all of Quebec with the exception of the Sherbrooke and Abitibi areas. In 1969, Shop & Save would become the property of the Toronto based Oshawa Group.

As neither Couvrette & Provost, nor Lamontagne, nor Denault was for sale, the players started thinking that there might be another way to pursue expansion and, most of all, put an end to the overtures of outside

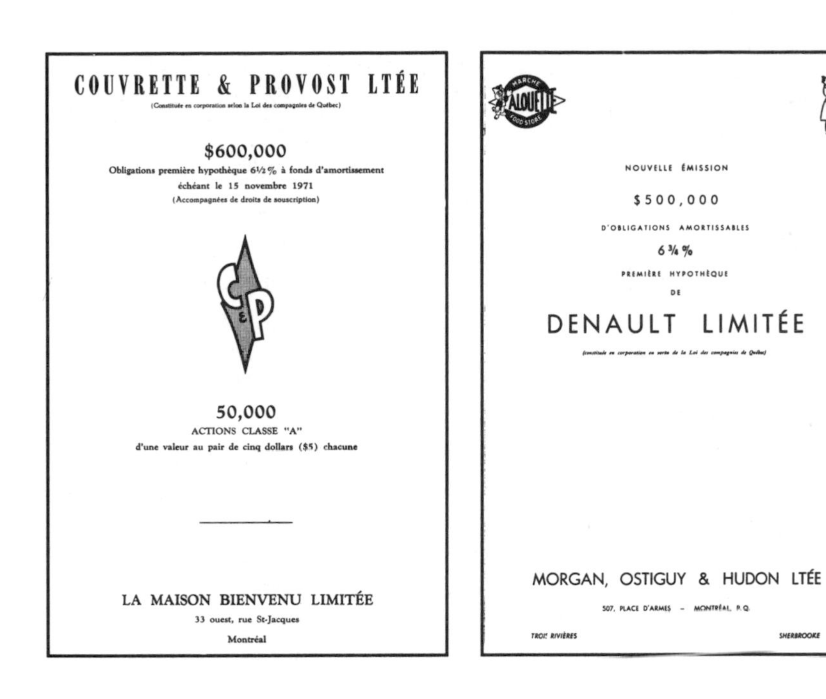

COUVRETTE & PROVOST LTÉE

(Constituée en corporation selon la Loi des compagnies de Québec)

$600,000

Obligations première hypothèque 6½% à fonds d'amortissement

échéant le 15 novembre 1971

(Accompagnées de droits de souscription)

50,000

ACTIONS CLASSE "A"

d'une valeur au pair de cinq dollars ($5) chacune

LA MAISON BIENVENU LIMITÉE

33 ouest, rue St-Jacques

Montréal

NOUVELLE ÉMISSION

$500,000

D'OBLIGATIONS AMORTISSABLES

6¾%

PREMIÈRE HYPOTHÈQUE

DE

DENAULT LIMITÉE

(constituée en corporation en vertu de la Loi des compagnies de Québec)

MORGAN, OSTIGUY & HUDON LTÉE

507, PLACE D'ARMES - MONTRÉAL, P.Q.

TROIS RIVIÈRES SHERBROOKE

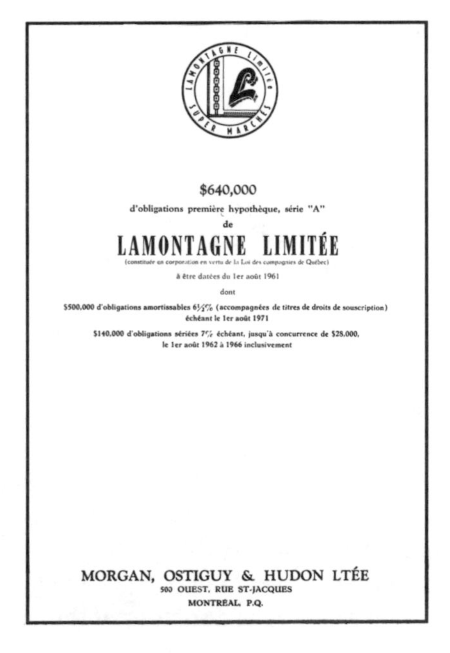

$640,000

d'obligations première hypothèque, série "A"

de

LAMONTAGNE LIMITÉE

(constituée en corporation en vertu de la Loi des compagnies de Québec)

à être datées du 1er août 1961

dont

$500,000 d'obligations amortissables 6½% (accompagnées de titres de droits de souscription)
échéant le 1er août 1971

$140,000 d'obligations sériées 7% échéant, jusqu'à concurrence de $28,000,
le 1er août 1962 à 1966 inclusivement

MORGAN, OSTIGUY & HUDON LTÉE
500 OUEST, RUE ST-JACQUES
MONTRÉAL, P.Q.

The 1961 prospectuses for the first public issues.

entrepreneurs, particularly the Oshawa Group and Loeb, who were determined to acquire the wholesale businesses developed by the three Quebec companies.

Large chains, especially in urban centres, were steadily increasing their market share. They could be found in strategic locations, particularly in shopping centres, which were fast becoming part of the suburban and regional landscape. Furthermore, Loeb and the Oshawa Group were increasing their presence in certain Quebec markets. Montreal was the main target. Also affected, although to a lesser extent, were the Sherbrooke, St-Maurice and Quebec City regions as well as the Saguenay/Lac-Saint-Jean area.

More than ever, the merger that everyone had been contemplating since 1961 seemed the most appropriate response to the increased competition. In the fall of 1968, Antoine Turmel took the opportunity of a trip to Montreal, where he was to attend a board meeting of the Provincial Bank,[1] to sit down and discuss the situation with René Provost.

Since both Couvrette & Provost and Denault belonged to the Montreal Grocery Buying Group, René Provost expected a run-of-the-mill business meeting. Not one to beat around the bush, Antoine Turmel informed René Provost of Denault's expansion plans with the emphasis on entering the Montreal market. He then went on to discuss the coexistence of Couvrette & Provost and Denault in the Trois-Rivières market, and also mentioned E.U. Limitée of Quebec City, which he had bought in 1967. Getting straight to the point, he asserted that his and René Provost's businesses, which were doing very well separately, would do even better together. With increased volume, greater purchasing power, greater concentration of skills and human resources, exchange of information and experience, and so on, the combined operations could more easily face changing market conditions and increased competition.

René Provost was already thinking along the same lines as Antoine Turmel. He knew that the Montreal market was even more threatened than Sherbrooke's.

After carefully thinking through the idea and making a few provisional calculations of the mutual benefits likely to stem from an association between the two companies, Antoine Turmel and René Provost agreed to disclose the project to their closest colleagues and submit the idea of a merger to their respective boards of directors. If the project was deemed interesting, they would request a mandate to continue the discussions with a view to negotiating the terms of a possible agreement.

Early in 1969, the two Presidents established the basic terms for a merger between Couvrette & Provost and Denault.[2]

Once submitted to the Directors and accepted by the Board of each company, these preliminary arrangements led to a formal letter of agreement, which was signed on February 25, 1969.

On March 1, a joint press release was issued by Antoine Turmel and René Provost to announce that an agreement to merge had been reached. According to the agreement, the shareholders of Denault were to be offered two common shares of Couvrette & Provost for each of their Class A or Class B shares.

The deal had been struck without Jean-Louis Lamontagne. Once he learned of the proposed merger, he refused to be left out. A fire at the Quebec City warehouse of E.U. Limitée, a subsidiary of Denault, gave Lamontagne the opportunity he needed to enter the negotiations.

Lamontagne owned a large, modern warehouse in Quebec City which could also accommodate the operations of E.U. Limitée. For Denault, it would be the solution to an urgent problem. For Lamontagne, this arrangement was not only a way to restore a money-losing warehouse to profitability, it also gave him a good argument for the integration of his company into the merger agreement.

But Antoine Turmel was reluctant to enter into a three-way partnership. This would mean starting all over again. Getting two parties to see eye to eye had been difficult enough; with three-sided discussions there would be no end of technical details and procedures to be sorted out.

Given his earlier designs on both Couvrette & Provost and Denault, Jean-Louis Lamontagne was not about to give up easily on the idea. To let such an opportunity pass him by was out of the question, even if his partner, J.-A. Tremblay, was far from convinced that it was a good deal.

Determined to bring about a three-way merger, Jean-Louis Lamontagne intensified his overtures to Denault and Couvrette & Provost.

Antoine Turmel and René Provost decided to go to Quebec City together in an attempt to convince Jean-Louis Lamontagne that a merger with him would be premature. In their view, it was preferable to let the duo play out its scenario before forming a trio. The purpose of the trip was clear: they would convince Jean-Louis Lamontagne that he should postpone his integration into the new company. As things turned out, it was Lamontagne who convinced them that a three-way merger would be even more beneficial to all parties. Antoine Turmel — more so than René Provost — had been convinced by Lamontagne's arguments. But, in the end, after thoroughly examining the situation, the three men pronounced themselves in favour of a partnership.

On March 25, 1969, a letter of intent co-signed by Antoine Turmel, René Provost, J.-A. Tremblay and Jean-Louis Lamontagne laid down the terms and conditions governing the integration of Lamontagne Limitée into the merger that Turmel and Provost had entered into on February 25.

Notes

1. Now the National Bank of Canada.
2. With the help of Antoine Geoffrion, Réjane Laberge Colas and Claude E. Leduc of the Geoffrion, Prudhomme firm of legal advisors, notary Jacques Lagassé, Marcel Caron, Jérôme Carrière, and subsequently Marcel Camirand of Clarkson Gordon, auditors.

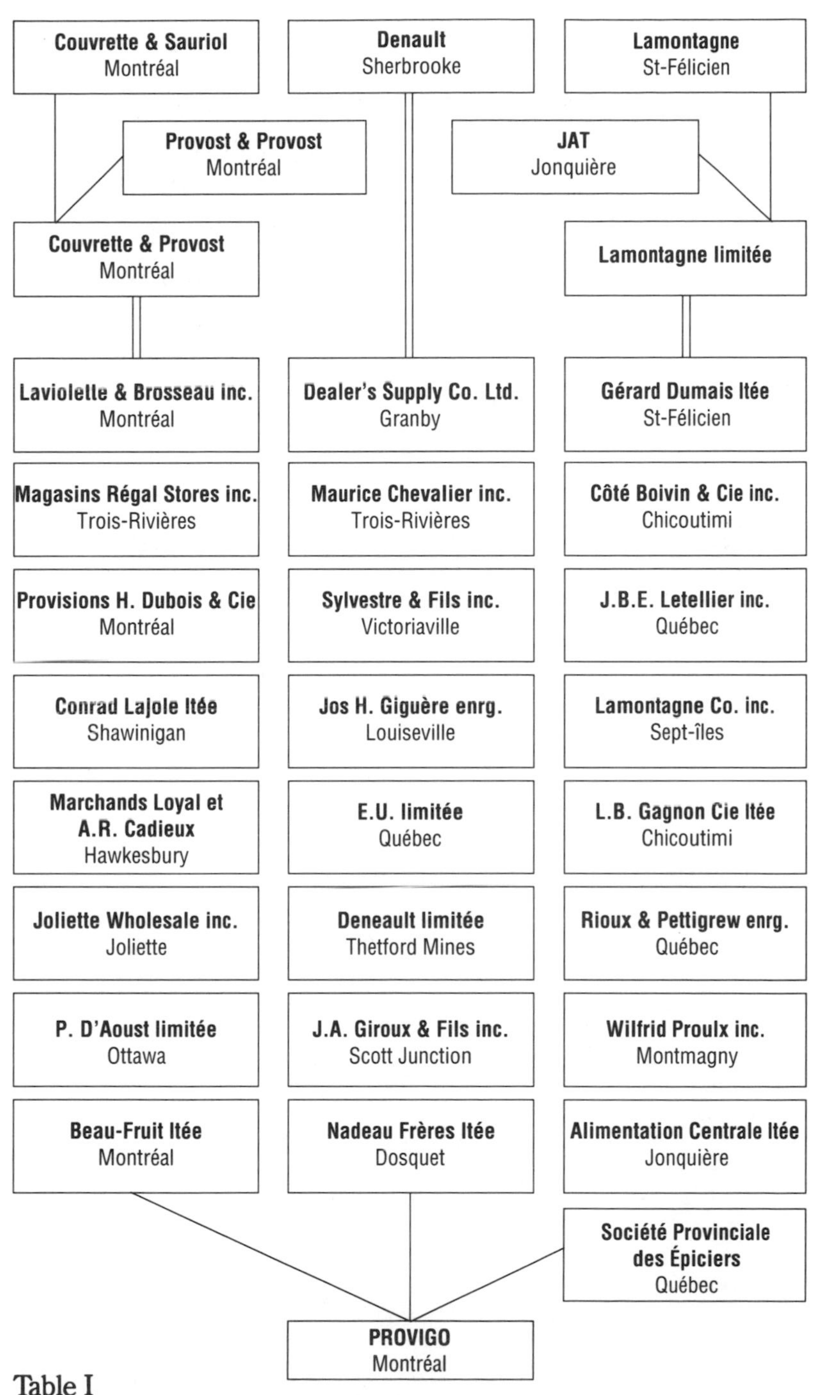

Table I
Provigo: The Pioneers and their Acquisitions (1961-1969)

CHAPTER FIVE

THE 1969 MERGER

The challenges facing Couvrette & Provost, Denault and Lamontagne during the first months of 1969 were considerable. The three companies were attempting to merge separate capital structures, operating methods, sales, profitability levels and human resources. They had to find ways to avoid possible duplications, eliminate self-competition in certain regions, establish new management structures and develop new operational plans. There was much to finalize before the merger could become a reality.

Yet the basics had been worked out in a letter of agreement when Couvrette & Provost Ltée — designated head of the project because of its size, capital structure and reputation — submitted the official offers to the shareholders of Denault Limitée and of Lamontagne Limitée on May 23, 1969.

Details of the Merger Offers

Through its President, René Provost, Couvrette & Provost separately and simultaneously offered to buy all the outstanding shares of the other two companies. Denault shareholders would receive two Couvrette & Provost common shares for every one of their Class A or Class B shares; Lamontagne shareholders would receive five Couvrette & Provost common shares in exchange for seven of their Class A or Class B shares.[1]

In effect, Couvrette & Provost offered 1,067,665 of its shares to

Aucune commission de valeurs mobilières ou organisation similaire au Canada ne s'est de quelque façon prononcée sur les mérites des valeurs offertes par les présentes et toute déclaration à l'effet contraire constitue une infraction.

Les présentes offres ne sont pas et ne doivent, sous aucune condition, être interprétées comme des offres faites à un résident quelconque des Etats-Unis d'Amérique ou de l'un quelconque des territoires ou possessions de ces derniers.

OFFRES

par

COUVRETTE & PROVOST LTÉE

Aux détenteurs
de toutes les actions classe "A" de la valeur au pair de $1 chacune et de toutes les actions classe "B" de la valeur au pair de $1 chacune du capital-actions de

DENAULT LIMITÉE

Aux détenteurs
de toutes les actions classe "A" sans valeur au pair et de toutes les actions classe "B" sans valeur au pair du capital-actions de

LAMONTAGNE LIMITÉE

i) L'offre aux actionnaires de Denault Limitée est:

2 actions ordinaires sans valeur au pair de Couvrette & Provost Ltée pour chacune des actions classe "A" de la valeur au pair de un dollar ($1) de Denault Limitée, et

2 actions ordinaires sans valeur au pair de Couvrette & Provost Ltée pour chacune des actions classe "B" de la valeur au pair de un dollar ($1) de Denault Limitée;

ii) L'offre aux actionnaires de Lamontagne Limitée est:

5 actions ordinaires sans valeur au pair de Couvrette & Provost Ltée pour chaque 7 actions classe "A" sans valeur au pair de Lamontagne Limitée, et

5 actions ordinaires sans valeur au pair de Couvrette & Provost Ltée pour chaque 7 actions classe "B" sans valeur au pair de Lamontagne Limitée.

Ces offres expireront le 27 juin 1969. Couvrette & Provost Ltée se réserve cependant le droit de prolonger la date d'expiration des offres au-delà du 27 juin 1969.

Une des conditions des offres est que Couvrette & Provost Ltée ne sera pas liée, à moins que ne soient déposées en acceptation des offres et non retirées:

i) 90% de toutes les actions classe "A" de la valeur au pair de un dollar ($1) chacune émises et en cours de Denault Limitée, et

90% de toutes les actions classe "B" de la valeur au pair de un dollar ($1) chacune émises et en cours de Denault Limitée;

ii) 90% de toutes les actions classe "A" sans valeur au pair émises et en cours de Lamontagne Limitée, et

90% de toutes les actions classe "B" sans valeur au pair émises et en cours de Lamontagne Limitée.

Couvrette et Provost Ltée se réserve le droit de renoncer à cette condition en totalité ou en partie.

Les offres formelles apparaissent respectivement aux pages 3 et 4, et aux pages 5 et 6 des présentes.

The offers that made the merger possible.

Lamontagne and 1,292,202 to Denault. If things worked out as planned, upon expiry of the bid Couvrette & Provost would have over 2,700 shareholders and more than 3.6 million outstanding shares listed on the Montreal and Toronto stock exchanges.

The advantages of this merger were succinctly described in the Couvrette & Provost annual report for the year ended March 29, 1969: "This larger capitalization should result in a greater and larger trading pattern for the shares, giving thus greater liquidity.

"Numerous programs and services will be combined. Merchandising, computer and information centers, private brands and diversification through horizontal and vertical growth will be possible.

"These are some of the reasons which permit us to foresee the future with great confidence. The joining of forces by the managements, directors and key employees of the three companies will enable the emerging company to play a predominant role in the food business, and to ensure its position as one of the leaders in business and industry in Quebec." So wrote Bernard Couvrette, Chairman of the Board, and René Provost, President of Couvrette & Provost, in their message to the shareholders dated June 16, 1969.

In retrospect, their vision was understated. The future would more than fulfill the expectations of the men at the helm of the three merging companies.

In early June of that year, the Montreal newspapers reported that Couvrette & Provost had garnered over 90 percent of the outstanding shares of the two companies and that the expiry date of the bids had been extended from June 27 to August 15, 1969.

By the end of June, this proportion had risen to 97 percent of the shares of Lamontagne and of Denault. It was announced that 2,300 people were shareholders in Couvrette & Provost and that 3,560,000 common shares were then outstanding. The goal had been achieved.

The Caisse de dépôt et placement du Québec, a major shareholder of the three merged companies, had encouraged and supported the merger project. With 17 percent ownership, it was the only shareholder holding over 10 percent of the common shares.

The Starting Point

In the course of the negotiations preceding the bids, certain arrangements had been concluded with regard to the directors and officers of Denault and Lamontagne.

According to a document dating from the period "the directors of Couvrette have agreed with those of Denault and those of Lamontagne that if the offers are accepted, the directors of the latter two companies will appoint seven directors to the Couvrette Board, which will then be made up of twenty one members." Antoine Turmel was appointed Chairman of the Board, Chief Executive Officer and Chairman of the Executive Committee; René Provost kept the post of President and General Manager; Jean-Louis Lamontagne and J.-Arthur Tremblay became Senior Vice-Presidents. As well, these directors would be members of the Executive Committee, which would comprise six members, two from each of the merged companies. Roland Provost (Vice-President, Institutional Division) and Gaston Roy (Vice-President, Marketing) were the other two members of the Executive Committee.

Other senior executives were to be assessed by food industry experts Daniel Bartz & Associates of Milwaukee.[2] Frank Magee of Philadelphia[3] was called upon to study the rationalization of warehouse and transport operations. The recommendations of these experts were used mainly as a frame of reference for subsequent decisions.

Next came the task of completing the selection of the top management team. From Couvrette & Provost came Ernest Provost, appointed Vice-President, Operations, Warehouse and Traffic; Jacques Couvrette, Vice-President, Cash & Carry Division, Gérard Carrière, General Secretary; and Gilles Brunet, Assistant to the President. The new Vice-President, Sales, was Alfred Martel, who had worked at Lamontagne. Jean Jutras, Data Processing Director, and Pierre H. Lessard, Treasurer and Controller, had both come from Denault.

One of the earliest priorities was to standardize the accounting methods of the three companies, establish coincident fiscal years and guarantee that budget forecasts were consistently formulated throughout the company. The engineer of this delicate task was Pierre H. Lessard, newly appointed Treasurer and Controller. He was the first holder of an MBA to work for the company, a fact in which Antoine Turmel, who had hired him at Denault, took great pride.

The Board of Directors consisted of 21 members (seven from each of the three companies): Marcel Bélanger, Paul Desruisseaux, Claude Genest, Jacques Lagassé, Gaston Roy, Antoine Turmel and George Vilim from Denault; Pierre Bergeron, Jean-Louis Lamontagne, Robert Lamontagne, J.P.W. Ostiguy, Marcel Robert, Guy Tremblay and J.-A. Tremblay

The founders: Antoine Turmel,

René Provost,

Jean-Louis Lamontagne

and J.A. Tremblay.

from Lamontagne; Bernard Couvrette, Jacques Couvrette, Dominik Dlouhy, H.N.R. Jackman, Ernest Provost, René Provost and Roland Provost from Couvrette & Provost.

The first meeting of Provigo's Board of Directors, July 1969.

Officers, executives and directors had to learn to work together efficiently from the start, and somehow forget that until then they had been their own masters. Some found this easier to do than others. Antoine Turmel, for his part, quickly showed that he possessed the leadership abilities long attributed to him. In fact, as Chief Executive Officer, he and his most trusted associates soon took up the reins almost entirely.

The merger, which had been finalized through an exchange of shares in the summer of 1969, quickly became a day-to-day reality. The first fiscal year to include the combined results of the three companies covered 44 weeks, ending January 31, 1970. On an annual basis, sales had reached $202 million, with net income of $1.6 million. Forecasts had targeted $200 million in sales.[4]

In theory, everything the pioneers had set out to do had been accomplished. The three companies had reorganized, restructured, relocated and had even decided to give the newly integrated operations a new name as soon as legal procedures would permit.

In reality, each of the three remained independent in terms of operations and management. And all three were growing steadily.

Notes

1. The offers were to expire June 27, 1969, but the company reserved the right to extend the deadline. One of the conditions stipulated that Couvrette & Provost would not be bound by its bids unless 90 percent of all Class A and Class B shares of Denault, and of Lamontagne, were deposited in acceptance. Couvrette & Provost reserved the right to waive this condition.
2. Daniel Bartz had acted as consultant for Couvrette & Provost and was one of the main consultants for the National American Wholesale Grocers Association.
3. He had in the past worked for both Couvrette & Provost and Lamontagne.
4. For the previous fiscal year, the combined sales of the three companies had totalled $182 million. Those of Denault and of Lamontagne amounted to slightly over $50 million each, and those of Couvrette & Provost exceeded $72 million, for somewhat different fiscal years.

CHAPTER SIX

PROVIGO : FIRST STEPS

The new company had 1,100 employees and 13 warehouses supplying 9,000 retail distributors. All were located in Quebec. To be successful, an organization of this scope and stature requires meticulous planning. The merger between Couvrette & Provost, Denault and Lamontagne had left many people sceptical, if not worried, about the new company's future prospects.

There were few changes during the first year. Couvrette & Provost still looked after the Montreal and Ottawa regions; Denault covered Sherbrooke and Trois-Rivières; Lamontagne served the Quebec City region, as well as the Saguenay/Lac-Saint-Jean and North Shore areas. Regional and subsidiary operations were independent, which "should enhance personal initiative, a sense of responsibility and the projection of each particular division's personality in its midst, with which it will remain identified. Such autonomy should also induce healthy competition between divisions."[1]

Head office, responsible for setting policies and providing general information, was located in the Couvrette & Provost offices on the premises of the Marché Central Métropolitain warehouse in Montreal. It had no more than the bare working essentials. At first, Antoine Turmel and other members of senior management worked there only on a part-time basis, since they were still in charge of operations in the regions. In time, however, these offices became their permanent headquarters.

This was a period of integration, reorganization and restructuring. Many aspects of the company's activities were affected. Nonetheless, the new company did continue to grow, develop and make new acquisitions. The Quebec City warehouse was enlarged to accommodate the operations of E.U. and those of Denault (Dosquet); Cash & Carry outlets were opened in Dolbeau, Lachute and Baie-Comeau.

Around the same time, the Company acquired J.V. Hallé Inc., a major Quebec City produce wholesaler. Through this acquisition, the new company became better acquainted with the perishable sector of the food business, which had become increasingly important to retailers. As well, it was at that time, on November 1, 1969 to be precise, that the first Aux Vraies Aubaines (AVA) store opened in Sherbrooke.

Aux Vraies Aubaines

This "discount store" project was dear to Antoine Turmel.[2] Based on his plans, Aux Vraies Aubaines was a no-frills, warehouse-style store covering a vast area of 20,000 square feet. Customers had to take the merchandise directly from containers. Prices — always the lowest possible — were not stamped on each item but were displayed nearby. There were no specials, no advertising.

Antoine Turmel's strategy called for a 10 percent profit margin; a traditional supermarket would have needed a 20 percent margin to make a reasonable profit.

All store spending was capped. Salaries, for example, could not exceed 3 percent of sales. Antoine Turmel aimed for sales of $40,000 a week, at a time when few independent stores could claim sales of more than $25,000.

When they heard of the new AVA store opening on Wellington Street in Sherbrooke, some Denault customers were angry with this new competition. Antoine Turmel offered them partnerships. They refused. As a result of this new venture, he lost a dozen retailers, who formed the Félix group. Almost immediately, however, the AVA store broke even, and took in some $50,000 in sales per week. Around 1972, that figure had reached $200,000 and several new outlets had sprung up. By 1976, there were seventeen AVA stores and they had become fairly sophisticated compared with the first one.

Corporate Objectives

Antoine Turmel described the objectives of Couvrette & Provost to a gathering of Montreal financial analysts on January 7, 1970, and, a week later, to their Toronto counterparts.[3]

In the first part of his address, he outlined the philosophy of the Company which would soon be known as Provigo. He discussed what we now refer to as corporate culture, and the flexibility which the structure of his new company would need because, as he put it, "it is impossible to predict what distribution patterns will be favoured by consumers in the future."

"It is essential that we be able to switch our operations from one type into another, whether it be from a traditional store to a warehouse store, a large supermarket or a convenience store, to wherever the needs and opportunities appear to be."

Convinced of the profitability of the new company, Antoine Turmel declared: "Our basic role is to supply our clients at minimum cost and maximum efficiency. Our profit is the measure of our efficiency, the efficiency with which we identify the requirements and patterns of our markets, and the efficiency of our operations in satisfying these needs."

To achieve such profitability, Antoine Turmel would rely on the employees' commitment to reduce operating costs and increase sales. He foresaw that sales would exceed $400 million within six years, an annual increase of 12 percent, while the net profit margin would rise from 0.9 percent to 1.1 percent per year to total $4.4 million. These income levels would entail earnings per share of about $1.20, compared with $0.47 the previous year. Thus, the growth rate of the profits would average 18 percent per year.

A further objective of the new company was to expand into other regions and provinces. Antoine Turmel could see certain trends taking shape; for example, "the consumption of frozen foods will grow and greater stress will be laid on specialty stores serving specialized products."

For Antoine Turmel, the food business was unique indeed: "it isn't cyclical; it is almost impossible to lose money on inventories;" and, from now on, "it is becoming more and more a cash business."

Even Antoine Turmel's expectations were surpassed. In 1976, Provigo reported sales of $478.1 million and a net income of $5.9 million; Antoine Turmel had predicted $400 million in sales and net income of $4.4 million.

"Provigo": The New Signature

The time had come to give the Company a name which would not be associated with any of the three founding companies. After an internal contest failed to produce satisfactory results, the graphics firm of Cabana Séguin[4] was commissioned to come up with a name and logo for the new company.

The name Provigo was adopted by the Executive Committee. 'Provigo' has visual appeal and sounds pleasing. It is neither too short nor too long. It has a multilingual flavour. The word itself is new but, separately or in combination, the various syllables evoke the words positive, professional (PRO); provisions (PROVI); vigour (VIGO); and suggest dynamism (GO).

As for the logo, the P was red, and its outline began and ended in two tapered strokes at the end. Within the loop formed by the P was an orange drop. The outline of the P represented a crossroads symbolizing transportation and distribution. The leg of the P resembled the type of ribbon awarded premium quality products in the agrifood industry. Contrasting with the bright red of the P, the orange drop represented a seed, symbol of all growth. Finally, even the script used in the name had a distinctive character in that it was formed by lower case letters which appeared to be linked.

On September 9, 1970, Couvrette & Provost announced the adoption of the new name, Provigo Inc., designed to "meet the basic needs of the Canadian market with an international flair." With its multilingual character, the new name was readily incorporated in advertising material. In no time, there were Provigo signs in Montreal, Sherbrooke, Quebec City, Chicoutimi and elsewhere, replacing those of the constituent companies and subsidiaries.

At Provigo head office, Antoine Turmel surrounded himself with some of his most trusted associates from Sherbrooke. These included Gaston Roy, Vice-President, Marketing; Pierre H. Lessard, Treasurer and Controller; and Jean Jutras, Director Data Processing Systems. Alfred Martel, from Lamontagne, rounded out the team as Vice-President, Sales.

Even though Provigo's head offices were in Montreal — in the former premises of Couvrette & Provost, now the Montreal Division — none of the Montreal Division's senior managers had been selected to work at the head office level. This omission led to frustration in certain quarters.

As planned, a private brand had been developed, and several products bearing the Provigo label were already on the market. All had been well

In 1970 the company becomes Provigo.

received by retail clients and consumers alike.

Even then, in keeping with its corporate agenda of establishing an integrated distribution network of food products, Provigo was working towards developing a convenience-store formula. The Annual Report published in May 1971 stated that "this type of store has the potential to appeal to many independent grocers." This marketing intuition would lead to the emergence of the Provi-Soir outlets, which began to appear in 1974 according to a carefully developed plan.

The objectives of the first year following the merger (reorganization and restructuring), as well as those of the second year (planning and consolidation), were rapidly attained. Indeed everything was going so well that by the end of the second year the Company was on its way to achieving its third-year objectives.

But to reach its goals, the Company needed additional funds. Management studied a number of financing methods. To increase capital stock and therefore to dilute earnings per share was out of the question; this response would reflect a fundamental principle of the Company in the years ahead.

Provigo's new signature appears across Quebec.

On April 24, 1971, the directors and senior executives of Provigo, who were the principal shareholders, held 1,092,997 common shares, or 29.3 percent of the outstanding shares. The Caisse de dépôt et placement du Québec held 786,700 shares, or 21 percent of the total. It was alone in holding more than 10 percent of the shares.

A Five-Million Dollar Debenture Issue

In July 1971 management decided to take out long-term loans in an attempt to reduce the bank borrowings of Provigo Inc. and its subsidiaries, to redeem certain bonds before their November 1971 maturity date, and to increase the Company's working capital. To these ends, $5 million in debentures were issued.[5]

This initial financing activity would enable Provigo to establish its credit rating even if it meant doubling its long-term debt. The latter rose from $4.4 million to $8.8 million between January 30, 1971 and January 29, 1972.

In January 1971, Provigo's debt was essentially that of Couvrette & Provost, or $1,128,000, plus that of Provigo (Sherbrooke), formerly Denault, which amounted to $1,006,000, and that of Provigo (Saguenay), formerly Lamontagne, which was $1,310,000. These figures do not incorporate promissory notes, mortgages and a number of other long-term debts. These previous debts were to be consolidated with the overall Provigo debt.

Sales were still progressively increasing. By year-end 1970-1971, they had reached $209 million, a five-year increase of nearly 60 percent over the combined sales of the three merged companies.

1971 — Ten Years Later

In 1971, the three companies which had formed Provigo had been public for ten years. Provigo now employed 1,500 people. It had some 8,000 clients, 1,400 of which were affiliated grocers. Its wholesale distribution network was vast: 15 major distribution grocery centres and 29 intermediate cash-and-carry warehouses; a frozen food and four produce warehouses; and a division supplying food products to the institutional sector. A fleet of 150 trucks ensured the reliable and efficient movement of the company's merchandise. At the retail level, Provigo owned 20 supermarkets and 4 AVA warehouse markets.

Throughout the years, Provigo never ceased to adapt its structures to the changing needs of the company. Management was always seeking the utmost efficiency and optimum profitability, while at the same time offering unsurpassed customer service.

To improve profitability, in 1971 Provigo sold its Primes Régal Inc. subsidiary to a similar trading-stamp company which, nevertheless, continued to serve Provigo's affiliates. The same objective prompted it to close two fruit and vegetable businesses, two retail stores and one self-service warehouse. The premises and equipment which were no longer needed were sold.

A New Head Office

In February 1972, Provigo Inc. moved into its present-day headquarters at 800 René-Lévesque Blvd. West in Montreal, where most of the Company's management staff were located. At the time Provigo Inc. played the role of a holding company to its operating companies: Provigo (Montreal), Provigo (Sherbrooke), Provigo (Quebec) and Provigo (Saguenay).

The redesigned organizational chart incorporated three main sectors, Retail, grouping the Company's supermarkets and discount stores;

Wholesale, which included the Presto self-service outlets; and Real Estate Development, represented by Placements Denault Inc. The Board of Directors was reduced to 12.[6] Pierre H. Lessard, who was Treasurer and Controller, retained the position of Treasurer and became Vice-President, Finance and Administration.

Provigain, Provibec and Provipop

The growing success of Provigo's private brand program had enabled the Company's affiliates to stabilize their profit margins, enhance their ability to compete with the big chains, and increase their sales.

But despite the success of its 250 products, this private brand program did not properly identify the merchants who were supplied by Provigo. What was needed was a more complete program, one which would group these merchants under a limited number of banners; there were 19 at the time.

A market study and in-depth research on the various categories of retail establishments revealed three main marketing and identification strategies which would be able to meet the needs of retailers belonging to a group of voluntary chains.

Provigo started a family of three. Before long, Provigain, Provibec and Provipop became household words in Quebec. The graphic designs identifying the three chains underscored the fact that all three belonged to the same family. The lettering and outline of the symbols were identical. The bright orange colour evoked a luminosity which was reflected from one banner to the next. As distinctive features within a unifying theme, the Provigain banner featured the sun; Provibec, foliage in dynamic growth; and Provipop, light in op-art movement.

Provigala

Provigo's new retail segmentation strategy was central to its first large-scale promotion campaign conducted in 1973. The Provigala contest, offering $150,000 in prizes, was launched during Beaux Dimanches, a popular French-language television program on Radio-Canada. As outlined in the annual report, the contest had three objectives:

— To acquaint consumers with the Provigo family and to increase traffic in affiliated stores.

- To make the consumer aware that Provigo affiliates were capable of offering top-quality products at competitive prices, along with extensive services that were the mainstays of independent grocers.
- To ensure maximum participation by making the contest accessible to everyone, locating intense promotion at all points of sale, and encouraging sustained, cordial communications between consumers and retailers.

From the outset it was clear that a sense of partnership between retailers and the wholesaler and concern with image were the priorities in Provigo's promotional efforts.

An Emphasis on Retail

During the 1972–1973 fiscal year, sales reached $251.9 million, up nearly $30 million from the previous year.

With the purchase on November 6, 1972, of Les Aubaines Alimentaires Ltée, a Trois-Rivières business operating four supermarkets in the St-Maurice region, Provigo acquired its first retail stores since the merger.

Les Aubaines Alimentaires had been applying the mass-and-discount-merchandising formula with considerable success for several years. The company, popular throughout the St. Maurice region, reported annual sales of some $12 million.

Aubaines Alimentaires in Trois-Rivières, one of Provigo's first acquisitions.

Les Aubaines Alimentaires dominated the market in Trois-Rivières, somewhat similarly to Jato in Quebec City, which Provigo would buy three years later.

Under the leadership of Gérard Bourget and Gérard Charette,[7] Les Aubaines Alimentaires could be considered the first successful venture into food discounting in Quebec.

Meanwhile, more and more AVA stores — whose formula was similar to that used by Les Aubaines Alimentaires — were opening. By the end of 1972, there were twelve such stores in operation and three under construction. Although the formula had been improved, the initial concept of selling food products at discount prices in a no-frills environment was retained.

The Move to Laval

Just about everywhere in Quebec, Provigo had enlarged, built or renovated its premises to keep pace with the growing needs of the Company. But it became increasingly evident that the distribution centre located in the Marché Central Métropolitain was too small, an eventuality which had not been foreseen at the time of the merger. New premises were planned.

This time, space would not be a problem. Built on property in Laval measuring close to 1,250,000 square feet, the new warehouse covered an area of 300,000 square feet, twice the surface needed at the time. Moreover, to avoid the necessity of a future move, this vast warehouse was designed in such a way that it could be enlarged to double its capacity.

The Laval complex was intended to accommodate distribution operations supplying retailers and institutions, as well as the distribution of frozen and non-food products for the Montreal division.

When construction began in June 1973, the move was scheduled for a year later, but it was not until the beginning of the 1975–1976 fiscal year that all the Montreal region distribution services could be completely integrated in the new warehouse.

In 1973, Provigo could boast a stable corporate family; it should be noted that J.V. Hallé Inc. had become Provifruit Inc.

A Turning Point

In November 1972, Roland Provost, the eldest of the Provost brothers and the man responsible for the idea of launching Provost & Provost, decided

Premier Bourassa at the official opening of Provigo's large distribution centre in Laval, May 30, 1975.

to retire. He was the first of the Provigo founders to do so.

From the time of the merger, he had contributed substantially to the success of Provigo in his dual capacity of Vice-President in charge of the Institutional Division, and member of both the Executive Committee and the Board of Directors. Now, without anyone to head the institutional food services, the operations were gradually abandoned. They would not be revived until the creation of Dellixo in 1987.

The co-founder of Provost & Provost, Roland Provost was a master entrepreneur. He had been one of the major figures in the creation of Couvrette & Provost following the merger with Couvrette & Sauriol. He had also chaired the Association des Épiciers en Gros du Québec (AEG).

A year later, Ernest Provost, another of the Provost brothers, retired. A co-founder of Provost & Provost, and one of the pillars of Couvrette & Provost, Ernest Provost had been Vice-President of Warehousing and Transportation since the 1969 merger. Owing to his highly developed sense of efficiency and productivity, he had been entrusted with the running of the Marché Central distribution centre from the start. Its smooth operation was a testament to his ability. No operational or financial detail escaped his keen eye.

During that same period, Jacques Couvrette, who had been one of the Company's directors from the beginning and, earlier, Vice-President of Couvrette & Provost and General Manager of Épiceries Presto, also decided to retire after having established the best organized and most prosperous network of cash-and-carry warehouses in Quebec.

Gérard Carrière also retired about the same time. He had been Bernard Couvrette's right arm for many years at Couvrette & Sauriol where he was head of procurement and merchandising. Appointed Secretary of Couvrette & Provost at the time of the Company's incorporation in 1961, Gérard Carrière had retained that position after the 1969 merger. He was also director of purchasing for the Montreal Division. Among his many initiatives, he made certain that all rebates and discounts be credited to his division. At the time, his staff had the best inventory turnover among wholesale grocers — some twenty five times a year.

After Gérard Carrière retired, Claude E. Leduc, the Company's legal counsel, was appointed Secretary of Provigo, a position he still holds.

On May 28, 1974, at the Annual and Special Meeting of the shareholders, bylaws were adopted to lower, from seventy to sixty-five, the age limit for eligibility for the position of director, reduce the number of directors from twelve to nine and set the quorum for a Board meeting at five directors. From this point, there would be five members of the Executive Committee rather than six.

In accordance with these amendments to the bylaws, the general meeting elected nine directors. The first four, Marcel Bélanger, Claude Genest, Henry N.R. Jackman and Jacques Lagassé, came from outside the company. The other five — Jean-Louis Lamontagne, René Provost, Gaston Roy, J.A. Tremblay and Antoine Turmel — were from Provigo Inc.[8].

Together, these directors agreed that the five Provigo officers to be appointed members of the Executive Committee would be selected from their own ranks. In addition, these five would make up the Board of Directors quorum.

Antoine Turmel had surrounded himself with a powerful and effective administrative and decision-making apparatus; except for one, the members of the Executive Committee were conveniently located in offices next to his.

The Importance of Human Resources

Senior management felt the need for a vice-president of human resources. The man chosen to fill that position, which he held from 1974 until 1986, was Jacques Lesage. Jacques Lesage, with a master's degree in industrial relations obtained in 1957, had already acquired a good deal of experience and knowledge of the food business managing Steinberg personnel for some twelve years.

His first task was to standardize the working conditions, fringe benefits and salaries of employees working for the once independent businesses in Montreal, Quebec City, Chicoutimi and Sherbrooke, now wholly-owned subsidiaries of Provigo.

Pierre H. Lessard, Controller at Provigo head office, had noticed various disparities in the way the subsidiaries remunerated their employees. Aware that such inequities would sooner or later have an adverse effect on the company, he persuaded senior management to hire a specialist in personnel, compensation and industrial relations who was well versed in the workings of the labour code.

With over 2,000 employees, it was imperative to apply a uniform human resources policy, particularly when it came to labour relations. The task was not an easy one, and it became even more complicated as Provigo continued to grow and acquire new companies. Eventually, management would have to negotiate some 130 different collective agreements governing the working conditions of over 20,000 employees, all the while taking into account the conditions and laws in effect in the various Canadian provinces and certain American states.

Even though objectives might differ from one union or union federation to another, and despite the fact that each company within the Provigo group had its own characteristics, it was imperative to have an across-the-board human resources policy to reflect the company's objectives and to establish a necessary balance among the various groups.

But human resource responsibilities did not end with labour relations; there were also the challenges of recruiting and integrating personnel, of training and professional development, and of devising a succession plan for senior management. The sensitive issue of fringe benefits had to be tackled as well. All these problems had to be resolved consistently and fairly in ways that promoted a sense of belonging to a winning team.

Over the years, Jacques Lesage surrounded himself with a small but efficient team of diversely talented people. Not only were they able to carry through every mandate entrusted to them by Head Office, but they also provided management of the various operating companies within the Provigo group with invaluable advice concerning their relations with personnel and every aspect of human resources, so essential to a company's success.

Jato: A Valuable Acquisition

Antoine Turmel had kept his eye on a Quebec City company called Jato for three or four years. Jato ran supermarkets and its performance was the envy of many. Even though Provigo's retail sales were on the rise, overall growth was not keeping pace with senior management's expectations. Jato was seen as the opportunity to take a giant leap forward.

The business had its humble beginnings in 1940, when Alfred Boiteau had paid some $800 for a 300-square foot grocery business in the Saint-Jean-Baptiste district of Quebec City.

But the company, as such, began in 1954 with the opening of a new store in Sillery owned by Alfred Boiteau's son, Jean. The store was destroyed by a fire, and Jean Boiteau was forced to rent a garage as temporary business premises so he could keep his customers. Later, in 1958, even though the store had been extended, its surface area covered only 4,000 square feet.

But this was just the beginning for Jean Boiteau. The one and only time he had borrowed from the bank was to build his first store. In later years, slowly at first, then at the rate of one store per year from 1964 to 1976, Jato outlets appeared everywhere on the outskirts of Quebec City. As soon as a suburb numbered about 2,000 families, a new Jato store would open, assured that its revenue would grow as the population was expected to increase to 5,000 families over the next five years. Thus, when national food chains set their sights on the new and profitable suburban market, Jato stores were already solidly entrenched in the local shopping centres and their clientele was well established.

In early 1975, Jato sales were just below $50 million. At the time, Steinberg had a 25 percent share of the Quebec City region market, while Jato had 16 percent and Dominion 12 percent.

For Jean Boiteau, quality was the number one priority. He offered his clients personalized service — which he referred to as "traditionally québécois'' — even though he admitted having lifted some of his ideas from competitors and others elsewhere in Canada and the United States. In Quebec City, as was the case in the Saguenay/Lac-Saint-Jean area, Steinberg often served as the model.

Jean Boiteau had opted for a particularly simple yet flexible structure. In 1975, with a company staff of 500, no more than 20 people worked at head office.

The important thing for Jean Boiteau was the quality and freshness of merchandise. Perishable goods accounted for 50 percent of his sales, clearly higher than the industry average.

Jato stores had limited storage space by design, so to guarantee freshness stock was turned over fifty, even sixty times a year. Customers were not the only ones to benefit. Since Jean Boiteau paid his suppliers every two weeks on the average, it was as if he had sold the merchandise twice before paying for it. This enabled him not only to enjoy discounts, but also considerable liquidity.

Jato halted the practice of giving trading stamps two or three years before Steinberg. The company was able to demonstrate dramatically to its customers that it offered price reductions greater than the 2 percent that such stamps represented.

Cheaper Without Stamps

Jean Boiteau launched his ''red spot'' campaign. These stickers contrasted the competition's price ''with stamps'', with the Jato price ''without stamps.'' The price of the products bearing red stickers could be reduced by as much as 20 percent to 25 percent. At various times, the campaign ticketed between 500 and 1,000 products.

Jean Boiteau's advertising clearly stated that, while Jato was selling merchandise at reduced prices, the goal was to make money, and the only way to do so was by increasing sales and reducing administrative costs. The campaign was a success; sales rose to new heights. And so did profits.

Jean Boiteau: A Born Operator

Jean Boiteau, the sole owner of Jato, combined management skills with a thorough knowledge of supermarket operations. Few details, no matter how small, escaped his attention.

Jato's Jean Boiteau.

The opening of a Jato store draws a crowd.

When the Provigo people began their negotiations with Jato, they were not dealing with an unknown quantity. Jean Boiteau had been director of Lamontagne, and Provigo was his Quebec City supplier.

Needless to say, Antoine Turmel and Pierre H. Lessard were interested in acquiring a high performance retail business with substantial liquid assets, while at the same time strengthening senior management by inviting Jean Boiteau to join them.

Provigo's interest in Jato was not new. In the early 1970s, it had already tried, unsuccessfully, to come to an agreement. In the meantime, other companies, like the Oshawa Group, had made their own bids.

The unionization of his employees had somewhat upset Jean Boiteau; they no longer seemed to have the kind of motivation and dedication to their work which had made the company a success. Provigo, on the other hand, had passed muster and his integration would be a guarantee of further success.

On March 4, 1975, Provigo acquired all the outstanding shares of Jato Inc. The cost was $7.5 million, which was paid partly in cash and partly in the form of instalments extending to 1981. At the time, the company operated nine supermarkets in the Quebec City area. In fact, Jato had sufficient liquid assets to prevent the transaction from leading to any major cash outlay on the part of Provigo.

Jean Boiteau agreed to accept a new challenge. Antoine Turmel entrusted him with the mandate to direct Provigo's retail network along the same lines as Jato's. He was to emphasize quality, service, marketing, volume and profitability.

After meeting with those in charge, Jean Boiteau prepared and had an initial expansion program adopted. It included the construction of new stores and renovation of the existing ones. Provigo was truly concentrating its efforts on retail expansion.

With the addition of the Jato supermarkets, Provigo now owned 31 conventional supermarkets and 16 AVA warehouse markets. Six new units were scheduled to open during the 1975–1976 fiscal year.

Antoine Turmel Targets a Billion Dollars for 1981

With strong and growing competition from the supermarket chains, many had doubted the success and viability of the new venture when Provigo first started out.

When Antoine Turmel had revealed his objectives to gatherings of financial analysts in Montreal and Toronto in January 1970, his pronouncements had been taken with a grain of salt by many. In April 1975, he addressed the same audience, and reviewed the results of the five previous years before making his new predictions.

In 1970, as we have seen, he had predicted that Provigo sales would reach the $400 million mark in 1976. Net income, in his opinion, would reach $4.4 million that year. In 1975, he could well rejoice:

"Today, just five years later, annual sales are close to $360 million and will exceed $400 million in the present fiscal year, well ahead of schedule. The net earnings projection of $4.4 million should be realized for fiscal 1975, and net margin is better than 1.2 percent."

"These objectives were met and exceeded despite the dislocations in the industry which attended the price war of 1970 and the company's multiple reorganization following the merger."

For 1981, Turmel predicted sales of one billion dollars:

"Total annual sales by all divisions in six years are projected at $1 billion, nearly three times the present level."[9]

He was mistaken! In 1977, sales exceeded half a billion; in 1978, they had exceeded one billion and in 1981, Provigo would report sales of over 2.6 billion.

In 1976–1977, Provigo had already undergone considerable change. It now employed over 3,000 people. Unions had become more powerful and labour relations more difficult. Traditional management methods could no longer guarantee satisfactory results.

Head office had become more and more important relative to the Montreal Division. More often than not, the former Couvrette & Provost organization saw its particular objectives overshadowed by those of the company as a whole. As a result, while the Montreal Division sometimes benefited from this state of affairs, it was rather frequently penalized and its profitability suffered as a consequence.

In the spring of 1974, René Provost experienced heart problems. By August, he was back at work to deal with the impending relocation to the new Laval Centre. No sooner had he returned than employees declared a work stoppage and their demonstrations were marked by violence. That year was extremely difficult for him, and he felt increasingly isolated.

In addition, various events had deeply disturbed him and strengthened his decision to leave his job to a younger man. For over thirty years, René Provost had worked in ever more demanding positions. His health had suffered as a result.

Pierre H. Lessard, the New President and Chief Operating Officer

In September 1976, Pierre H. Lessard — Antoine Turmel's right arm ever since his early days with Denault in 1967, who was then Provigo's Vice-President, Finance and Administration, and Treasurer — succeeded René Provost as President and Chief Operating Officer. The latter assumed the responsibility of Vice-Chairman of the Board and Director of Corporate Affairs. Simultaneously, Pierre H. Lessard was appointed to the Board of Directors.

The man selected to fill the position left vacant by Pierre H. Lessard was his assistant, H. Paul Gobeil, who had assumed a managerial position since December 1974 and who was also acting as Assistant Secretary.[10]

The Company took this opportunity to restructure senior management. Gaston Roy, who was Vice-President, Marketing, became Vice-President, Procurement, in charge of coordinating all purchasing departments. Alfred Martel, who had been Vice-President, Sales, became Vice-President, Marketing, in charge of the Company's advertising strategy; as well, he was responsible for promoting the private-brand program, which was becoming more and more important.[11]

Gaston Roy

Gaston Roy remained Vice-President, Procurement, at Provigo until his retirement in 1982. On the eve of his departure, Antoine Turmel paid him an unusual tribute.

After recalling Gaston Roy's 43 years of experience in the food industry, 30 of which were spent at Denault and Provigo, Antoine Turmel said:

"On many occasions the food industry has sought out Mr. Roy's knowledge and expertise.

"Mr. Roy has applied his talents mainly to marketing and related areas; from sales to procurement, he has demonstrated his ability as a skilful strategist and patient negotiator.

"The food industry is witnessing the departure of a legendary figure — the company, a loyal colleague. A hard worker, Mr. Roy always devoted both time and energy to his responsibilities."[12]

The tribute was well deserved. Antoine Turmel was losing a close colleague who had been his first and most trusted associate since the days of Denault.

Gaston Roy continued to sit on the Provigo Board of Directors and Executive Committee until his retirement in 1982.

He had learned well the lesson that manufacturers pay to have their products advertised and promoted by granting numerous and diverse allowances to distributors in the form of cash and volume discounts, allowances for special displays, performance, etc. He took full advantage of these and other incentives, first for Denault, then for Provigo. His prowess in such dealings enabled the Company to sell at lower prices, offer various services to retailers at a reduced cost and achieve greater profits.

Gaston Roy combined in-depth knowledge of the food industry with a straightforwardness, open mindedness and integrity which had earned him the confidence and respect of everyone he did business with.

Ready for the Next Stage

In 1976, when René Provost left the position of President and made way for Pierre H. Lessard, and while senior management was being restructured, Provigo could be proud of having built a successful organization. The three pioneering businesses had truly merged into a single company capable of taking on any challenge.

Everything was in place and ready for Provigo to move into its expansion and diversification phase.

Provigo's development would be swift and spectacular. Nothing could stand in the way of its progress.

Notes

1. Excerpt from the 1969–1970 Annual Report.
2. He had planned the project in a hospital while recovering from a serious automobile collision in the winter of 1968.
3. See the Epilogue for the complete text of his speech.
4. Cabana Séguin had just produced a new, highly praised logo and signature for the Provincial Bank of Canada.
5. Three million dollars in 8.25 percent Serial Debentures to mature as to $375,000 on July 15 in each of the years 1974 to 1981 inclusive, and $2 million in 9.5 percent Sinking Fund Debentures, Series B, to mature on July 15, 1991.
6. The departure of Pierre Bergeron, Jacques Couvrette, Dominik Dlouhy, Robert Lamontagne, J.P.W. Ostiguy, Ernest Provost, Marcel Robert, Guy Tremblay and Georges Vilim ended the original balance of representation set by the founding companies.
7. Both would later join Provigo's management team.
8. Paul Desruisseaux and Bernard Couvrette had retired, while Claude E. Leduc, who had replaced Roland Provost, resigned to satisfy the new bylaw limiting the number of directors to nine.
9. Excerpt from an April 1975 presentation by Antoine Turmel before The Montreal and The Toronto Society of Financial Analysts.
10. A chartered accountant, Paul Gobeil had been a senior partner of the firm that had audited Denault.
11. Alfred Martel left Provigo in 1977 to start a successful advertising firm.
12. Excerpt from Antoine Turmel's message to the shareholders (Annual Report 1983).

CHAPTER SEVEN

THE FIRST DIVERSIFICATIONS

We expect to find not only regular grocery items in supermarkets but also soft drinks, beer, wine, dairy products, frozen foods, produce, meat and fish. Such variety did not always exist. Each breakthrough into a new sector was an adventure for grocers. New products were constantly added in response to the demand from affiliated merchants.

Ever since the merger, Provigo had owned medium-sized wholesalers of produce and frozen foods. As outlined in the first annual report, the objectives, in addition to the sale of fresh produce, included a frozen food program and the eventual integration into the distribution system of fresh and cooked meat products. These innovations were in keeping with the Provigo policy to provide the consumer with "one-stop shopping."

Provi-Fruit

Provigo's first diversification was into the fresh produce sector. In 1969, Provigo bought J.V. Hallé of Quebec City. The following year, the Company acquired Beau Fruit of Montreal, which from the outset was steered into the rapidly growing sector of frozen food products.

After the acquisition, J.V. Hallé experienced a substantial drop in sales to Provigo competitors like Steinberg, Dominion, IGA and even Jato. The man chosen by Jean-Louis Lamontagne to remedy the situation and effect the smooth integration of the future Provi-Fruit's operations into the

Provigo system was Richard Constantineau, who started working April 1, 1974.[1]

A number of companies owned or integrated by Provigo were not even purchasing their supplies from J.V. Hallé. A skilful negotiator, Richard Constantineau did wonders not only with clients but also with suppliers.

Provi-Fruit supplies come from all over the world.

With Jean-Louis Lamontagne he set up an information system; the first of its kind in North America. Particularly adapted to the wholesale produce trade, this new system enabled Provi-Fruit to sell and bill the goods even before they were stocked at the warehouse. In this way it was possible to adjust gross margins to market fluctuations and establish general profit levels without delay.

Provi-Fruit was the first Quebec company to import and sell Moroccan clementines to compete with Japanese mandarins. When one considers how popular this fruit has become in Quebec, it was quite a coup. Richard Constantineau was so successful with Provi-Fruit that, in 1977, he was offered a new challenge — the integration of the Jato stores into the Provigo system. Before accepting this responsibility, he arranged to spend one year working closely with former Jato owner Jean Boiteau. Constantineau was such a brilliant student, and Boiteau such an efficient teacher, that the situation eventually became awkward. Later, when Jean Boiteau was about to retire, he said half-jokingly that the pupil had outdistanced the master, and since there was nothing more he could teach Constantineau, the only thing for him to do was to retire.

As expected, Constantineau succeeded Jean Boiteau. After his stay at Jato, in 1979, he was made Vice-President of Provigo's Retail Operations. He would later play a key role in the acquisition and absorption of the Dominion stores in this position.

Provi-Fruit was integrated into Provigo (Distribution) and became the company's produce division. From its distribution centres in Quebec City and Montreal, the division soon served nearly all of Quebec. It is still growing steadily. Thanks to the hard work and dedication of its General Manager, Jean-Claude Desrochers,[2] Provi-Fruit has become the largest produce wholesaler in Quebec.

Provi-Viande

It soon became obvious that a move into the meat sector would be essential if the Company was to offer retailers the widest possible array of supply services. In an area so crucial to the profitability of retail stores, it was essential to be independent of outside suppliers. Provigo created its own subsidiary, Provi-Viande, and set up all the support services. Claude Dufour, a specialist with proven abilities in this field, was recruited in 1975 to undertake this task. His experience in the food business, particulary in the meat sector, reached back to 1949.[3]

The first task of the new general manager was to draw up plans for the future Provi-Viande distribution centre. Built in Laval in 1975, the new centre cost $4.5 million and covered an area of 85,000 square feet. Here, Provi-Viande Inc. quartered fresh carcasses — primarily beef and pork — and vacuum packed butcher cuts. Veal, lamb, poultry and frozen fish were available as well. The meat plant was also equipped to produce smoked meat and delicatessen items bearing the Provigo and Royal labels.

Of course, every product displayed the "Canada Approved" seal and the plant's operations were under the constant supervision of a government inspector. But in addition to complying with the stringent standards in force, Claude Dufour set up a quality control laboratory where a microbiologist would ensure that the entire production was uniform and of superior quality. All products would also be regularly submitted to taste tests before company approval was given.

Provi-Viande operations did not start until November 1976, four months behind schedule. As a result, the volume of sales was lower than forecast and losses were significant. Profitability depended a great deal on recruiting new retailers, on increasing the concentration of purchases of existing clients and, of course, on the superior sales performance of supermarket meat counters. But these were innovating times for the meat distribution sector. As Provigo management put it: "Our entry into this business comes at a time when revolutionary changes are beginning to take place with the distribution of beef in vacuum-packed primary cuts."[4]

Agriculture Minister Jean Garon officially opens the Provi-Viande Distribution Centre in Laval (May 6, 1977).

These changes would result in lower transportation costs and labour savings due to simplified work techniques. Vacuum-packed beef keeps longer and loses less weight. Operating results of meat departments in supermarkets could only improve. Provi-Viande guaranteed not only a stable supply but a healthy quality-to-price ratio as well.

In 1978, the company was profitable. Provi-Viande, now the new meat division of Provigo (Distribution), had expanded its markets by exporting over eight million pounds of pork. Trade with Japan was a major factor. That year, the Company had to increase the variety of its products and step up the plant's capacity to over 100 million pounds. The plant was expanded at a cost of one million dollars, and Claude Dufour, still General Manager of the Meat Division, was appointed Vice-President, Meat Operations, and made a member of senior management. During 1979–1980, the domestic clientele was widened and exports increased. At its height, Provi-Viande's sales fluctuated between 2 and 3 million pounds of meat a week and brought in annual sales of $125 million — with gratifying profits.

Working closely with federal and provincial authorities, Claude Dufour helped set up various programs for the Quebec agriculture department designed to promote self-sufficiency across the province in meat products and encourage the marketing of new products.

Provi-Viande, for example, was responsible for the marketing of grain-fed veal in Quebec. Today, this tender, tasty meat, available nearly all year round at affordable prices, attests to the success of the undertaking. It was an achievement that benefited producers, wholesalers, retailers and consumers alike.

In November 1980, Provigo decided to buy all the shares of Abattoir St-Valérien. Finalized in February 1981, the transaction enabled Provigo to integrate slaughtering operations with a weekly capacity of 12,000 hogs and 300 head of beef and veal cattle. The abattoir was located in the heart of an agricultural region noted for raising and fattening livestock. For Antoine Turmel, this acquisition marked "the company's first step towards vertical integration."

As there were very few slaughterhouses from which Provi-Viande could buy carcasses cut to its own specifications, this acquisition appeared to be entirely logical.

Despite an unstable and highly competitive market, 1980–1981 was once again a year of satisfactory growth. But the 1981–1982 period was a difficult one for Abattoir St-Valérien; the pork industry had been affected by a cycle of overproduction and prices dropped. Nevertheless, the meat division's sales rose by 19 percent. Exports, for their part, had reached 15.5 million pounds, an appreciable increase.

The pork market started to recover in 1982–1983; sales rose a further 16 percent and good profits were reported. But there were problems ahead.

Because of a major labour conflict, which shut down Provi-Viande from June 3 to December 5, 1983, the meat division underwent an extremely difficult year, incurring substantial losses. Provi-Viande had suffered the irremediable loss of a sizeable share of its market.

In addition, under new government standards, the Quebec environmental authorities demanded the installation of a more extensive filtration system to treat waste at Abattoir St-Valérien. The cost of such an installation would have been prohibitive. The slaughterhouse was doomed.

In 1984–1985, the meat division experienced further difficulties. As a result, its administrative methods were completely reassessed and its organizational structure was modified. On top of the St-Valérien setbacks, the Laval meat division had become a money-losing proposition.

As part of a rationalization project, Abattoir St-Valérien was shut down in April 1985; $1.6 million was reported among the Company's extraordinary items for that year as a loss stemming from the shutdown. So ended Provigo's first effort at vertical expansion. The meat division, even after Abattoir St-Valérien was abandoned, continued to experience difficulties.

The Provigo retail merchants — those fully-owned as well as the affiliates — were not really convinced of the wisdom of buying boxed beef, the distribution method advocated by Provi-Viande. They preferred to buy beef carcasses. Even more so when other meat wholesalers, in order to attract Provigo merchants, offered them reduced prices on the most popular cuts.

In 1986, under Pierre-Paul Léger, meat cutting and production of smoked meat and delicatessen products were halted to convert Provi-Viande into a specialized centre for the distribution of fresh meat as well as private and national brand delicatessen products. The change would mark a turnaround for Provi-Viande's profitability.

There is no doubt that the creation of Provi-Viande has been beneficial to Provigo, and even more so to the retailers who can rely on stable supplies, uniform quality and a good quality/price/service ratio.

Notes

1. An agronomist with a Master's in biochemistry and an MBA, Richard Constantineau was a graduate of Université Laval in his native Quebec City. Before joining Provigo, he had worked for five years as a special projects officer for the Quebec Ministry of Agriculture.
2. Jean-Claude Desrochers took over from Richard Constantineau as Manager of the Quebec City Division in 1977. He then became General Manager of the Quebec City and Montreal Produce Divisions, before becoming Vice-President of the Provigo (Distribution) Produce Division in January 1986 and is currently Vice-President, Fresh Products.
3. He had worked in the meat distribution sector before joining Steinberg as a butcher in 1950. Five years later, he was in charge of meat purchasing for Épiceries Richelieu. In 1965, when Boeuf Mérite was created as a joint venture between Épiciers Métro and Richelieu to distribute wholesale meat, Claude Dufour was promoted head of purchasing for the new company, and became General Manager in 1967. He is currently the owner of a successful Provigo supermarket.
4. Excerpt from the 1976-1977 Annual Report.

CHAPTER EIGHT

WITH LOEB: SALES TRIPLE TO $1.5 BILLION

Ottawa-based M. Loeb Limited had been active in the national capital region for many years. The company was also known in Quebec. Loeb's history is reviewed in some detail in this chapter to shed some light on Provigo's acquisition of Loeb in 1977. With the integration of Loeb, Provigo's sales reached the $1 billion mark and the company entered a new phase of national importance. It was the most significant acquisition in Provigo's history.

Founded by Moses Loeb in 1912, the company sold confectionery items — its only business at the time — from a 160-square foot storeroom. In 1916, the premises were expanded to 900 square feet and tobacco was added to the list. Loeb was incorporated under Ontario legislation in 1928. Several of its sales representatives started to travel through western Quebec and the Ottawa and St. Lawrence valleys, selling cigarettes, tobacco, and confectionery products. In October 1951, Loeb obtained the IGA[1] franchise, which enabled it to organize and serve a voluntary group of food retailers in the Ottawa Valley.

Since then, this territorial franchise had continued to expand, at times directly, at times through the acquisition of wholesalers operating in another territory. In 1964, for example, Loeb bought G.T. Armstrong & Sons Ltd. of Sherbrooke in the very territory served by Antoine Turmel.[2]

From a modest storeroom...

to a corporate giant

The modern warehouse built by A.A. Drouin in Amos, in 1971, to serve the immense James Bay hydroelectric project, attested to the scope of Loeb's operations in Quebec. The Ottawa wholesaler was making great profits from Quebec's glorious dam builders!

Loeb in 1961

In 1961, when Couvrette & Provost, Lamontagne, and Denault became public companies, Loeb had already made its debut in the Montreal market by buying Georges Painchaud Inc., the largest wholesale distributor of tobacco and confectionery products in Canada.[3] At the time, Loeb's sales stood at $81.6 million, compared with $64 million the previous year. Net income exceeded half a million.

From its head office in Ottawa, Loeb operated several divisions: grocery, meat, produce, frozen products, retail stores, tobacco and confectionery, health and beauty products, and non-food products. It also had a cash & carry division in Sudbury, and subsidiaries which included Georges Painchaud in Montreal and Casselman Creamery Ltd. in Casselman, Ontario.

The Company boasted some 3,000 customers in over 350 locations, including Ottawa, Hull, Kingston, Brockville, Cornwall, Lachute, Hawkesbury, Pembroke, North Bay, Parry Sound, Sudbury and Sault-Sainte-Marie. The IGA franchise covered a number of Ontario regions, plus the

Quebec counties of Gatineau, Pontiac, Papineau, Labelle, Argenteuil and Hull.

In Ottawa, Loeb started to operate superstores (45,000 square feet). In 1961 it inaugurated Shoppers City, the first discount shopping centre in the Ottawa region and supplied the Foodmart and other departments of the Freemart store in the centre. The company initiated a policy of selling its merchandise to drugstores and department stores at very low mark-ups.

Bertram Loeb, the prime mover of M. Loeb Limited

To finance expansion of its retail outlets and cash & carry warehouses, and to increase its inventory, in 1961 Loeb issued $2.5 million in 6.5 percent debentures with share purchase warrants.[4]

With sales nearly twice the combined total of Couvrette & Provost, Lamontagne and Denault, Loeb was considerably ahead of the Provigo forerunners in those days.

Between 1962 and 1964, Loeb bought Foodway Distributors Ltd. of London, Capital City Cartage (1962) Ltd. of Ottawa and Allied Record Corp. of Montreal.

In 1969, the year of the merger, the three Provigo constituents reported sales of $182 million, while those of Loeb were $390 million.

In January 1976, after the acquisition of Jato, Provigo would reach $478 million in annual sales. Loeb, for its part, had topped the billion mark.

It should be noted that throughout the sixties and seventies Loeb's sales were consistently double those of Provigo.

Taking the Lead in the Pharmaceutical Sector

In May 1964, with the acquisition of the controlling interest in the Montreal-based National Drug and Chemical Company of Canada, Loeb became the largest pharmaceutical products distributor in Canada.

At the time, National Drug had sales of approximately $60 million with branches in 17 Canadian cities. Among other activities, it served a network of 500 pharmacies under the name Associated Retail Pharmacists (ARP).

On January 30, 1965, Loeb owned 22.8 percent (an investment of $1,658,873 according to its financial statements) of all National Drug shares and was in a position to control up to 35.8 percent if it chose to exercise its purchase option.[5]

A Foray into the United States

At this time, Loeb held an option[6] on all the shares of M. Loeb Corporation of Chicago — a company owned by Bertram Loeb, President of M. Loeb Limited — which held the IGA franchise in most of Illinois and parts of Indiana and Iowa. Later, M. Loeb Corp. acquired Washington Wholesale Grocery Company of Washington, D.C., the largest food wholesaler in the region, whose distribution network covered the east coast of the U.S.

In January 1968, the Company acquired from Bertram Loeb all the common shares, plus 6,000 of the 16,450 outstanding preferred shares of Loeb Corp. of Chicago for $500,001. Under the agreement, 10,000 of the other preferred shares would be purchased in instalments between June 30, 1969 and June 30, 1972 at a cost of one million dollars. One of the terms of the agreement was that the seller should make a capital contribution to the company equal to the amount of any operating loss incurred during the fiscal year ended January 27, 1968.[7] That particular condition was inserted into the agreement before the auditors had completed their task.

The following year, disaster struck. For the first time since 1912, Loeb's profits dropped below the previous year's level. Consolidated net earnings before taxes had fallen from $5 million to $4.4 million, a decline of 12 percent.[8] After-tax earnings amounted to $1.6 million, compared with $2.4 million the previous year, this was a drop of 33 percent. Losses incurred by its U.S. subsidiaries were responsible for this sharp decline.

The Chicago operations had never been successful. Around the end of 1968, four corporate stores opened in Chicago, three of them in shopping centres. By the end of the fiscal year, they were out of business. Client-retailers were finding it difficult to cope with rising labour costs. As a result, more and more bad accounts had to be written off. It became increasingly obvious that the Chicago operation would never make it.

Westward Expansion

In the summer of 1958, Bertram Loeb became interested in Edmonton Associated Wholesale Limited and, in March 1959, along with John F. Damore, he acquired a controlling interest. At the same time, Edmonton Wholesale purchased the assets of Horne & Pitfield Ltd. and both operations were merged under the name of Horne & Pitfield Foods Limited, which became a public company. By 1965–66 a close working arrangement had developed between Horne & Pitfield Foods and Loeb.[9]

No more was heard of Horne & Pitfield until January 23, 1973, when Loeb offered to exchange all the shares of Horne & Pitfield Foods for shares of Loeb, on the basis of one Loeb common share for one Horne & Pitfield common share.[10] The estimated cost of the operation totalled some $7 million.[11]

The reason behind this arrangement was Bertram Loeb's suspicion that Horne & Pitfield was on the verge of being taken over. At the time, Horne & Pitfield was negotiating the acquisition of Market Wholesale Grocery Company of California.[12] In March 1973, Horne & Pitfield Foods Limited paid $9.25 million for all the shares of Market Wholesale Grocery Company, the largest independent wholesale distributor in the northern California food sector.

On May 22, 1973, the share exchange proposed by Bertram Loeb was effected. Loeb now owned 90.5 percent of Horne & Pitfield, which was at the time the largest food wholesaler in Alberta and which held the IGA franchise for the province.

For Loeb, and later for Provigo, Horne & Pitfield Foods and Market Wholesale Grocery would be excellent investments; they would also pave the way for expansion into the Canadian West and the United States.

Back in Ottawa

Loeb's gradual inroads into the distribution of pharmaceutical products and its expansion to the Chicago area, followed by Washington, D.C., then Western Canada and California, did not slow the company's development on the home front. Throughout this period it continued to grow in Ontario and Quebec.

In 1965, for instance, Loeb created Loeb-City Product Ltd. in a joint venture with the Illinois company City Products. It combined the marketing and merchandising techniques, developed in the U.S. by City Products, with Loeb warehouses and equipment to launch a chain of specialty retailing stores under the name Cartier.

In January 1968, Loeb offered to buy all the outstanding shares of Shoppers City Ltd. for $5.50 a share. By April 1968, Loeb held 88 percent of the outstanding capital stock. Shoppers City operated six IGA supermarkets and eight Top Valu service stations in Ontario, and had sales of $24 million. With this capital investment, Shoppers City outlets became captive clients for Loeb.

In 1970, Loeb owned, operated, or supplied not only IGA stores, but also a number of K-Mart Food Stores, Warehouse Market outlets, M/M Stores, Silver Star Stores and Top Valu Gasmarts. Under the direction of Bertram Loeb, the company's sales increased dramatically. But profits didn't keep pace. In fact, some years they were dropping. In 1967–1968, with sales of $251.5 million, net income after taxes had been over $2.4 million. In 1971–1972, Loeb sales exceeded $531.4 million but its net after-tax income barely exceeded one million.

Loeb changed its management team in February 1972; Bertram Loeb became Chairman of the Board, leaving the post of President to Robert Norris.[13] Norris served only two years as President, after which Bertram Loeb assumed the threefold responsibility of Chairman of the Board, President and Chief Executive Officer.

In 1973–1974, with the acquisition of Horne & Pitfield, and its subsidiary, Market Wholesale, Loeb sales climbed to $810.9 million, a jump of nearly $265 million. Net operating income, before taxes, rose from $1.4 million to nearly $3.2 million.[14]

Reaching the Billion-Dollar Target

By January 31, 1976 sales had reached $1,048,338,000, up 17 percent over the previous year. But rather than increasing, net income decreased by 9 percent.[15]

For some years, the Board of Directors and principal shareholders had been finding Bertram Loeb's approach too single minded; he had a tendency to increase sales without taking the necessary steps to ensure that profits followed suit. The Board felt that Bertram Loeb should give up the reins of the company. This had become obvious to everyone, except to Bertram Loeb himself, who wanted to save his company at any cost. But he kept making the wrong moves.

Towards the end of 1975, Frank M. Warnock[16] became President and Chief Operating Officer at Loeb. His mandate was to turn the situation around and moderate the influence of Bertram Loeb, who was still Chairman of the Board.

Meanwhile, the company's operations in the Chicago area were going through difficult times; Loeb had lost two large customers and many accounts receivable had to be written off. In the fall of 1976, the division was sold and the company absorbed a one-time loss of $980,000. Still, it was less than the operating loss incurred over the previous twelve months.[17]

By early 1977, sales had improved somewhat, but net income had dropped by some $2.6 million, or 45 percent. Bertram Loeb resigned as Chairman on December 6, 1976. He remained a member of the Board for several months.

In August 1977, Provigo acquired control of M. Loeb Limited with all its subsidiaries. Loeb's 50th annual report, published in 1978, was its last.

A Billion for Provigo

In 1975, before a gathering of Montreal and Toronto financial analysts, Antoine Turmel had projected Provigo's annual sales growth rate for the following six years at 18.6 percent, compared with 12.2 percent for the previous five years. This growth pattern translated into a one billion-dollar sales objective for 1981.

Between the 1976–1977 and 1977–1978 fiscal years, the forecasts were completely overturned. Sales shot up from $512.2 million to $1.2 billion. But these figures do not give an accurate portrait of the situation. A note to the Provigo financial statements for 1977–1978 was more revealing: the income figures included the operating results of Loeb for the 26 weeks since its acquisition.

More explicitly, a second note stated that the consolidated financial statements included the accounts of all the subsidiaries. It went on to report that the Company owned 80.1 percent of the outstanding common shares of Loeb which, in turn, owned 51.9 percent of the outstanding common shares and 25.8 percent of the outstanding preferred shares of National Drug and Chemical Company of Canada and 85.5 percent of the outstanding shares of Horne & Pitfield Foods. All other subsidiaries of the company were wholly owned.

These notes, in a few terse words, sum up the results of an acquisition which, against all odds, made the 1977–1978 fiscal year the most extraordinary and important in Provigo's history. Aptly, perhaps not coincidentally, the name Provigo on the annual report's white cover was printed in gold.

Notes

1. IGA (Independent Grocers' Alliance) is a voluntary group created in the United States in 1925. It consists of thousands of independent grocers, as well as wholesalers who hold exclusive regional or territorial franchises and from whom they get their supplies. In Canada, IGA served as the model for various groups of affiliated food stores which followed the American example.
2. This was not Loeb's only acquisition in Quebec. In 1960, it had bought Georges Painchaud of Montreal, and from 1964 to 1966, A.A. Drouin and Trudel & Ayotte of Amos, Maison Zenith of Saint-Jean and Raymond Poupart of Montreal.
3. From the M. Loeb 1961 Annual Report. This report marked the 50th anniversary of the company founded by Moses Loeb in 1912. After his death in 1951, the Company was directed by his sons (Bertram, Norman and David), one of whom, Bertram Loeb, was President and Chief Executive Officer.
4. M. Loeb Limited prospectus, April 13, 1961.
5. In fact, Loeb had paid for 92,173 common shares and 20,905 of the company's convertible preferred shares, in addition to obtaining an option for a further 100,000 non-issued common shares at $14.50 per share. The option was valid until June 15, 1967.
6. M. Loeb Limited Annual Report for the year ended January 30, 1965.
7. M. Loeb Limited Annual Report for the year ended January 27, 1968.
8. M. Loeb Limited Annual Report for the year ended January 25, 1969.
9. M. Loeb Limited Annual Report for the year ended January 29, 1966.
10. M. Loeb Limited Annual Report for the year ended January 27, 1973.
11. Message from the Chairman of the Board, Bertram Loeb, in the M. Loeb Limited Annual Report for the year ended January 26, 1974.
12. From notes by Kenneth W. Quinn (October 1986). Mr. Quinn had made a career at Horne & Pitfield Foods where he was President until his retirement in 1987.
13. An American, Robert Norris had acquired vast experience as Executive Vice-President of The Fleming Co., the second largest food distributor in the United States.
14. M. Loeb Limited Annual Report for the year ended January 26, 1974.
15. M. Loeb Limited Annual Report for the year ended January 31, 1976.
16. Frank M. Warnock had long worked at Scott Paper Company before becoming President of Dominion Dairies Ltd. As these two large companies supplied food wholesalers and retailers throughout Canada, he was a well-known figure in the food sector.
17. M. Loeb Annual Report for the year ended January 29, 1977. The company was obliged to honour its leases until 1986.

CHAPTER NINE

AGAINST ALL ODDS

It seems almost inconceivable that Provigo succeeded in acquiring control of a company as large and as important as Loeb. Throughout the previous decade Loeb's sales had doubled Provigo's and its operations extended through all of Canada and part of the United States. In addition to the food sector, Loeb was active in the distribution of pharmaceuticals and petroleum products.

The Caisse de dépôt et placement: An Important Player

Towards the end of 1968, the Caisse de dépôt et placement du Québec began to acquire shares in Loeb.

As early as 1971, the Caisse foresaw the potential advantage of a merger between Provigo and Loeb. The President of the Caisse, Claude Prieur, along with Michel Paris, its Assistant General Manager, and Pierre Arbour, Senior Advisor, Corporate Investments, all shared this perspective. So the Caisse continued to purchase Loeb shares until, in 1972–1973, it had nearly reached its statutory 30 percent ceiling on share ownership in an individual company. The Caisse was so close to this 30 percent limit that it dared not buy a block of 200,000 shares that was available at the time. The shares were offered to Antoine Turmel, as Chairman of Provigo. To keep Loeb or any possible competitor from finding out about the transaction, Turmel gave instructions that the 200,000 shares be delivered to a blind trust administered by the Provincial Bank of Canada, a common practice in such circumstances.

To keep an eye on its investment in Loeb, the Caisse was represented indirectly on the Board of Directors by Lucien Massé, President of Société Gazifière de Hull, Inc.[1]

At the time, the Caisse owned more than 27 percent of the Loeb shares and about 26 percent of Provigo's shares. It was widely thought that the Caisse would eventually combine these two major investments. The Caisse was by far the largest among the Loeb shareholders. Bertram Loeb, the Chairman of the Board, owned some 18 percent of the shares, his ex-wife, Blanche, about 7 percent, and his two brothers approximately 4 percent each. George Weston Ltd., which controlled Loblaw Companies Ltd., held 18.5 percent of the shares, but the federal government had ordered it to dispose of them in order to comply with anti-combines legislation.

Loeb's sales figures were colossal, but its profits were slim, due mainly to the losses incurred by the company in the Chicago area. As well, Bertram Loeb's volatile management style was beginning to make a lot of people nervous.

Paul Lacroix[2] also represented the Caisse on Loeb's Board for a few months. But he soon resigned, finding that the atmosphere at board meetings was not agreeable and that the tenacious Bertram Loeb would not listen to any arguments but his own.

Marcel Cazavant, who had succeeded Claude Prieur as President of the Caisse, then proposed Pierre Arbour and Mary Lamontagne to represent the Caisse on the Loeb Board of Directors.

Pierre Arbour's mandate, once he was on the Board, was to safeguard the interests of the principal shareholder, which was becoming impatient with Bertram Loeb's independent behaviour. He was entrusted with the delicate task of telling Bertram Loeb that he should step down and find a president and chief executive officer for the company's operations.

The Board of Directors issued strict instructions stipulating that Bertram Loeb was to refrain from making any further acquisitions in the United States without the Board's express consent.

But early in 1976, Bertram Loeb bought twelve Loblaw stores in a poor area of Chicago. As was his style, he had not sought the Board's authorization. That was the final straw.

At an informal but extremely important meeting, some members of the Board devised a strategy designed to obtain Bertram Loeb's resignation.

An official meeting of the Board followed and Bertram Loeb was told that he had no choice but to resign. His resignation became official on December 6, 1976. Bertram Loeb nevertheless remained a member of the board and one of the principal shareholders.

The Caisse Sells its Stake in Loeb

Frustrated with the constant negotiating and bickering, the Caisse was willing to sell its Loeb shares to Provigo. What was only a dream in 1971 was on the verge of becoming reality.

Provigo made an offer that the Caisse accepted. Provigo acquired 1,147,000 common shares of Loeb at five dollars each, paid in cash. The sale became official on June 23, 1977. Antoine Turmel had pulled off a master stroke.

The transaction had come as a total surprise to most people and made headlines in all the papers the following day. 25.3 percent of Loeb's shares had cost Provigo $5.7 million. Practically before the ink was dry, Provigo announced that it would proceed with an offer to purchase the outstanding common shares of M. Loeb Limited for $5 a share.

The deal seemed to please both parties. Speaking for Provigo, René Provost called it "an investment for the time being. If the takeover bid succeeds, we'll take it from there...". Marcel Cazavant, President of the Caisse, asserted simply that it was "a good transaction for the Caisse de dépôt et placement."[3] In fact, shares that had been acquired for an average of $4.69 were sold for $5.00. And the Caisse was rid of an investment that lately had become a nightmare. For the Caisse, the greatest dividend was perhaps its investment in Provigo, whose shares soon shot up.

Opinions on the share offer were not so unanimous. One analyst[4] declared that the $5 purchase offer was not particularly generous even though the price listed on the Toronto Stock Exchange on the eve of the transaction was $4.45. He emphasized that the book value of a Loeb share was $6.50 and, in his opinion, Provigo could hope for no more than 50 percent of the outstanding shares. As he put it: "They're dreaming, if they think they can get 100 percent at $5.00."

George Weston Ltd., for its part, had paid $6.03 for each of its shares. When the federal government ordered the company to sell its holding in Loeb, it was granted a period of grace since the shares were worth no more than $4.00 at the time. Would Provigo be able to obtain Weston's block of shares at $5.00? In an interview with *The Gazette*, Bertram Loeb declared: "Provigo's offer to buy Loeb is ludicrous."[5]

Bertram Loeb had even declared that he would not sell his shares (which accounted for 14.1 percent of the total) to Provigo for any consideration, adding that a Provigo-directed management could change many things in the Ottawa operations and that he felt responsible towards his employees.[6] In reply, Provigo spokesman René Provost made it clear that there would be no major changes. "Provigo has never been known to disrupt the operations of the companies it has acquired. On the contrary, we have encouraged managerial autonomy in every instance."[7] Indeed, one of the cardinal rules of Provigo in all its acquisitions has been to leave in place the teams who have obtained good results and complied with the general guidelines set by head office.

Bertram Loeb refused to sell his shares for less than six dollars. He felt that Loeb's earnings for that year would amount to $1.25 per share, and that an offer of $6.25 per share would represent barely five times that gain. Naturally, the issue was hotly debated. Bertram Loeb declared that the federal government could very well react to Provigo's acquisition of Loeb the way it had in the Weston deal. However, the regulators responsible for combines investigations subsequently deemed the transaction acceptable. By contrast, many suppliers were alarmed at the thought of how big Provigo would become should the Loeb acquisition go through.

On June 27, Loeb shares having already gained $0.80 to close at $5.25, the consensus was that Provigo might well up its offer. Loeb shares had had a volatile history. Various setbacks had caused them to plummet to $2.00 at the end of 1974; these same shares had also fluctuated between $8.00 and $16.00 from 1967 to 1970. However, on June 29, Provigo officially announced that it would not increase its offer despite the most recent rise in the price of shares, which had not affected the number of transactions to any significant degree.

The previous day, Provigo had not intervened at Loeb's annual general meeting and all directors had been reappointed, including the former representatives of the Caisse, Pierre Arbour and Mary Lamontagne.

Poised to Enter New Markets

As a direct result of buying the Caisse's shares in Loeb, Provigo was acquiring a supplier for some IGA stores as well as the opportunity to break into markets outside Quebec. The *Financial Times* was the first to raise the point (July 5) and suggested that Provigo could well become one of the most powerful distributors of food products in Canada, and even expand into the United States.[8]

Another article entitled "New confidence in Quebec stocks"[9] claimed that the Provigo-Loeb transaction marked a turnaround of the current economic situation, which had seen the paper value of many Quebec stocks drop significantly after the election of the Parti Québécois in 1976. The Weston holdings were undoubtedly the key to the transaction, since Provigo already owned 28 percent of the shares — 25 percent purchased from the Caisse and 3 percent acquired on the open market. Without wasting a moment's time, Antoine Turmel met with Weston's Vice-President, Richard Currie, at the end of June.

The Official Offer

The offer to purchase all of Loeb's common shares was ready on July 15.[10] It did not apply to the 837,005 common shares of Loeb owned by George Weston Limited, which Provigo had agreed to purchase for the same price under a private agreement.

The success of the entire transaction depended on the agreement with Weston. On July 13, 1977, Provigo bought 837,005 common shares of Loeb from Weston at $5 a share. The same day, Provigo signed a separate agreement with Loblaw Companies Limited under which a number of Provigo subsidiaries purchased various assets of nine Dionne supermarkets in the Montreal region. Weston held Loblaw, which held Dionne. Once these transactions were completed, Provigo owned 2,123,115 common shares of Loeb, or 47 percent of all outstanding shares.

Weston, which had paid $6.03 for its shares in 1973, lost about $850,000, a loss that was softened by the sale of the Dionne supermarkets.[11]

Bertram Loeb Strikes Back

But Bertram Loeb was not ready to concede victory. With his brother David, he still controlled 22 percent of the outstanding shares. On July 22 newspapers reported that the Loeb brothers would make their own offer to shareholders in an attempt to acquire 53 percent of the shares. As a result of this eleventh-hour move, trading in Loeb shares was suspended on the Montreal and Toronto Exchanges pending further information.[12] But the Loeb brothers' intended offer seemed to stand little chance of success. A spokesman for Weston declared: "Our agreement has been signed. We are legally bound and that's it."[13] On July 23, realizing that they could not get their hands on the shares held by Weston, the Loeb brothers gave up their attempt to thwart Provigo.

On August 8, when its offer expired, Provigo owned 3,213,950 common shares of Loeb, or 69.2 percent of the total. The offer was extended and, by September 12, Provigo's interest had grown to 79.8 percent. The remainder would be more difficult to acquire. Somewhat later, Bertram Loeb sold the shares he had sworn he would never sell to Provigo to the Sobey Group. The Sobey family would have its own part to play in Provigo's history.[14]

Loeb's 50th Annual Report

Throughout this tumultuous period, Loeb continued to operate under the direction of Frank M. Warnock, President and Chief Executive Officer. His was the only signature on the annual report for the year ended January 28, 1977, Loeb's 50th and last. Sales had gone up by 9.2 percent over the previous year, reaching $1,164,861,000, an increase of nearly $100 million and profits had increased by 12.7 percent. Loeb's successful comeback had already begun under the direction of Frank M. Warnock.

On September 30, 1977, the Board of Directors accepted the resignations of Bertram and David Loeb. Antoine Turmel and Pierre H. Lessard from Provigo were appointed Directors of M. Loeb Limited. Antoine Turmel succeeded J. Lorne Gray as Chairman of the Board.[15] On November 18, Hyman Solaway also resigned and was replaced by René Provost, Provigo's Vice-Chairman of the Board.

As of July 30, 1977, M. Loeb Limited, its subsidiaries, National Drug and Chemical Company of Canada Limited and Horne & Pitfield Foods Limited and its Market Wholesale subsidiary were part of the Provigo Group, and their results were consolidated in the financial statements of Provigo Inc.

Provigo had reached its goal: it had conquered new territories and broadened its operational horizon. The new Quebec billionaire had joined the ranks of the Canadian and foreign elite. The transaction had cost no more than $18,487,000. For Antoine Turmel, it was "a smart move." In everybody else's eyes, it was a master stroke.

Notes

1. He was an accountant by profession and served on Loeb's Board from 1974 until his retirement in July 1976.
2. President of Lacroix Inc.
3. *La Presse* (June 24, 1977).
4. Quoted in *The Globe and Mail* (June 24, 1977).
5. Gazette headline (June 25, 1977).
6. *The Gazette, La Presse, The Globe and Mail* (June 29, 1977).
7. *La Presse* (June 29, 1977).
8. *The Gazette* voiced the same opinion: ''Aggressive and acquisitive Provigo Inc. has almost no experience in the English-speaking market, but the Montreal-based company could become a major force in the Canadian food industry and extend itself into the United States... .'' The article then went on to wonder how Provigo would finance the operation.
9. From the Financial Post News Service, published in *La Presse* (July 6, 1977).
10. On a rush order from Antoine Turmel to Claude E. Leduc, the company's legal counsel.
11. Apparently, Dionne's profits were marginal and, according to Richard Currie, President of Loblaw and Vice-President of George Weston, the sale was in keeping with Loblaw's policy of divesting itself of any operations which did not have a strategic importance in the company's plans.
12. *The Globe and Mail* and *La Presse* (July 23, 1977).
13. *The Globe and Mail* (July 23, 1977).
14. See Chapter 17 for further developments of this aspect of the story.
15. Mr. Gray stayed on as a Director.

CHAPTER TEN

LOEB IS NOW PROVIGO

On July 30, 1977 Provigo held 70 percent of Loeb's common shares. Provigo had become a different company, with new horizons. It now ranked among the largest companies in Canada. The boundaries that originally confined Provigo's operations to Quebec and the food industry had been swept away with the acquisition of Loeb.

However, it is no easy task for a company to absorb another business whose sales have for some time been twice as high. Many things are bound to change when, in less than two years, total sales climb from half a billion to over two billion dollars.

At Provigo, for instance, English was more widely used since it was now imperative to communicate with the managers of the newly acquired companies. Until this time, bilingualism had been needed to deal directly with a number of individuals among clients, suppliers, investors and shareholders.

Although Loeb personnel had remained unchanged after the acquisition — and management still enjoyed a large measure of autonomy — it was clear that the only way to achieve more efficient, better coordinated management performance was to restructure the constituent companies, consolidate certain operations and, above all, streamline the organizational chart.

It was no longer practical to maintain the separate identities of the major companies' fifty different subsidiaries.[1] In 1978, twenty-four were regrouped. Provigo, which alone had twelve subsidiaries, ended with only four: Provigo (Distribution) Inc., Provigo (Détail) Inc., Provi-Soir Inc. and Les Placements Denault Inc. Loeb retained six out of its sixteen subsidiaries, National Drug five out of eleven and during the following year six of the eleven Horne & Pitfield subsidiaries were amalgamated.

In its annual reports for the first three years, Provigo included separate financial reviews for each of its major subsidiaries in order to keep track of their respective progress. These covered Provigo itself and its operations in Quebec; Loeb, with operations in Ontario, Quebec and Washington; Horne & Pitfield, established in Western Canada; California-based Market Wholesale Grocery; and National Drug, which distributed wholesale pharmaceutical products in Canada.[2]

The figures for the first complete fiscal year following these acquisitions give a better idea of the relative scope and profitability of each company within the Provigo Group.[3] At the time, out of total sales exceeding $2 billion, Provigo sales accounted for $771.8 million, Loeb's for $647.3 million, Horne & Pitfield for $228.2 million, those of Market Wholesale, its subsidiary, totalled $293.6 million, and National Drug's $160.4 million.[4]

The Provigo Group's consolidated net income for the same period exceeded $14 million.

As of 1981, in keeping with the standards recommended by the Canadian Institute of Chartered Accountants regarding disclosure of a company's activities on a segmented basis, Provigo's annual report would group results on the basis of the Company's principal activities:

(1) Wholesale food distribution;
(2) Retail food distribution;
(3) Drug distribution;
(4) Other operations.

In this breakdown, one can see that Provigo's current structure organized by group of activities was already beginning to emerge some seven years ago.

Changes at Loeb

By September 1977, Provigo had increased its holdings in Loeb to 80 percent. But it was not until June 16, 1979, nearly two years later, that all outstanding common shares of Loeb would belong to Provigo. Until then, some minority shareholders would be monitoring the situation closely.[5]

While biding its time, Provigo took Loeb's business firmly in hand in an attempt to improve its performance and generate more profits. For one thing, it was vital to stop the hemorrhaging in the U.S. operations.[6]

In August 1981, H. Paul Gobeil, Provigo's Vice-President, Finance, was appointed President and Chief Operating Officer of M. Loeb to succeed Frank M. Warnock, who had just resigned. While he maintained his head office position, H. Paul Gobeil moved to Ottawa to devote all his time and attention to his new duties.[7]

H. Paul Gobeil concentrated on improving Loeb's performance in the shortest time possible. This goal entailed intensifying sales efforts, tightening financial controls and moving toward retail store franchising. Profitability became a day-to-day concern.

M. Loeb Corporation, Loeb's American subsidiary, continued to experience difficulties. During 1982 the company's activities were streamlined through the sale of certain assets and the termination of costly leases. These transactions entailed an additional write-off of $1.6 million,[8] but they put an end to losses which would have otherwise recurred indefinitely.

Once rid of its money losing operations, M. Loeb Corporation turned its attention to the Tidewater division in Virginia, whose operations centred on supplying military bases along the eastern seaboard.

In 1980, Loeb bought the seven Raymond stores in Hull and, toward the end of 1983, five more stores in the same region. The stores were sold as IGA franchises to retailers who would buy all their supplies from Loeb. A few distributors and several outlets for petroleum products were also acquired by Loeb.

In 1983, M. Loeb Limited became Loeb Inc. Its major subsidiaries were now directly held by Provigo. These included Horne & Pitfield, Market Wholesale and Loeb Corp. (formerly M. Loeb Corporation).

To mark this restructuring, H. Paul Gobeil, who remained President and Chief Operating Officer of Loeb, was elected to the Provigo Board of Directors, where he was appointed Executive Vice-President. William Kipp, one of Loeb's vice-presidents until 1983, became Executive Vice-President. He later succeeded H. Paul Gobeil as President in 1985.

It would be impossible to recognize in Loeb today the firm acquired by Provigo in August 1977. Without the excess baggage of its former subsidiaries, Loeb, already dominant in the Ottawa market, was able to improve its position, expand its markets and achieve greater earnings.

Loeb had changed by franchising its corporate stores to the benefit of some one hundred independent retailers who expanded and modernized their stores with Loeb's encouragement and support. This marketing and merchandising program was both innovative and aggressive. Loeb retailers eventually attained productivity levels — and a level of sales per square foot — higher than the food industry average.

Under the able direction of H. Paul Gobeil and his successor William Kipp, and with the help of competent, motivated management and staff, Loeb experienced prodigious growth. Its largest group of stores, under the IGA banner, took full advantage of the merchandising formula known in the trade as "everyday low prices" and doubled its share of the market within a few years. This turning point in Loeb's history proved so beneficial that Loeb achieved a remarkable performance among Provigo's Food Group.

Not surprisingly, with its position secured in Ottawa-Hull, London, Sudbury, Northern Ontario, Abitibi and northwestern Quebec, Loeb started to entertain expansion projects. Why, for example, should it settle for only part of Ontario?

Loeb's current logo.

Notes

1. Provigo Inc. Annual Report for the year ended January 28, 1978.
2. Provigo Inc. Annual Report for the year ended January 27, 1979.
3. *Ibid*.
4. Profitability varied among these companies. Provigo's sectorial income was $7.1 million, Loeb's $1.9 million, Horne & Pitfield's (with its subsidiary Market Wholesale) $7.1 million, and National Drug's $1.1 million.
5. See Chapter 17.
6. In January 1980, for example, the closing of the Landover (Maryland) warehouse alone had resulted in an extraordinary loss of over $1.6 million according to Provigo's Annual Report for the year ended January 26, 1980.
7. A number of changes followed in Provigo management. Yvan Bussières, who had been Vice-President, Real Estate Development, was appointed Vice-President, Administration and Treasurer, while Jean-Claude Merizzi, Vice-President, Development and Expansion, also assumed the additional responsibility for real estate development.
8. Shown as an extraordinary item in the January 29, 1983 financial statements. According to one of the notes, it represents the final cost associated with the termination of the leases for two unused warehouses.

CHAPTER ELEVEN

TERRITORIAL EXPANSION: HORNE & PITFIELD MARKET WHOLESALE TIDEWATER WHOLESALE

By acquiring Loeb at a good price, Provigo had accomplished more rapid territorial expansion than most people would have believed possible. In addition to Ontario, it had established itself in Western Canada and some parts of the U.S. through Horne & Pitfield. Horne & Pitfield and its American subsidiary, Market Wholesale, had a very good track record in the western provinces and California. Its profits were higher than Loeb's or Provigo's even though the company's sales volume was lower.[1]

In fact, with sales short of Loeb's by more than $125 million and some $190 million below Provigo's, the profits of Horne & Pitfield and its subsidiaries for 1978–1979 were 3.7 times those of Loeb and even matched Provigo's. Horne & Pitfield's sectorial income was $7.1 million for sales of $521.9 million.

In 1979, together with Market Wholesale, its wholly-owned subsidiary, Horne & Pitfield had 1,405 employees. Its Canadian distribution network consisted of eight distribution centres; six cash-and-carry warehouses; 348 IGA, M/M, Mayfair and Triple S affiliated retailers; and

75 franchised Red Rooster convenience stores. Its American subsidiary acted merely as wholesaler, with a network of seven distribution centres and nine cash-and-carry warehouses. All in all, it was a large, well-managed company.

Horne & Pitfield's Beginnings

Horne & Pitfield Foods, incorporated under Alberta legislation in Calgary in 1910, became a public company in 1959. But its origins can be traced back to 1882, to the city of Winnipeg.[2]

At the time, the founders of this modest business — James Sutherland, Robert Campbell and Robert Wilson — supplied settlers on their treks through Manitoba, Saskatchewan and Alberta in search of new destinies in the "last best West." John Horne did not join the team until 1906, when the corporate name became Campbell, Wilson & Horne.

From 1910 to 1959, distribution centres were set up in such places as Lethbridge, Edmonton, Red Deer, Grande Prairie, Peace River, Medicine Hat, St. Paul and Dawson Creek, and the company name was changed to Horne & Pitfield Ltd.

In the early days of Horne & Pitfield, another wholesaler was making its debut in Edmonton. Initially a cooperative owned by retailers, it was incorporated in 1945 under the name Edmonton Associated Wholesale. It started business in an old Air Force hut on the Edmonton Exhibition Grounds. Sales for 1949 amounted to a mere $384,839. Operations remained small and business difficult until 1952, when John A. Clarke took over the company.

Under Clarke's direction, Edmonton Associated Wholesale enjoyed considerable growth from 1952 to 1956. But the building chosen to replace the Air Force hut in 1947, as the centre of operations, was itself a one-storey affair with a basement which had already been flooded twice. It was clearly unsuited to the company's burgeoning needs.

In 1956, Clarke faced two choices: incur considerable debt for a new distribution centre with sufficient capacity to support the firm's growth, or sell the business.

He was analyzing his options when John F. Damore, vice-president at IGA headquarters in Toronto, expressed his interest in buying the company and establishing a network of IGA franchises in Alberta. Damore was head of a group of five Chicago businessmen.

In February 1957 the transaction was concluded and in June the IGA

Horne & Pitfield yesterday...

and today.

program was launched in the Edmonton area with 20 independently owned and operated stores. Sales were then $4 million a year.

To ensure continued growth, the company had to use three different warehouses located in various parts of Edmonton. It was obviously not an efficient way to operate. So management decided to build a new distribution centre for September 1958. As well, the directors of Edmonton Wholesale were seeking suitable acquisitions. Two possibilities developed: Jenkins Groceterias and Horne & Pitfield Ltd., both Calgary-based companies.

But Edmonton Wholesale itself had already attracted the attention of Bertram Loeb.

Edmonton Wholesale Becomes Horne & Pitfield Foods Limited

After lengthy negotiations, a double transaction changed the entire situation in March 1959. John F. Damore and Bertram Loeb purchased the Chicago group's shares in Edmonton Wholesale which, in turn, acquired the assets of Horne & Pitfield. The new company was called Horne & Pitfield Foods Limited. Simultaneously, the company went public.

At the time of the acquisition, Edmonton Associated Wholesale had annual sales of $6 million, but with losses of $50,000. As for Horne & Pitfield, it showed sales of $27 million a year with $260,000 in profits. The combined sales of the two companies — $33 million — ensured a surplus. The net worth of the new company was $2.2 million.

As often happens at the time of an acquisition, new projects were launched while consolidation was still in progress. Thus between 1959 and 1962, Horne & Pitfield established itself in the retail trade, using the programs previously developed by IGA and M/M. The opening of 15 corporate stores, however, resulted in heavy operating losses. The company still showed profits in its wholesale operations but was losing money overall as a result of the abysmal retail performance. In 1962–1963, sales reached $39 million while losses totalled $735,099. The accumulated operating deficit stood at $2.4 million.

The situation was grim. Something had to be done.

The first step involved changes in senior management. Kenneth W. Quinn was appointed Vice-President and General Manager towards the end of 1962.

Horne & Pitfield's head office in Edmonton

A chartered accountant, Quinn had been responsible for the external audit of Edmonton Associated Wholesale in 1957 when the company was bought by John Damore and his Chicago group. He had worked on the transaction and, after the acquisition, John Damore asked him to join the team.

In the fall of 1957, Quinn left private practice to become assistant to the General Manager of Edmonton Associated Wholesale. In 1959, he devoted his time almost entirely to studying possible acquisitions and preparing the transaction that, as he has written, would "resurrect the corpse." That same year he was appointed to the Board of Directors and given the position of Secretary-Treasurer of Horne & Pitfield. He became Vice-President and General Manager in 1962, and President and Chief Operating Officer in 1968. In 1975 he was made President and Chief Executive Officer, a position he kept until his retirement in May 1987.[3]

Kenneth W. Quinn spent part of 1962 tidying up the affairs of Horne & Pitfield Foods. The company sold a number of corporate stores to independent retailers. Others were shut down. Spending was closely watched in an effort to revitalize the company. These measures had a direct and immediate impact. The operating deficit, which had reached $735,099 by the end of fiscal 1962–1963, gave way to net earnings of $290,265 the following year. This considerable difference of over one million dollars in just one year marks an amazing turnaround in a short period of time.

During the years that followed, management continued to improve the company's financial position and increased the number of independently owned and operated IGA and M/M franchises throughout its territory, particularly in rural areas. By April 1968, the long-standing operating deficit had been eliminated and the earned surplus reached $225,000.

Kenneth W. Quinn. An entrepreneur in the Provigo tradition.

The Seventies: A Period of Adjustment

After having jettisoned its retail stores and subsequently recovered its profitability, Horne & Pitfield realized that its growth during the seventies would depend on its ability to meet emerging consumer preference for larger stores located in shopping centres that offered a wider selection of products.

In those days it was difficult to find qualified independent retailers not only willing to reorient their businesses in keeping with new industry trends but also able to invest considerable capital in the process. So a new division was formed to run the larger corporate stores. In effect, this move was a second retail debut. These new supermarkets operated in tandem with Zellers and Woolco in Calgary, Simpson-Sears in Lethbridge, and K-Mart in Medicine Hat.

The division was a success. Ten years after the difficult 1962–1963 period, the company that was on the verge of ruin had established a solid operational basis once again. By March 31, 1973, the end of the fiscal year, sales had climbed to $94 million and net income to $840,000.

As early as 1972, Horne & Pitfield was itching to make new acquisitions. After surveying potential markets to the north, east and west, the company decided that the best opportunities lay south of the border. For Horne & Pitfield, that meant California. After a year of negotiations, it bought Market Wholesale Grocery Co. for $9,250,000 on March 31, 1973.

Market Wholesale: A Prosperous Subsidiary

The core activities of Market Wholesale Grocery consisted primarily of wholesale food distribution in Northern California.

With head office in Glendale, California, the company was originally part of Arden Farms, which had operated three different types of businesses: wholesale, under the name Market; retail, under the name Mayfair; and dairy operations, under the name Arden.

Market Wholesale's largest distribution centre (California)

In 1962, Arden Farms decided to dispose of its wholesale business. Two of its executives, H. Edward Moore and Carl R. Goslovich, together with several other associates, bought the wholesale division. Edward Moore became Market Wholesale's President and Carl R. Goslovich, its Executive Vice-President.[4]

From 1962 through 1973, these two seasoned directors also proved to be highly capable managers. They initiated significant expansion plans which resulted in considerable increases in the company's sales and profits. Annual sales had reached $120 million when Horne & Pitfield began to show an interest in their operations.

Carl R. Goslovich, President and CEO, Market Wholesale, from 1977 to 1988.

At the time of its acquisition by Horne & Pitfield, on March 31, 1973, Market Wholesale had distribution centres in Eureka, Fresno, Glendale, Modesto, Sacramento and, of course, Santa Clara, where the company later established its head office.

Loeb Takes Over Horne & Pitfield

While Horne & Pitfield and Market Wholesale were concluding their transaction, Loeb decided that the time had come to make a breakthrough in Western Canada and, while it was at it, in the American West as well.

On January 23, 1973, Loeb made an offer to holders of common shares of Horne & Pitfield Foods in the form of an exchange of one common share of Loeb for each Horne & Pitfield share.

Bertram Loeb, Chairman of the Board and President of M. Loeb Limited, was on familiar ground. With John F. Damore he had purchased in 1959 Edmonton Associated Wholesale Limited — which would become Horne & Pitfield Foods Limited. At the time of the earlier transaction, Bertram Loeb was Chairman of the Board of both Horne & Pitfield and M. Loeb Limited.

On April 17, 1973, a little over two weeks after the acquisition of Market Wholesale by Horne & Pitfield, 1,503,662 Horne & Pitfield common shares had been tendered. With the shares it already owned, Loeb now held 86 percent of the common shares. Both Horne & Pitfield and Market Wholesale were firmly in its grasp.

All in all, it was quite a coup for Bertram Loeb.

A Future Asset for Provigo

Market Wholesale had reached sales of $170 million in 1974. This was an impressive figure since, apart from the large chains, there were few voluntary groups in California. The wholesaler's clientele was entirely made up of independent stores. At the time, Market Wholesale did not operate any corporate stores.

In 1974, the company built a 160,000-square-foot warehouse in Modesto to replace its old one. The same year, it set its sights on Lucky Wholesale Food of Redding. A little later, headquarters were transferred to Los Angeles before they were finally established in Santa Rosa.

In the meantime, Market Wholesale had opened a second distribution centre in Fresno and several cash-and-carry warehouses in the California cities of Chico, Fresno, Madera, Merced, Porterville, Salinas, Stockton and Visalia.

As a result of the distribution, merchandising, and financing services, which were available to client retailers, sales continued to grow at Market Wholesale.

At the time of Provigo's acquisition of Loeb and its subsidiaries, in July 1977, the Market Wholesale network consisted of nine distribution centres and eight cash-and-carry warehouses. By fiscal 1977–1978, sales were bordering on $246 million, far ahead of its parent company, Horne & Pitfield, whose sales were $191 million.[5]

At the end of May 1982, Market Wholesale opened a new 245,000-square-foot distribution centre in Santa Rosa, as the old one was no longer suitable. The high cost of setting up these new premises caused only a momentary decline in overall performance.

Market Wholesale was growing at such a rapid pace that, in 1985–1986, it ranked second among food wholesalers in Northern California, where competition is far from relaxed.[6]

After forming groups of affiliated stores for several years, Market Wholesale has recently entered the retail business and started to operate its own outlets.[7]

Market Wholesale Grocery is now one of the two Provigo Corp.

divisions and oversees Provigo's U.S. operations in the food sector.

Provigo in Western Canada

When it was acquired by Provigo in 1977, Horne & Pitfield owned eight distribution centres and six cash-and-carry warehouses in western Canada. It supplied 340 affiliated customers grouped under the IGA, M/M, Mayfair and Triple S banners. There were 52 stores in its Red Rooster convenience-store network. As well, Horne & Pitfield directly operated eleven corporate IGA supermarkets in Alberta in addition to holding half of Canadian Shopping Malls Ltd., the proprietor of three shopping centres in Alberta.

On November 1, 1978, the Horne & Pitfield shareholders approved its amalgamation with a wholly-owned subsidiary of Loeb, which at the time held 85 percent of the common shares. The company continued to operate under the same name. According to the terms of the transaction, minority shareholders received preferred shares in exchange for their common shares. Since the preferred shares were redeemable for $15.50 each, Loeb was able to recover the lot and hold all of Horne & Pitfield's shares.

That same year, Antoine Turmel was elected Chairman of the Board of Horne & Pitfield and Pierre H. Lessard was elected Director; Kenneth W. Quinn retained the position of President and Chief Executive Officer.

In the past, a 100,000-square-foot warehouse would have seemed enormous. In May 1981, Horne & Pitfield decided to build a 325,000-square-foot distribution centre in Edmonton.

But it was easier said than done. Competition ran high in Alberta and, in 1982 and 1983, the economic situation was less than favourable. Since the outlook for 1984 was scarcely more promising, rationalization and control programs were undertaken in the interest of better results. Certain IGA stores were expanded, others renovated.

By 1985, Horne & Pitfield realized that its retrenchment efforts had not been futile. It had the largest network of affiliated stores in Alberta and its chain of Red Rooster convenience stores was in top position in western Canada. As well, there was expansion into profitable territory. In 1986, there were 172 Red Rooster outlets, 76 of them twinned with self-service gas stations. The year Provigo had acquired the company there had been only 52. It was indeed a period of remarkable growth in this sector.

Tidewater in Virginia: A Prosperous Subsidiary

For Provigo, not only did Loeb represent expansion into Ontario, Horne & Pitfield into Western Canada and Market Wholesale into California, it also meant market opportunities along the eastern seaboard.

As described in Chapter 8, the Chicago experience had been a disaster for M. Loeb Corporation. In fact, operations had to be abandoned. The Washington D.C. facilities — later renovated and transferred to Virginia — showed positive results.

M. Loeb Corporation had acquired Washington Wholesale Grocery Co. of Washington D.C. in 1964 in an attempt to return its American operations, continually burdened by the Chicago setbacks, to profitability. There was every chance of success, since Washington Wholesale was the largest food wholesaler in the region with a distribution network extending to the east coast of the United States.

When Loeb was acquired by Provigo, it operated a distribution centre in Washington (Landover-Maryland) from which it supplied 14 Foodlane supermarket concessions, and a warehouse located in Tidewater, Virginia, which primarily served the large military bases in the area.

In 1980, the Landover warehouse, in the red ever since losing its best retail client, was closed. Provigo then concentrated its efforts on the Tidewater distribution centre and the Washington cash-and-carry warehouse, both of which were profitable. But the relative position of these two operations had changed considerably over the years. While Tidewater's sales in 1977 amounted to $10 million, a fraction of Washington's $60 million, Tidewater now ran ahead of the Washington operation.[8]

In 1982, the Washington warehouse was sold and the costly leases of unused warehouses terminated. These transactions were financially burdensome but they effectively put an end to losses which would otherwise have continued indefinitely.

All that is left of Loeb Corporation today is Tidewater Wholesale, a division of Provigo Corp., the U.S. Provigo group. Its distribution centre, located in Chesapeake, Virginia, supplies the stores managed by the U.S. Defense Department for servicemen stationed on the Armed Forces' bases of Southern Virginia and South Carolina.

With Market Wholesale in California and Tidewater Wholesale in Virginia, Provigo sales in the food sector in the U.S. market totalled $455 million in 1987–1988, generating income of $6.9 million.[9] Along with the results of recent acquisitions, these figures are expected to reach $800 million in 1989, perhaps even higher. Provigo now serves 15 percent of the Northern California market.

Throughout North America

Provigo, which today owns Horne & Pitfield, Market Wholesale, Tidewater Wholesale and, of course, Loeb, has truly become a giant in food distribution with operations on both sides of the border.

Early in 1988, in addition to thousands of independent clients, the Canadian network of the Provigo Food Group comprised 1,601 stores throughout Canada, most of which were operated by local entrepreneurs who owned their businesses.[10] Provigo's food sales are first in Quebec, second in Canada, and still growing.

In 1988 the Food Group alone oversaw 45 distribution centres and 67 cash-and-carry warehouses throughout Canada and part of the U.S. At the time of the Loeb acquisition, Provigo had no more than 11 distribution centres and 33 cash-and-carry warehouses, all of which were in Quebec.

There are still many markets to conquer, both in Canada and the United States. Although Provigo is originally a Quebec success story, it clearly intends to develop new markets and export its goods, services, and expertise far and wide.

Notes

1. Provigo Inc. Annual Report for the year ended January 27, 1979.
2. From *This is the story of Horne & Pitfield*, by Kenneth W. Quinn, President of Horne & Pitfield.
3. He was succeeded by Wayne A. Wagner.
4. From March 1977 until his retirement in early 1988, Carl R. Goslovich was President and Chief Executive Officer. He was succeeded by Keith H. Thye.
5. In 1978–1979, Market Wholesale reported sales of nearly $293.6 million and Horne & Pitfield $228.3 million. The following year, their respective sales were $323.6 million and $262.8 million. (Provigo Inc. Annual Reports for 1979 and 1980). Thereafter, the results of Market Wholesale, which acted solely as wholesaler, were integrated into those of the Wholesale Food Group.
6. Provigo Inc. Annual Report for the year ended January 25, 1986.
7. The first Better Buy warehouse store was officially opened on October 16, 1987. In June 1988, Market Wholesale acquired a chain of eleven supermarkets operating under the name Petrini in the San Francisco Bay area. This upscale chain of traditional supermarkets had annual sales of $180 million.

On August 1, 1988, Provigo announced the acquisition of 15 traditional supermarkets on the outskirts of San Francisco. These stores (Lucky Stores and Alpha Beta) had sales of some $150 million.

8. In Provigo's 1978–1979 Annual Report, the subsidiaries' restructured organizational chart already showed Tidewater Wholesale Grocery Co. Inc. as the exclusive property of M. Loeb Corporation, the American subsidiary of M. Loeb Limited.
9. Provigo Inc. Annual Report for the year ended January 30, 1988.
10. Provigo Inc. Annual Report for the year ended January 30, 1988.

CHAPTER TWELVE

FROM NATIONAL DRUG TO MEDIS

A quick sketch of Provigo in 1977 would show a food distribution company whose sales and territory had increased considerably. But such a picture would be far from complete. Soon, National Drug and Chemical Company of Canada Limited would enable Provigo to enter the drug distribution business, the first key element in a carefully planned diversification.

At the time of the Loeb acquisition, National Drug, one of its subsidiaries, reported annual sales of over $146 million and net income of $1.11 million. The company had 721 employees. Its network consisted of twelve distribution centres, two agencies, 323 pharmacies affiliated to voluntary groups and 20 franchised stores. There were also nine corporately-owned pharmacies: the Good Neighbor Drug Mart outlets in the Atlantic provinces, and three Charmco convenience health and beauty aid stores.[1]

In Canada, National Drug is the most important wholesale distributor of pharmaceuticals and related products serving pharmacies, hospitals, and various government and private organizations.

When it joined the Provigo family, National Drug was more than a simple distributor. It offered its client pharmacists a merchandising and marketing program as well as various support and manpower services. It also owned a division specializing in the sale of surgical instruments, owned and operated pharmacies in the Maritime provinces and owned a few subsidiaries like Laurentian Laboratories Limited. With its headquarters in Montreal, the company had operation bases and offices across Canada. Gordon J. Odell had been National Drug's President and Chief Executive Officer since 1964, a position he would retain until his retirement in 1986.

A Long History

As with many of the Provigo constituent companies, National Drug's history goes back a long way. Its incorporation date is recorded as November 9, 1905. But an article published in a historical album on the occasion of Canada's Centenary in 1967[2] reveals that the 18 Canadian wholesalers who almagamated as National Drug represented a continuity of service extending back to 1809. And if we include Lymans Limited, which was acquired in 1962, the company's history goes further back to 1800.

The laboratories of Lymans Limited, a constituent of National Drug, at the turn of the century.

The idea of a merger among Canadian wholesale druggists is attributed to Charles W. Tinling, President of Dominion Drug Company of Hamilton. He was joined in this venture by D.W. Bole, owner of Bole Drug Company of Winnipeg, and Theo H. Wardleworth of Montreal-based Evans & Son Limited. Together they toured the country to convince other colleagues that such a partnership would be mutually beneficial.

D.W. Bole, first President of National Drug, from 1906 to 1922.

Back in 1905, the objective behind such a merger was essentially the same as today. Amalgamation brought countrywide operations and resulted in savings through consolidation of purchases. Distribution and sales networks would be rationalized, and management could be more efficient. All these advantages, they argued, would help them better serve pharmacies and dispensaries throughout the country.

The new firm, with D.W. Bole as President, bought various assets and businesses from Halifax to Vancouver,[3] and set up its head office on Saint-Gabriel Street in Old Montreal.

National Drug had branches in every major Canadian city. Better still, in some cities, two or three wholesalers agreed to become part of the company. In such cases the offices and warehouses were combined in larger, more efficient premises.

A number of the amalgamated businesses were subsidiaries of British companies, and for years the majority vote on the National Drug Board of Directors was controlled by holders of preferred shares who lived in England. In 1946, Wood, Gundy & Co. Ltd. of Toronto, repatriated these shares. It was now possible to restructure the capital stock, a transaction which was approved in August 1946. From then on, the capital stock would be made up of common shares and new preferred shares, both with a par value of five dollars.[4]

This simpler, more flexible structure made it possible to dispense with the trust set up to protect preferred shares — particularly the British ones — and to distribute shares more widely in Canada. The company became truly Canadian.

Until then, National Drug's financial statements had been published with figures in both Canadian dollars and pounds sterling. In 1945, for instance, net profits were shown as $241,875 or £49,700, and assets as $4.7 million or £975,867.[5]

Naturally, any company doing business from coast to coast and operating a dozen subsidiaries must offer a variety of services. Among National Drug's subsidiaries, the wholesale sector included National Canadian Drugs Limited in the Maritimes, Johnston & Boon Co. Limited in Fort William, Ontario, National-Drugs Limited in Manitoba and Saskatchewan, Alberta-National Drug Company Limited in Alberta, and B.C. Drugs Ltd. in British Columbia.

Laurentian Laboratories Limited looked after manufacturing activities in Montreal, while Can-Wide Distributors Limited of Toronto, along with Preferred Brands Limited and Laurentian Agencies Limited — both from Montreal — took care of sales representation for various health products.

This group of companies made up a rather complex structure that would undergo numerous changes and additions over the years.

In 1962, for example, National Drug bought all the common shares of Lymans Limited, a Montreal wholesaler. The transaction also involved the purchase of two subsidiaries, Specialty Pharmaceuticals Ltd. and Beck Bros. & Turner Ltd. Lymans served Quebec, chiefly the Montreal area. The operations of National Drug's Montreal subsidiary were later consolidated with those of Lymans.

Loeb Enters the Picture

Despite these various transactions, National Drug's profits had been declining for several years. In 1964, the company experienced a loss of over half a million dollars on sales of $56.2 million. The earnings surplus was rapidly disappearing, dropping from $5.7 million in 1960 to $3.9 million in 1964. Nothing seemed to be going right.

When Gordon J. Odell took up the position of President of National Drug in August 1964, he became the company's seventh president in 18 months. His predecessor, C.P. Haynes, had initiated a number of reforms, but his tenure as President had been short-lived. During this period, the traditional pharmacy business was totally disrupted by the exodus to the suburbs, the sudden proliferation of shopping centres and the growing popularity of discount supermarkets and drugstores.

National Drug decided to revise its traditional structures and management methods as well as redesign store layouts. Gordon J. Odell took up the reforms initiated by his predecessor, C.P. Haynes, and carried them even further. To ensure the company's profitability, he began by closing down the operations that were losing money. He had been hired in July 1963 as a management consultant and sales specialist to act as manager for Ontario. A remarkable performance had earned him the confidence of the company's directors and with it the position of president.

In April 1964, a few months before Gordon J. Odell became President of National Drug, Loeb had offered to buy no less than 100,000 common or preferred shares at $14.50 each. The offer, which expired on May 25, was over-subscribed. Loeb also obtained a purchase option from National Drug for 100,000 unissued common shares at the same price. This option was valid until June 15, 1967.

At year-end 1964–1965, Loeb owned 22.8 percent of all outstanding shares, an investment that had cost the company $1,658,873.[6] This investment grew from year to year. At the end of 1971–1972, Loeb held 52.1 percent of National Drug's common shares and 25.8 percent of its convertible preferred shares.[7] This holding enabled Loeb to include National Drug's results on a pro-rata basis in its consolidated financial statements. Loeb's interest in National Drug had thus far cost $3,524,000. That year, National Drug sales exceeded $91.7 million or 17.3 percent of Loeb's consolidated sales.

The Deficit Disappears

Many changes were taking place at National Drug during the days of its takeover by Loeb. In 1964, as mentioned earlier, the company had to take a loss of over half a million dollars. The following year, the hemorrhage was stopped. Sales of slightly over $60 million bolstered net income to $109,757, a recovery of some $625,000 in one year.[8]

But there was still plenty of room for improvement. While he was manager in Ontario, Gordon J. Odell had closed the London, Hamilton and Windsor centres, maintaining only those in Toronto and Ottawa. Once president, he shut down operations in Sydney, Victoria, and even Montreal. He then instituted a program of belt-tightening and cutbacks throughout the company. These included giving up the prestigious Place Ville-Marie offices[9] where the company had set up its headquarters after the sale of its premises at 442 Saint-Gabriel Street in Old Montreal (today, the Vieux Saint-Gabriel restaurant).

In the Maritimes, the wholesale operations of National Drug and Estey & Curtis Company were merged in 1966 to create a new company — Eastern Drug Services Limited. National Drug held 50.1 percent of its shares for itself, Estey & Curtis the remainder. That same year, Eastern Drug acquired Provincial Wholesale Drugs Limited of Halifax.

In 1969, National Drug liquidated a number of manufacturing operations in Montreal along with certain assets of Laurentian Laboratories Limited. Future policy would entrust the manufacture of its products to specialized laboratories. However, the company continued to act as manufacturing agent and exclusive distributor of these products and numerous others that would later be added to its product list.

The bankruptcy of Pharmacies Modernes in Montreal gave Bertram Loeb the idea of having National Drug resume its wholesale activities in that city. Gordon J. Odell was against it. He felt that Georges Painchaud, a subsidiary of Loeb, would have the inside track. Nonetheless, Bertram Loeb ordered a warehouse to be built in Montreal. A few months later, he changed his mind and, in 1969, National Drug sold the barely completed premises to Georges Painchaud, which converted the building into a successful cash-and-carry warehouse.

In 1970, Eastern Drug became a wholly-owned subsidiary of National Drug, which had paid $1,060,000 in cash for the second portion of the shares. In 1973, Eastern Drug bought the business and assets of McMurdo Wholesale Drug Company of St. John's, Newfoundland. Finally, during 1978–1979, Eastern Drug Services Limited ceased to operate as a subsidiary and became a division of National Drug.

Around the same time, in 1974, National Drug took over Western Wholesale Drug Limited of Vancouver, which became a division — Western-National Drug Services. In 1976, however, all activites in British Columbia were abandoned because of labour conflicts. Employee demands would have put the company in the red.

Much More Than a Wholesaler

National Drug, whose sales and profits had started to grow in 1964 when Gordon J. Odell became President, had undergone many changes by July 1977, when it joined the Provigo fold as part of the Loeb acquisition.

Not only did its sales border on $150 million, contributing over a million dollars to net income, it had also become much more than a wholesaler. It was now exploring every possible marketing approach and taking advantage of any opportunity to ensure that the products it distributed — particularly those for which it enjoyed exclusivity — reached the largest possible number of retail outlets. National Drug was constantly developing new services and improving existing ones to counteract the trend of manufacturers selling directly to retailers. In keeping with this approach, National Drug encouraged the creation of voluntary groups of pharmacists such as ARP (Associated Retail Pharmacists).

With the help of its agencies and, notably, Laurentian Agencies, which operated independently of the parent company, National Drug offered the same services to all clients. Laurentian was the Canadian representative for several foreign manufacturers, offering them marketing and distribution services.

Few Canadians realize that such popular patented medicines as Gin Pills, Vitonol, Paradol, the entire range of Dr. Chase products and Snap hand cleaner are brands that belonged to National Drug. Some of them still do. The first to be surprised were undoubtedly Antoine Turmel and Pierre H. Lessard when they began to sit on the Board of Directors and Executive Committee of National Drug in 1977.

The Deal Gets Even Better

The two positions of Chairman of the Board and Chief Executive Officer of National Drug — previously held by Bertram Loeb — were now occupied respectively by Antoine Turmel and Gordon J. Odell. The latter had risen from President and Chief Operating Officer to President and Chief Executive Officer. Gordon Odell enjoyed the greatest independence in his dealings with National Drug's new owner. National Drug was his baby.

In 1977, National Drug Limited was only partially owned by Provigo through Loeb, which held 51.9 percent of the common shares and 25.8 percent of the preferred shares.

To comply with the interests of minority shareholders, National Drug continued to publish annual reports from 1977 to 1980.[10] They make for interesting reading. For example, the reader will learn of the acquisition of Top Drug Mart of Toronto, a company affiliated with Koffler Stores Ltd. This transaction enabled National Drug to rationalize its distribution network in Ontario and increase sales.

The reports also reveal that in January 1980, National Drug acquired the remaining 16 percent interest in National-Drug Limited, a separate company which served Manitoba and Saskatchewan.

Above all, a perusal of these reports shows that National Drug's annual sales were steadily rising and that progress was evident on every front.

In 1980, National Drug celebrated the 75th anniversary of its incorporation. Provigo marked the event in a special way. First of all, it decided to give the company's name a slightly more French flavour by adding the designation Compagnie National Drug Limitée;[11] Loeb as well could now be referred to as M. Loeb Limitée. This was a symbolic gesture. There were more fundamental changes in store.

Gordon J. Odell, President of National Drug from 1964 to 1986.

Provigo Becomes Sole Owner of All Common Shares

In mid-December 1980, the Boards of Directors of Provigo and National Drug approved Provigo's project to acquire all National Drug shares. Concurrently, Provigo created Nadruco Holdings Limited, a company in which it was the sole shareholder. Nadruco then acquired all of National Drug's common and preferred shares belonging to Loeb. On January 30, 1981, the general meeting of National Drug shareholders approved the merger between Nadruco and National Drug Limited, which came into effect the following day.

National Drug Limited, born of the merger, became a wholly-owned subsidiary of Provigo. Minority shareholders were compensated with preferred shares redeemable for $16 for each of their common shares. There were 366,465 such shares outstanding. On February 15, 1981, National Drug redeemed these shares at the price offered for a total cost of $5.8 million. Provigo was now the sole holder of common shares.

But this transaction was far from finished. A while later, a dissident minority shareholder went to court to claim that $16 was not a fair price for his shares. After a lengthy trial, he won his case, and an additional $10 per share was awarded. As he held 1,000 shares, Provigo was forced to pay him $10,000.

Because these proceedings had been extremely costly and time-consuming, and because the amount at stake was relatively small, Provigo decided not to appeal, despite its conviction that the initial offer was fair. This decision would cause Provigo further headaches.

Dissatisfied with the settlement of $10,000, the dissident shareholder persuaded one of his acquaintances to file a request for permission to launch a class action suit on behalf of all minority shareholders, even though they had accepted Provigo's offer of $16 per share. The contention was that every shareholder should obtain the additional $10 awarded by the court.

Matters had taken a more serious turn. It was no longer a question of 1,000 but 365,465 shares. The amount at stake now exceeded $3.5 million, not to mention all the expenses related to the case. Provigo, which had already disbursed more than $5.8 million to buy these shares in early 1981, was running the risk of having to pay an extra $4 million. The motion prompted a lengthy debate and multiple legal procedures until, in June 1987, the Superior Court of Quebec decided to dismiss the request to launch a class action suit.

The claimant filed an appeal within the prescribed time limit. The affair is still pending.

Half a Billion Surpassed

In 1984–1985, Provigo's pharmaceutical sector activities registered net sales of over $532 million with operating profits of $13.2 million.[12]

In addition to serving 248 pharmacies affiliated with Associated Retail Pharmacists (ARP), National Drug supplied over 3,000 other clients — pharmacies, sundry businesses and hospitals — from its 10 distribution centres located throughout Canada.

During the year, National Drug sold its seven Maritime-based Good Neighbor Drug Mart pharmacies to Shoppers Drug Mart, a subsidiary of Imasco. Shoppers was one of National Drug's major clients. The Sobeys Group had also made an offer, feeling that its significant interest in Provigo would give it the edge. The Sobeys were greatly disappointed.

In the pharmaceutical sector it was still Loeb, Montreal Division (Painchaud), rather than National Drug, which served Quebec. Under the Promoprix banner, the Greater Montreal area had 81 affiliated pharmacies served by Painchaud at the time. The Promoprix voluntary group of pharmacies had been set up in 1979 by Painchaud.

Gordon J. Odell's tenure as President and Chief Executive Officer of National Drug ended in 1986. He had taken the helm of a leaky vessel in 1964 and left behind a profitable company when he retired in 1986. Henri A. Roy of Provigo became Chairman of the Board and Chief Executive Officer. In the summer of 1986 William H. Brown was made President and Chief Operating Officer of National Drug, which was now part of the Health and Pharmaceutical Group, a recent Provigo creation.[13]

Newly-Born MEDIS

Early in 1987, the Provigo Health and Pharmaceutical Group became Medis Health and Pharmaceutical Services Inc., consolidating all related activities into a single subsidiary.

At its formation, Henri A. Roy, Chairman of the Board and Chief Executive Officer of Medis, could announce that this wholly-owned subsidiary of Provigo was the only company in Canada distributing pharmaceutical products from coast to coast and that its sales should soon exceed one billion dollars.[14]

From $650 Million to $1 Billion Within a Year

In less than two years the pharmaceutical products group grew very rapidly, doubling its sales and attaining the goals formulated by Henri A. Roy when he assumed responsibility for the Health and Pharmaceutical Group in the fall of 1985.

According to Henri A. Roy, Medis had three primary objectives: to complete the national distributional network, to increase and diversify the range of services offered to pharmacies and to maintain expansion through recruiting new clients. It was clear that coast-to-coast operations depended on re-entering the British Columbia market, which National Drug had abandoned in 1976. With 11.4 percent of the population at the time, British Columbia accounted for 13 percent of the market, no doubt because of its large retirement community. Pharmacy retail sales were estimated at $743 million for 1986.

Why Not Go for the Largest Wholesaler?

Southwestern Drug Warehouse Ltd. dominated the pharmacy wholesale business in British Columbia with sales of $53 million in 1985. The company sold neither tobacco nor cigarettes, which resulted in a better overall profit margin. Its major client, Shoppers Drug Mart, accounted for approximately 40 percent of its sales. Southwestern had built a modern 90,000-square-foot warehouse for its operations. In addition to supplying products, it offered its clients data processing services.

At Provigo, plans were afoot to buy Southwestern. Not only would this acquisition have secured a dominant position for Medis in British Columbia, it would at the same time have enabled Provigo to acquire a subsidiary of Southwestern, called Express Pharmaceuticals, a growing competitor of Alberta National Drug. In one stroke, Medis would become number one in Alberta and British Columbia.

In the view of Medis' senior management, the fact that Southwestern was on the verge of entering into an agreement with another chain of pharmacies, which would add some $30 million to its sales figures, made the prospect of this acquisition all the more interesting.

A deal was finalized in October 1986. For approximately five million dollars, National Drug, now Medis, regained a foothold in British Columbia and consolidated its business in Alberta.

Conquering Quebec

With Southwestern Drug in British Columbia, Alberta National Drug in Alberta, National Drug in Ontario, Manitoba and Saskatchewan, and Eastern Drug Services in the Atlantic Provinces, Medis and its subsidiaries served virtually all of Canada. Quebec, still served by a division of Loeb (Painchaud), was the only element missing in the network, even though Medis had its head office in the province. So in January 1986 it created a new division, Médi-Service, after signing supply agreements with Uniprix, the largest group of independent pharmacists in Quebec, and the Maxi-Santé Group.

The agreement led to a $150-million increase in Provigo's pharmaceutical products sales in Quebec and considerably enlarged its territory. Such expansion necessitated the construction of a 50,000-square-foot distribution centre in Quebec City, an investment of $6 million. Since Loeb did not have a clientele in Quebec City, Médi-Service started serving that territory before acquiring the assets of Painchaud, Loeb's pharmaceutical division in Montreal, which Médi-Service replaced.

Médi-Service serves over 1,000 clients which comprise affiliated members, independent pharmacies and corporate chains such as Uniprix, Maxi-Santé, Jean Coutu, Cumberland, Superpharm and Kanes.

In addition to ensuring better distribution of products in Quebec, Médi-Service offers affiliated pharmacists such services as financial assistance, location research and leasing advice, and assistance in store layout, merchandising and advertising. Médi-Service expected to achieve sales of over $300 million as of 1987, which would confirm its predominant role in Quebec in the distribution of health-care and pharmaceuticals products and services.

Medis was now in a position to distribute its products and offer its services from coast to coast. The priority was to achieve national excellence through offering a wide variety of quality products with first-rate service. In Quebec, Médi-Service has become the number one pharmaceutical wholesaler by expanding its network of retail clients. In Ontario Medis supplies over 800 pharmacies, including large chains like Shoppers Drug Mart, K-Mart, Super X and Zellers. Medis has also entered into supply agreements with Lawton's in the Atlantic Provinces and Boots Drug Stores (Canada) Ltd. in Ontario and Western Canada.

As befits a leader, Medis was determined to establish its presence throughout Canada and, above all, to enlarge its range of services offered on the basis of social and demographic factors in each region of Canada.

The extremely rapid pace of change that Medis was experiencing took its toll. Profitability declined, calling for a serious reconsideration of the strategy pursued. Strong measures were taken during 1988 after an exhaustive review of operation.

Medis clearly holds a specific position within the Canadian pharmaceutical sector, and its long-term profitability and competitiveness depend to a large extent on its ability to increase systematically its productivity in terms of procurement, logistics and distribution, aspects which can also be found in most of Provigo's operating companies, particularly those in the food sector. In other words, Medis has at its disposal the internal resources to improve its performance, provided that efforts are concentrated on the critical aspects. The pursuit of this new orientation is the challenge facing the Medis team in the years ahead.

Notes

1. Provigo Inc. Annual Report for the year ended January 28, 1978.
2. *Centennial/Anniversary Souvenir, a commemorative volume celebrating Canada's Centenary and National Drug's 60 years of service.*
3. Brown and Webb, Simson Brothers and Hattie & Mylius in Halifax; T.B. Barker & Sons and Mc Diarmid in Saint-John; Harry Skinner & Company in Kingston; Elliot & Company and Lyman Know & Clarkson in Toronto; J. Winer & Co. and Dominion Drug Company in Hamilton; London Drug Company in London; Bole Drug Company in Winnipeg; Canada Drug & Book Co. in Regina; Bole Drug Company in Calgary; Henderson Brothers in Vancouver; Canada Drug & Book Co. in Nelson, B.C.; and Evans & Son Limited, Kerry Watson & Company and Lyman Knox & Company in Montreal.
4. National Drug Limited (revised October 6, 1980) The Financial Post Information Service.
5. National Drug and Chemical Company of Canada Annual Report for the year ended December 31, 1945.
6. M. Loeb Limited Annual Report for the year ended January 30, 1965. Loeb had bought 92,173 common shares and 20,905 convertible preferred shares.
7. M. Loeb Annual Report for the year ended January 29, 1972. Loeb owns 347,457 common shares and 21,605 convertible preferred shares.
8. National Drug and Chemical Company of Canada Annual Report for the year ended January 4, 1966.
9. It was much cheaper for National Drug to set up headquarters in 1965 in Pointe-Claire on the outskirts of Montreal.
10. Provigo would take into account the results of National Drug in its own annual reports of 1978, 1979 and 1980.
11. This change became official on June 2, 1980 by an amendment to the Letters Patent of National Drug and Chemical Company of Canada Limited.
12. Provigo Inc. Annual Report for the year ended January 26, 1985.
13. Both were succeeded in 1988 by Pierre Lortie and David R. Friesen, a long-time Provigo executive.
14. Medis presentation by Henri A. Roy, February 5, 1987.

CHAPTER THIRTEEN

PROVI-SOIR: THE IDEA CATCHES ON

The idea behind the Provi-Soir network of franchise convenience stores is not new. As early as 1968, Antoine Turmel was thinking of opening convenience stores, at the same time as he was planning his AVA discount-store project. Little did he know just how successful Provi-Soir would be. At first, the idea was to form a voluntary group of associated store owners. But what emerged from the project was a system of franchise stores which has become the envy of many, not only in Quebec but throughout Canada.

By April 30, 1973, Antoine Turmel was ready to implement this new approach to retailing: "As a result of several market studies, Provigo intends to develop a chain of convenience stores called 'Provi-Soir', with the first units opening in 1974. In addition to operating during conventional hours, these stores will respond to consumer needs by remaining open Sundays and every night. Industry statistics indicate that this market offers excellent potential; in the past year, convenience stores sales increased by 19 percent and store openings by 14 percent. The objectives of this endeavour are to generate additional sales, increase our share of this market and to permit several grocers to operate a business which promises an interesting future."[1]

With convenience stores showing the largest growth in sales in the retail food industry today, these predictions could hardly have been more accurate. The next year the concept was perfected: "The company will launch its 'Provi-Soir' convenience store franchising program this year. These stores will have a floor area of approximately 2,000 square feet, with a range of some 2,000 items including a variety of grocery products and a limited choice of fresh produce and prepared meats. Provi-Soir stores will be open 7 days a week with minimum operating hours of 9:00 a.m. to 10:00 p.m., and will be eligible for permits to sell beer. In collaboration with the major oil companies, several will also sell gasoline through self-service pumps.

"These convenience stores will be located in densely populated districts and many will use service stations converted and adapted to this type of operation. We expect to open 15 Provi-Soir stores in the Montreal and Quebec City areas during 1974, of which at least 10 will be in cooperation with major integrated oil companies."[2]

And a few months later, the project became reality: " 'Provi-Soir' convenience stores began operations: three franchise stores were open by January 25, 1975; another six units were about to be completed. Although fifteen stores had been planned for 1974, development was delayed as a result of certain difficulties encountered in obtaining the permits necessary for this type of operation. The problems have been largely overcome and some twenty-five stores are expected to be operational by the end of the present fiscal year. At least half of these will feature self-service gas bars. Master agreements for the sale of petroleum products have been signed with Shell Canada Limited and Murphy Oil Quebec Ltd., and negotiations with other oil companies are in progress."[3]

These few paragraphs from three successive annual reports sketch the story behind Provi-Soir's bold new formula to combine food and gas-station services in a franchise network of convenience stores. The stores would be licensed to sell beer and, later, would remain open 24 hours a day, 365 days a year.

Speaking about Provi-Soir at the second Provigo presentation to Montreal and Toronto financial analysts, in April 1975, Antoine Turmel emphasized that "another rapidly growing operation is the Provi-Soir convenience store. Convenience stores have multiplied in Canada over the last ten years but are relatively new to Quebec. Provigo planners worked three years to achieve an advanced concept and design, and a strong public image."

Jean-Claude Merizzi was entrusted with the project. A graduate of

École des Hautes Études Commerciales in Montreal, he had spent five years in the commerce branch of the Quebec Ministry of Industry and Commerce before joining Provigo in September 1973.

At Provi-Soir he set out to learn all he could about North American convenience-store trends. He went to Florida to attend a convention on the subject. Self-serve gas stations had also begun to appear about the same time. During his trip, Jean-Claude Merizzi saw how the convenience-store business had been successfully paired with gas-station operations and he was convinced that the formula had a lot to offer.

For him it was evident that the Provi-Soir banner should signal this dynamic merchandising formula. What was needed was a comprehensive network of new stores, based on the franchise principle. Provigo would first have to acquire the site, and then fit out both the store and gas station, since such an investment would be too large for most future Provi-Soir retailers.

Naturally, Jean-Claude Merizzi had to convince everyone at Provigo that his vision was worth pursuing. This was no easy task. People agreed on the overall concept, but not on his particular application, which would place new demands on the retail operator. In the end, Jean-Claude Merizzi won Antoine Turmel's approval and the project was given the go-ahead. The first step was to approach the large oil companies to obtain their support in pairing the Provi-Soir outlets with service stations. Yet in 1973–1974, even though Provigo's sales were around $300 million, the company was not well known outside of Quebec and the head offices of the major oil companies were all located in Toronto. The concept still needed to be sold.

Furthermore, with the oil embargo, the times were hardly propitious for developing new concepts. Even when the oil companies were sufficiently convinced that the project was worth pursuing, they argued that the oil shortage prevented them from going along. It took a full year of negotiations before the first company, Shell, decided to take a chance on an association with Provi-Soir. At the time, the two companies agreed on five locations. This first trial proved immensely successful. Today, there are 135, and every large oil company is participating: out of 233 Provi-Soir outlets, nearly 60 percent are twinned with a self-serve gas station.

But winning the support of the oil companies did not spell the end of Merizzi's labours. He had to obtain permits to operate businesses which combined food and gasoline operations. Here again, victory did not come easy. Most frustrating was the political unwillingness of certain municipal administrations to allow this type of business on their territories. Above all, the reluctance of Montreal, Ville LaSalle, Laval and Ste-Foy delayed considerably the establishment of Provi-Soir outlets paired with gas stations. Provigo wanted to offer combined services, particularly in Quebec's major urban centres.

One-Stop Shopping

The first Provi-Soir opened in September 1974, in Charlesbourg, on the outskirts of Quebec City; the first one to combine gas-station services opened in Longueuil, near Montreal, in November 1974. The aim was to offer the consumer a place to find a wide variety of products any time of day or night. This convenience would distinguish Provi-Soir from the competition. To be sure, there were several successful American models, but everything had to be adapted to conform to Quebec laws and regulations, as well as to suit the differences in consumer tastes and preferences.

The first three Provi-Soirs were set up in existing grocery stores or service stations. Soon, however, Provigo decided to start from scratch. There were no real savings to be derived from renovating and fitting out existing outlets. A move into a new store was also a way to avoid comments about "your gas station starting to sell groceries." As well, this approach would enable Provi-Soir to project a uniform image and establish a characteristic presentation format across the province.

Provi-Soir wanted to project itself as a convenience store offering gas-station services rather than as a food store located on the site of a gas station. Variety, cleanliness and service — these were the quality standards to be met by each Provi-Soir outlet. In this context, a choice had to be made between the corporate-store formula versus a network of franchise stores.

The franchise system made all the difference. The turn-key franchise formula was the one selected. Provigo purchased the site and would then build or have the future franchise facilities built. The fact that Provigo was owner or primary lessee of the premises and equipment would ensure its complete control over the franchised establishment. A typical store would cover 2,400 square feet. Similar exterior cladding material, decor, lighting, and layout would be used for every store.

It should be recalled that, at the time, only independent merchants were granted a licence to sell beer, cider and, later, wine. Thanks to Antoine Turmel's determination, Provi-Soir was the first chain of stores to obtain such a licence for its merchants. Given the sensitive nature of this issue, it was a hard-won victory, but the permit enabled the Provi-Soir retailer to compete on an equal footing with the independent merchant.

In February 1975, when the implementation of the Provi-Soir concept was just under way, Jean-Claude Merizzi experienced heart problems and had to undergo surgery. Fortunately, he had recently convinced Claude Perrault, who was Director of Marketing at Provigo (Sherbrooke), to join him in this exciting but demanding project.

As Operations Manager, Claude Perrault immediately took up the task of expanding the Provi-Soir network. He remained Jean-Claude Merizzi's assistant until the latter's appointment, in March 1979, to the position of Vice-President, Planning and Business Development, at Provigo head office. Claude Perrault then became General Manager of Provi-Soir. His long practical experience in the field gave him a thorough knowledge of the organization. His successor, Pierre N. Gagné, also had that invaluable experience.

Under Claude Perrault, the number of Provi-Soir outlets grew from 3 at the beginning of 1975 to 19 a year later, 34 in 1977, 78 in 1978, 110 in 1979, 140 by year-end 1979–1980 and 200 in November 1985. A vigorous development pace had been set.

7 Days a Week, 24 Hours a Day

One of the models used in the creation of Provi-Soir was the American chain of Seven Eleven convenience stores,[4] whose very name stands for service available from 7 a.m. to 11 p.m.

Initially, the Provi-Soir stores were to remain open from 7 a.m. to 9 p.m., then 10 p.m. and, finally, 11 p.m. From the outset, there was an exception. One of the sites acquired from Shell in Saint-Jérôme north of Montreal included round-the-clock gas-station operations. The status quo had to be maintained as one of the conditions of the agreement.

When senior management of Provi-Soir suggested across-the-board 24-hour-a-day service, people were incredulous. Who could possibly want to operate such a franchise? How can one exercise efficient control 24 hours a day? Arguments against the project ran the gamut from petty theft, waste, and shortage of customers to the risk of armed robbery.

It was in the fall of 1976 that the first Provi-Soir began to offer round-the-clock service. One by one, the franchisees grew convinced that the system was a good one. Today, with the exception of two outlets, all Provi-Soir stores are open 24 hours a day, 7 days a week, 365 days a year, even on Christmas and New Year's Day.

Where you can find anything at any time.

Round-the-clock service has become Provi-Soir's trademark. Night traffic represents 14 percent of Provi-Soir's business on average. There is no question that the Provi-Soir formula of extended hours has been a success.

Improving the Formula

Today's Provi-Soir is slightly different from the 1974 version. But the goal of offering the consumer virtually every last-minute shopping item within easy distance remains unchanged. These days, Provi-Soir provides more than simply food products and a few basic non-food items; it carries beer, cider, wine, magazines and newspapers, plus a variety of household necessities and, of course, gas is available wherever possible. Worthy of note is the fact that grocery items account for only 15 percent of sales. The lion's share of the business comes from a variety of additional services and departments.

The Hibouf fast-food service, opened in Laval in June 1984, is a case in point. It offers hot coffee, sandwiches, pizzas, delicatessen items and the like. After four years, this formula is now part of 173 outlets and growing in popularity.

Several Provi-Soir stores have automatic banking machines,[5] plus dry cleaning, photo developing and video rental counters; some also house a mini-bakery. Various other services will probably be added in the near future. For instance, Provi-Soir customers will be able to purchase in-store tickets for cultural and sports events.

In many ways, the needs of the residents of a particular area determine what services are offered. We know, for example, that consumers in the 18-to-35 age bracket make up a large part of the clientele and spend on average three minutes per visit to a Provi-Soir outlet; as a result, their particular demands have to be met promptly.

One of the key factors behind the success of a Provi-Soir store is its location. Ideally, it should be at the intersection of two heavy traffic arteries. Needless to say, interesting and available property is becoming rarer all the time, as well as more expensive, but the investment is worth it. Nowadays, few people balk at the high price of a choice location. Twenty dollars a square foot is no longer considered exorbitant. This is a far cry from the two dollars a square foot of the early acquisitions, a figure that had taken aback Antoine Turmel and Pierre H. Lessard, who headed Provigo's Real Estate services at the time.

Credit must go to Jean-Claude Merizzi and Claude Perrault for convincing everyone that their formula would make Provigo number one in a market undergoing prodigious growth.

In 1973, Antoine Turmel had taken a number of measures to support the new venture. He convinced Provigo's wholesale divisions that they should supply Provi-Soir at advantageous terms with a fairly low profit margin. In the end, the project's success exceeded even Antoine Turmel's most optimistic forecasts.

1980-1981: New Developments

Until 1980-1981, Provi-Soir was a series of franchise stores mentioned as so many units in Provigo's annual report, as were the Pinto convenience outlets serviced by Loeb, and Horne & Pitfield's Red Rooster stores.

In 1980-1981, Provigo adopted a new method of grouping its various activities. Sales to convenience-store retailers were now to be included in wholesale distribution operations. That year, there were 393 Provi-Soir, Pinto and Red Rooster stores, compared with 343 a year earlier.[6] Sales of gasoline sold in stations were reported under "Other Activities," along with Top Valu's service-station sales and the real estate activities of Provigo and its subsidiaries.

During the same period, these "Other Activities" sales were slightly over $118 million, with income of some $9.75 million. Despite showing the lowest sales among all activities, this sector was relatively the most profitable.[7]

In 1981, Provigo's large petroleum sector consisted of two divisions. The first comprised 188 gas stations, 87 of which were paired with Provi-Soir outlets — all of them in Quebec — and whose sales volume totalled 196.3 million litres. The second consisted of the 101 Top Valu Gasmarts operated by Loeb in the Ottawa valley and Ontario, which sold 227 million litres of gas that year. The acquisition of the assets of Able Oil Inc. in September 1980 enabled Top Valu to get a foothold in the lucrative Toronto and Southwestern Ontario market, as well as to increase the number of its stations from 67 to 101 within a year.

The Convenience Group Becomes C Corp.

From 1980 to 1985, the "Other Activities" sector of Provigo expanded in new directions. In addition to the sale of petroleum products and real estate management, this sector also included sales of sports and recreation equipment, and do-it-yourself home improvement and renovation products, as well as revenue from restaurant operations.

In 1985, Provigo decided to restructure its activities. The "Other Activities" sector was replaced by the Convenience Group and the Development Group. The Convenience Group would include all convenience-store store operations.

A year later, the Convenience Group became C Corp. Inc., which began to oversee all the Provigo groups of convenience stores on a national level.

Jean-Claude Merizzi, Executive Vice-President of Provigo, became Chairman of the Board and Chief Executive Officer of C Corp. as well. Claude Perrault was appointed its President and Chief Operating Officer. The team that had set up Provi-Soir was now in charge of guiding C Corp. to the top of convenience sector retailing. As emphasized in a recent Annual Report: "Traditionally considered a food outlet, the convenience store has broken new ground even though the formula's success has enabled the sector to account for more than 10 percent of current food retail sales.

"The concept of convenience stores as defined by Provi-Soir in Quebec corresponds to lifestyle changes engendered by socio-demographic trends as well as changes in the labor market, consumer behavior and spending habits."[8]

In Ontario, the Winks network, introduced in autumn 1986, is based on the Provi-Soir concept adapted to the specific conditions of the Ontario market.

There are now 233 Provi-Soir stores in Quebec and 23 Winks, 3 Winks Express and 20 Pinto outlets, as well as 73 Top Valu gas stations in Ontario. The Canadian West has 175 Red Rooster convenience stores.[9]

Sales for the entire C Corp. network are close to half a billion dollars and well over that figure if we include those of the Red Rooster outlets. With income of $10.2 million, the Convenience Group has already proven to be a profitable and promising sector.

Open 24 hours a day, 7 days a week, the Provi-Soir stores, whose concept is the model for all C Corp. convenience stores, have become veritable service centres on which consumers rely more and more. The term 'service station' has indeed acquired new meaning.

Notes

1. Provigo Inc. Annual Report for the year ended January 27, 1973.
2. Provigo Inc. Annual Report for the year ended January 26, 1974.
3. Provigo Inc. Annual Report for the year ended January 25, 1975.
4. With some 7,000 outlets, Seven Eleven is the world's largest chain of convenience stores.
5. There were already 62 such machines in August 1988.
6. Provigo Inc. Annual Report for the year ended January 31, 1981.
7. The figures for the various other sectors were: Pharmaceutical — sales $276 million, income $6.5 million; Food, Retail — sales $351.2 million, income $3.7 million; Food, Wholesale — sales close to $2.2 billion, income $50 million.
8. Provigo Inc. Annual Report for the year ended January 31, 1987.
9. Provigo Inc. Annual Report for the year ended January 30, 1988.

CHAPTER FOURTEEN

THE RETAIL BATTLE FOR MONTREAL

The acquisitions throughout the 1970s had transformed the Company. By 1980 Provigo held a dominant position in food distribution in Quebec. The company was developing a presence elsewhere in Canada and even in some parts of the United States. Provi-Soir was expanding rapidly and successfully, and Provigo had broken new ground by distributing petroleum products. A subsidiary, National Drug, was now a major player throughout Canada in the distribution of health and pharmaceutical products. The 1980s promised new successes for the maturing Quebec prodigy.

At Montreal head office, senior management was made up of Quebeckers who were particularly sensitive to the growth of food operations in the province but who monitored and coordinated the activities of its subsidiaries in other regions at arm's length.

With the acquisition of Jato in early 1975, and especially since 1978 when both wholesale and retail operations had been entrusted to two executive vice-presidents, Jean-Louis Lamontagne and Jean Boiteau respectively, Provigo had begun to chart a new course in its food operations.

The pioneers, who were primarily wholesalers, had decided to explore the retail business more fully, to the point of developing a friendly rivalry or even competition between the wholesale and retail operations.

In April 1979, Richard Constantineau, who had made his mark during his five years with the Provi-Fruit Division and as General Manager of the Quebec Region Retail Division, was transferred to head office and appointed Vice-President, Retail Operations, to succeed Jean Boiteau who was about to retire.

In 1980, Provigo already owned 46 corporate stores, 9 AVA discount stores and 140 Provi-Soir outlets, all in Quebec, plus 657 affiliated retailers operating under the Provigo, Provibec and Provipop banners. Two years earlier, Provigo had bought the seven Hudson's Bay Company food stores on the North Shore; the famous trading company had once controlled all food distribution in that region. This purchase, which had been overshadowed by the Loeb and Dionne transactions, was the final victory in the invasion of the North Shore that had been initiated by Jean-Louis Lamontagne in the 1960s. At the very beginning of the 1980s, Provigo determined that it was time to concentrate on Quebec's main market. Since Montreal represented some 60 percent of the total retail food business in the province, Provigo could hardly continue to grow everywhere else without turning its attention to this important market where it was virtually absent but for its headquarters and wholesale operations.

For senior management, there were two approaches to the Montreal market. One was to start from scratch by purchasing property and by building or renting stores throughout the Montreal region. The snag was that it would take Provigo 15 years to carve out a major share of the greater Montreal market where, over the years, Steinberg and Dominion had already secured the majority of prime locations.

The other approach was to buy sites complete with facilities or, to put it plainly, to acquire Steinberg or Dominion. Provigo decided on this course to save precious time.

Rumour had it that Steinberg was for sale. Since its stores were particularly well located, the possibility of acquisition was considered but not for long. The purchase of Steinberg would have been rather costly (perhaps half a billion dollars), not to mention the logistics of integrating the company, sorting out differences and absorbing headquarter operations and vast wholesale warehouses. As well, the operating philosophies of the two companies contrasted sharply. While Provigo was primarily a wholesaler which serviced affiliated retailers, Steinberg's corporate retail stores were the backbone of its operations.

On the other hand, there was Dominion, with operations concentrated primarily in Montreal. And it was for sale at a price that suited Provigo's objectives.

On December 17, 1980, Provigo bought 87 of the 89 Dominion stores in Quebec. The news came as a surprise to most people. Indeed, it was no small accomplishment which achieved the company's primary goals: 71 of these stores were located in the Montreal region.

The agreement had been finalized the previous day at the Château Champlain in Montreal. On the Dominion side were Thomas G. Bolton, Deputy Chairman of the Board and Chief Executive Officer, and Allen C. Jackson, President and Chief Operating Officer; Provigo was represented by Chairman of the Board Antoine Turmel and President Pierre H. Lessard.

The Purchase of the Dominion Stores

For some months, the Fédération des magasins COOP, which had bought four Dominion stores in Alma, Jonquière, Chicoutimi and Rimouski, had been negotiating the purchase of all the other Dominion outlets in Quebec. The offer of purchase was backed by the Caisse centrale Desjardins, the Société de développement coopératif, Soquia (Société québécoise d'initiatives agro-alimentaires) and the Caisse de dépôt et placement du Québec. COOP had made a deposit of five million dollars.

But the negotiations seemed to take forever.

Dominion wanted to end its Quebec operations. People in the industry knew that the overall situation of the group was not particularly satisfactory and that its performance was average at best. Out of more than $2.66 billion in sales in 1979–1980, $500 million came from Quebec, despite the fact that 89 of its 337 stores were located in the province. Moreover, the number of Dominion stores in Quebec had dwindled from 105 three years earlier.

Increased competition from well-entrenched independent and affiliated retailers selling beer and wine, combined with the strong presence of Steinberg in urban areas, had forced Dominion to close many of its stores in Quebec. By jettisoning its Quebec operations, the company would recover some of its assets and be able to consolidate its Ontario operations.

It was against this backdrop that Provigo management took matters in hand and made a direct proposal to the top management of Dominion to purchase its Quebec operations. Details were brushed aside and the deal was closed in less than six weeks. The newspapers reported a price of $100 million. It was, indeed, Provigo's largest transaction to date.

Dominion's top man in Quebec, Réal Brouillette, was surprised and declared that he was not in a position to explain the reasons why Argus Corporation, headed by Conrad M. and G. Montegu Black, had made the deal with Provigo. As for the Fédération des magasins COOP, it refused to comment on the sale, which had been conveyed by telegram.[1]

In *Le Devoir* (December 19, 1980), Denis Ouellet, an analyst with Lévesque-Beaubien, argued that the transaction would obviously strengthen Provigo's activities in Montreal. He added that Dominion had been losing ground to its competitors because its image was weaker than both Métro-Richelieu's and Steinberg's, and that Provigo was well perceived by francophones. He concluded that the purchase was a golden opportunity for Provigo to penetrate the Montreal market, but how this purchase would be financed or the new operations integrated remained to be seen.

Others observed that the Dominion purchase would be detrimental to Provigo's short-term profitability although it would ensure greater profitability in the long run.

Pierre H. Lessard put the sales figure in some perspective. Although $100 million in assets were involved, the real investment was less than that since the in-store and warehouse inventory could be sold rapidly.[2]

He also sounded the general consensus in an article published in the *Globe and Mail* (December 19, 1980): "This is one way we can increase our market share in the Montreal area in one swoop." He added that the integration of Dominion stores, along with the rationalization of operations and economies of scale, would make the deal profitable.

For Antoine Turmel, this transaction gave Provigo a substantial share of the Montreal market and a presence which it could not otherwise have achieved for another fifteen years.

In Love with Provigo

Investors responded quickly and favourably to the news of the deal and Provigo's share price rose accordingly.

The agreement was concluded late on December 17, 1980 and was announced the following day. On the 18th, the quoted share price rose by $3.50 to close at $55.50 per share. On December 20, the shares had increased by $8.75 or 19 percent in a week, closing at $55.75.

This level was almost double the $28 the shares had attained earlier that year. By June 1981, the quoted market price would rise to $71 per share.

At the Annual and Special General Meeting held May 26, 1981, the shareholders approved a special bylaw stipulating that all common shares would be subdivided on a 4:1 basis and that, subsequently, the common share capital would be increased by 12 million shares.

To finance in part the purchase of some assets of Dominion Stores in Quebec, Provigo issued two million newly-split common shares. These were offered on June 29, 1981 at $16.50 per share and were eligible as investments in a Quebec Stock Savings Plan.

The share offering was made six months after the Dominion agreement. All financial analysts had been positive about the purchase, and all agreed that Provigo had a brilliant future.

Discussing the Provigo shares, analyst Martin Kaufman of Nesbitt Thomson Bongard declared: "It's selling a little ahead of itself, but I still love the stock on a long term basis." Donald Tigert of Burns Fry added that Provigo had "the best growth record among food merchandisers" and that "its shares are difficult to buy because they are so tightly held."[3]

In fact, at the time of the transaction, the Sobey family held 24 percent of the common shares of Provigo, the Caisse de dépôt et placement 21 percent and senior management 15 percent; the remaining 40 percent were divided among the other 2,400 shareholders.

One last accolade from the financial press: "[Provigo's] record for the past 10 years has been nothing short of spectacular, with sales and earnings growing 31 percent annually and return on equity averaging 21.4 percent. Dividends have been raised at a 25 percent compounded rate during the 1970s."[4]

In short, the acquisition of the Dominion stores would continue Provigo's ascendancy, provided the company knew how to operate them profitably. Gérard Virthe, an expert with the Cogem Group, expressed the opinion that in a sector as competitive as food, there was no way to succeed without reinvesting, adding that if Dominion had not dawdled, it would have completed its breakthrough on the Quebec market.[5]

Owning Is Only Part of the Challenge

Between the time the agreement in principle was signed and the moment Provigo took possession of the 86 Dominion supermarkets and 6 Dominion distribution centres, many things had to be settled. In April 1981,

Antoine Turmel wrote: ''This contract will be completed in a few weeks, and we will take possession in stages beginning in May, integrating the warehouses and stores into our system over a period of three to four months.''[6]

When Provigo took over the 86 Dominion supermarkets, it had yet to determine what orientation they would be given. First it wanted to study the current performance and actual potential of each store. At the time, it was believed that some 40 stores would be sold to affiliated retailers while others would remain corporate stores operated by Provigo. Some might be sold outright or closed. The challenge and responsibility of integrating and operating the Dominion stores fell to Richard Constantineau, Vice-President, Retail Operations.

On February 20, 1981, *La Presse* quoted René Provost: ''As of May 1, the Dominion supermarkets will become corporate stores. Later, some of these will be offered to independent merchants. The major part of Provigo's activities centre on the wholesale business, but 25 percent of our retail business does come from corporate stores. With them, we can move towards larger formats in less time. Such a move would pose too great a risk for some independent merchants during the early transition years towards profitability.''

But first all the leases had to be renegotiated, inventories taken, human resources integrated and facilities appraised. These tasks were undertaken store by store. In other words, a ''Dominion'' would become a ''Provigo'' only when the new sign went up.

Negotiations were laborious. The first stores to be transformed were in the Quebec region. At the time, the operation was expected to be completed by September.[7]

In its annual report, Dominion pointed out that the $100 million it would receive from Provigo represented between 25 to 30 million dollars more than the book value of assets.[8]

Steinberg did not even wait for the takeover of the Dominion stores to launch an all-out attack against Provigo. Full-page ads proclaimed: ''89 Dominion stores left town — 155 Steinberg supermarkets on your side!'' ''Can ex-Dominion shoppers find happiness in a Steinberg store? Yes, yes, yes...'' And ''Steinberg is still the freshest idea in supermarkets however you slice it.''

Steinberg also seized this opportunity to slash its prices.

Naturally, Provigo launched a counter-attack with its own full-page ads

When do Dominion stores become **Provigo** Supermarkets?

Many people are still confused about the transaction between **Provigo** and Dominion here in Quebec. The fact of the matter is, **Provigo** will own most of Quebec's Dominion stores, as it was announced publicly a few months ago. However, between the purchase and the actual taking of possession of each store, there will be a small but necessary delay.

To avoid any more unnecessary confusion, we'll give you one sure way to tell exactly when your

local Dominion store has become **Provigo** supermarket: the day you see a **Provigo** sign on the front of your supermarket, you can be sure that **Provigo** is operating the store, but not before.

When that happens, you'll begin to notice **Provigo's** efforts to provide economy, quality and variety - and a special effort to provide personal service. All these things have helped make **Provigo** one of the leaders of the Quebec supermarket business. But don't forget, it's the **Provigo** sign that will signal **Provigo's** ownership of your local Dominion store.

For stores in the metropolitan Montreal area, allow approximately 8 weeks for the conversion from Dominion to **Provigo** to be completed.

provigo SUPERMARKETS

Dominion stores became Provigo supermarkets in the summer of 1981.

with messages to reassure Dominion's former customers, particularly the 50 percent of anglophones who were generally unfamiliar with Provigo's history and dominant presence throughout the rest of Quebec.

The Métro supermarkets also entered the race. In Richard Constantineau's opinion, Métro was a more dangerous competitor than Steinberg because independent merchants are more aggressive.

Notwithstanding the media campaigns of the rival retailers, Steinberg's Vice-President, Marvin Biltis, summed up the situation in more basic terms: "In the supermarket world, what matters first is the location, closely followed by the customer's experience while in the store. The war will be fought through advertising, but it will be won in the stores."[9]

It was indeed a pitched battle, but Provigo took the time to do things right. And prevailed.

1981: A Difficult Year

After an acquisition, however promising, the bill must still be settled. A bank loan provided the bridge-financing, which amounted to $95 million. The ultimate financing was broken down as follows: $31 million from the new issue of common shares, $34 million from working capital and $30 from various long-term bank borrowings during 1981.

The issue of two millions shares at $16.50 at the end of June 1981 was greeted with enthusiasm and was rapidly subscribed. The demand even exceeded the offer. However, in the weeks that followed, interest rates reached 20% — the highest in the entire modern-era economic history of Canada — and the quoted market price dropped appreciably. By the end of August, the quoted price was down to $12.50 and still falling.

The integration phase of the stores began in June and lasted until August, some three months behind the initial projections. Still to come was the task of implementing training, communications and management programs to familiarize management and staff with Provigo's structures and methods. The immediate priorities were to improve customer service, enhance productivity and increase profitability.

The integration of the retail stores may have been slow and occasionally painful but the takeover and integration of the wholesale operations proceeded smoothly, thanks to the action plan designed and fine-tuned by Jean-Louis Lamontagne and Reynald Gagné.

With the acquisition of the Dominion stores, Provigo saw its food sector sales go up from $2.24 billion to $2.76 billion in 1981; sectorial operating income, however, dropped from $53.8 million to $50.5 million.[10]

The renovation of the Dominion stores was essential, no matter how costly. It was a demanding task. And when the work was completed in 1987, it was already time to upgrade the renovated stores.

At the end of fiscal 1981–1982, Antoine Turmel wrote in his annual message: "It was a year of expansion, and indeed an expensive one. But we are convinced that our new commitments will generate earnings potential in the medium and long term for Provigo Inc. as a whole."[11]

The figures in subsequent annual reports showed that he was right.

A year later, Pierre H. Lessard wrote: "The retail division, which has undergone a great deal of expansion with its acquisition of 86 new stores in 1981, has just completed an eventful and difficult year. First of all, we had to analyse the viability and potential of each individual store within the Company's criteria."[12]

These statements did not reveal that the purchase of Dominion, conducted by Antoine Turmel, Pierre Lessard and Richard Constantineau, had not lived up to their initial expectations.

The process of converting and modernizing Dominion, and even more so the sale to affiliates, was hampered by interest rates of 21% as well as the poor condition of several stores.

Along with new sites, higher sales volume, greater market share and assured clientele for Provigo's wholesale business, Provigo's senior management thought they were also acquiring a certain know-how comprising the skills, expertise and experience of those in charge of Dominion in Quebec.

As Provigo took possession of its new acquisition, management was dismayed to find that the anticipated resources were not in Montreal but in Toronto, where all policies were formulated and all strategic decisions taken. To be sure, there were some talented people in Montreal, but they had been generally confined to a subordinate role for several years; on the whole, Quebec middle management showed little initiative or enterprise.[13]

As well, in the six months between the agreement in principle and the initial takeover, the operating situation had deteriorated at Dominion. In some ways, these six months had been a dangerous waste of time which to some extent compromised the potential of the acquisition.

The division in charge of integrating the Dominion stores did not see eye to eye with the one looking after the other Provigo supermarkets in the Montreal region. Because of such differences, the transformation of the stores one by one took an additional six months.

In short, nothing was going as expected and operating losses were mounting.

The Price War Resumes

It goes without saying that Provigo could have done without Steinberg's campaign to siphon the former Dominion clientele from the new Provigo stores. It certainly made it more difficult to integrate the new acquisition's operations in a smooth and carefully considered way.

To make matters worse, in March 1983 Steinberg and Provigo fought a price war that lasted for 15 weeks. The surprise attack had been prepared long beforehand by Steinberg, which wanted to solidify its clients' loyalty and attract new customers by offering discount coupons. It distributed coupons worth 5 percent of a customer's total purchase, applicable to a subsequent purchase. Reaction was swift. The next day, Métro responded with a similar offer. The ball was now in Provigo's court.

Forty-eight hours after the price war was declared, Provigo announced an automatic reduction of 6 percent on any purchase except tobacco, beer and the like. The rebate could be applied immediately rather than against a subsequent purchase. Even more dramatically, coupons issued by the competition would be accepted.

The ads were flashy: Provigo grants 20 percent more reduction (6 percent instead of 5 percent). The discount was immediate — no more lost or mislaid coupons.

This time Steinberg was caught off-guard.

Provigo's surprise move met with resounding success and its supermarkets gained considerable favour as a result. In the advertising and merchandising world, the Provigo program was considered a smash hit and received extensive press coverage. It had been a costly battle for the opponents, with Steinberg the biggest loser.

As Antoine Turmel saw it: "Provigo faced strenuous competition from the very outset of its fiscal year as a major competitor launched a price war in Quebec that lasted 15 weeks — from early March to mid-June — and which proved to be an extremely costly one for all concerned. There was no choice but to maintain our position as market leader and retain our market share. Not only were these objectives achieved but the reputation of Provigo stores was enhanced. There is a lesson to be drawn from this experience: a retailer cannot rely solely on pricing to attract consumers who

1 A **6%** rebate will be granted on the sales price of any item in the store, except those subject to government pricing regulations.

2 The rebate will be given directly to the customer, **in cash,** at the checkout counter of your supermarket.

3 This exceptional 6% offer represents 20% more than the rebate offered by competitors.

PLUS

We will gladly exchange the special coupons issued by our competitors **FOR CASH** with the purchase of an identical or similar product.

The 1983 price war. Provigo came out on top.

seek, in addition to good prices, well located and well kept stores that offer an interesting variety of products and adequate service. The public is very much aware of both retail marketing and product merchandising.''[14]

In other respects 1983 was a turbulent year. Provigo suffered two major work stoppages. The first affected 45 Montreal-area stores for six weeks; the second paralyzed six stores in the Quebec City region for five weeks. Competition was becoming increasingly intense. New types of stores, such as the superstores, had appeared in an already saturated market.

In April 1984, Richard Constantineau, who, as vice-president of retail operations had been in charge of the Dominion project, tendered his resignation.[15] Many of his colleagues felt that he was somewhat responsible for Provigo's setbacks in this drawn-out affair which had turned out to be more costly than anticipated. They wondered why Provigo's Chief Operating Officer, Pierre H. Lessard, had for so long accepted the weak performance of the man primarily responsible for the Dominion affair. For some colleagues, the attitude of Antoine Turmel, known to be quite demanding with managers who performed poorly, was even more of a mystery. Perhaps Pierre H. Lessard and Antoine Turmel, who were both aware of the enormous difficulties encountered by Richard Constantineau, felt that others could not have done better under the circumstances.

It must be said that without the Dominion stores Provigo could not have penetrated the Montreal market for several years and at enormous expense to boot. Today, most people do agree that the deal was a good one, and that it was the correct way to secure certain strategic locations.

Some thirty Dominion stores were closed; as many were sold to affiliates and five of them became Heritage or Maxi stores. The others continued to operate as corporate stores until 1986.

The Dominion Affair Will Long Be Remembered

Dominion had been on the Provigo agenda for quite some time. The acquisition had delayed other projects, and the entire operation had required a great deal of money and demanded extensive human resources in support.

The Provigo people admit to mistakes in the sales of the first stores. But market conditions, interest rates and high rental costs of certain locations conspired to make success that much more difficult.

Even though senior management believed that the problems caused by the transaction had been settled once and for all, the Dominion affair was back on the Provigo agenda every year following the acquisition. Since 1981, all annual reports have mentioned the positive and negative spinoffs of the Dominion acquisition. Until 1987, shareholders questioned the wisdom of the December 1980 decision at every general meeting.[16]

In the 1986 and 1987 annual reports, there were notes to the financial statements explaining extraordinary items related to losses stemming from the sale and closure of old Dominion supermarkets.[17]

It would seem that the Dominion affair is now part of Provigo's history. When all is said and done, the purchase of the Dominion stores was in fact an advantageous and, in the long run, profitable move.

As well, thanks to the initiative of Jean-Louis Lamontagne, Provigo enhanced its position in the Montreal market by acquiring in 1984, for some $7 million, eleven A&P supermarkets which it was already supplying.

With these stores and with the final integration of the Dominion stores, Provigo had acquired a strong foothold in greater Montreal. Perhaps the early dificulties in establishing itself have led to a more secure future in Quebec's metropolis. The competition tested Provigo's determination and retail expertise, and gave the company an opportunity to show its strengths to a new clientele. After this success, Provigo never looked back.

Notes

1. *La Presse* (December 19, 1980).
2. Quoted in *Le Devoir* (December 19, 1980).
3. *The Globe and Mail* (December 29, 1980).
4. *Ibid*.
5. *Finance* (December 9 1981).
6. Provigo Inc. Annual Report for the year ended January 31, 1981.
7. *La Presse* (June 11, 1981).
8. *La Presse* (June 12, 1981).
9. *The Globe and Mail* (August 11, 1981).
10. Provigo Inc. Annual Report for the year ended January 30, 1982.
11. Provigo Inc. Annual Report for the year ended January 30, 1982.
12. Provigo Inc. Annual Report for the year ended January 29, 1983.
13. Michel Robin, who later set up the Super Carnaval markets in Quebec, was part of the talented pool tapped by Provigo. See Chapter 22.
14. Provigo Inc. Annual Report for the year ended January 28, 1984.
15. H. Paul Gobeil, Executive Vice-President, succeeded him as head of retail operations.
16. In the Provigo Inc. Annual Report for the year ended January 30, 1982, a note to the financial statements indicates that the cost of this acquisition totalled $95,040,000.

17. In the Provigo Inc. Annual Report for the year ended January 25, 1986, a note puts at $12.2 million the "losses and provisions for losses on the sale and closing of supermarkets net of income tax recovery." The following year, a note on the same subject indicates a further loss of $2.3 million. This would be the last.

CHAPTER FIFTEEN

SPORTS AND LEISURE: A PROMISING SECTOR

In the early 1980s, Provigo was essentially a wholesaler and retailer of food products and related goods. But with National Drug, the Company had acquired a taste for diversification and Jean-Claude Merizzi, Vice-President, Planning and Business Development, sought to widen Provigo's scope of operations and expand its range of products. An investment in a new sector would be acceptable as long as it was consistent with Provigo's prior experience in distribution and in sales and marketing.

But Provigo's decision to enter the sporting goods sector came as a total surprise.

On December 4, 1980, Provigo Inc. entered into an agreement with Sports Experts Inc. to purchase its voting shares in return for a cash consideration of approximately $2 million. As the transaction was not expected to be finalized before March 1981, Antoine Turmel refrained from elaborating on the subject in the Annual Report for the year ended January 31, 1981. He did observe, "We believe that this is an interesting form of diversification in the promising field of sports and leisure time activities."

However, the report does not reveal that this diversification was more or less the result of chance events.[1]

Jean-Claude Merizzi was looking for a promotion to celebrate the opening of the 100th Provi-Soir store on June 15, 1979. He met with

Claude Beaulieu, President of Sports Experts, after a tennis match, to persuade him to give Provi-Soir 100 bicycles to be drawn in a contest. In return Sports Experts would gain some valuable publicity. After some discussion, Beaulieu sold him the bikes at cost.

So began a series of meetings which led to the acquisition of Sports Experts by Provigo two years later.

The Early Days of Sports Experts

Sports Experts was established in 1966. Drawing his inspiration from the formula adopted by Ro-Na in the hardware sector, Claude Beaulieu gathered a dozen sporting goods merchants to form a buying group.[2]

Beaulieu later discovered from the National Sporting Goods Association that the application of this formula to the distribution of sporting goods would be a first in Canada, if not in North America. At first, he thought simply of grouping purchases; in this way they could order directly from manufacturers or their agents and avoid the middleman, and so reduce procurement costs. The idea was to have an office which would serve as a base of operations, but with no inventory, since merchandise would be delivered directly to each store.

This was only half of the right formula. It would make it possible to buy directly from manufacturers, but without truly benefiting from the best prices, which could only be obtained by volume purchases from a central distribution centre. Another solution had to be found.

Finally, 2,000 square feet of space on St. Lawrence Blvd. in the north end of Montreal was rented. Staff was kept to a minimum — one secretary, one bookkeeper and one dispatcher. A manager was hired, then replaced. But the results were still unsatisfactory. At the request of those who had joined him in his project, Claude Beaulieu agreed to take the reins as full-time manager. He entrusted his Saint-Jérôme store, north of Montreal, to an associate.

Suppliers were very sceptical. They felt that the new group, whose rationale was to buy wholesale at low prices and then re-sell to individual members at cost plus 5 percent, had little chance of success. The suppliers even insisted that the members give individual and joint guarantees for the payment of merchandise.

It is not easy for a small company to get started, especially when it runs contrary to conventional business practices. But the founders clung to their principles; at times stubbornly. The first year, the group sold $452,000

spéciaux **sports** **experts** *specials*

BOTTINE À BOUCLES – BUCKLES BOOT

5 BOUCLES – 5 BUCKLES

Fabrication Européenne. Cuir de qualité, rebord élasticisé, intérieur et languette capitonné, semelle moulée, boucle solide et résistante.

– High quality leather, padded, sealed sole, quality buckle. Made in Europe.

VALEUR $62.95 VALUE

PRIX **sports** SPECIAL **experts** $49^95

BOTTINE DOUBLE LACÉE – LACED DOUBLE BOOT

Fabrication Européenne. Laçage rapide, intérieur coussiné, fait à la main, cuir de bonne qualité.

– Made in Europe, speed laced, padded, hand made, high quality leather.

VALEUR $45.00 VALUE

PRIX **sports** SPECIAL **experts** $29^95

APRÈS SKI – AFTER SKIING

En véritable loup-marin, intérieur doublé mouton, semelle en crêpe naturel.

– Lined with top quality sheepskin fur, insulated soles of natural crepe rubber.

VALEUR $45.00 VALUE

PRIX **sports** SPECIAL **experts** $34^95

SKI EN FIBRE DE VERRE

CADRES D'ACIER ENTRECROISES

GARANTI 1 AN. Base kofix et de résine epoxy, rebord du dessus en plastique, couleur attrayante noir, blanc.

FIBRE GLASS SKIS

– 1 YEAR GUARANTEE. Kofix base, micro glass fibre and epoxy, plastic top edges, interlocking steel edges, color black and white.

VALEUR $65.00 VALUE

PRIX **sports** SPECIAL **experts** $49^95

HABIT D'AUTO-NEIGE

100% nylon extérieur, isole thermos, capuchon bordé et doublé de peluche d'orlon, avec fermeture éclair ajustable au collet. Fermeture éclair [illegible] en diagonales des épaules à la cheville, 2 poches avec boutons à pression, poignet de laine au manche, élastique à chaque jambière, ajustable à la taille. Homme et femme.

SNOW SUIT

– Self-adjusting waist, centre-back action pleat vents, full length shoulder-to-toe two-way zipper, elastic stirrups - all features that assure comfort and wearability. Waterproof coated nylon outer fabric. Zippered split fur hood doubles as high collar. Two slash pockets at chest and large patch pockets on legs with snap fastener closing. Storm cuffs at wrists, knee length zipper on right leg. Pure white synthetic thermal fill, quilt lining. Men and Ladies.

VALEUR $35.00 VALUE

PRIX **sports** SPECIAL **experts** $26^95

BOTTES POUR AUTO-NEIGE

Fabrication Canadienne. Housse en nylon, lacées au mollet, base caoutchoutée, lanières ajustables. Chaussette intérieure feutrée. Hommes et femmes.

SNOW BOOT

– Made in Canada. Nylon upper, blue felt liner, adjustable strap on instep, ribbed outsole and heel. Men and Ladies.

PRIX **sports** SPECIAL **experts** $14^95

VOUS TROUVEREZ AUSSI CHEZ LES MARCHANDS MEMBRES SPORTS EXPERTS PLUSIEURS SPECIAUX CONCERNANT TOUS GENRES DE SPORTS POUR LES GENS DE 1 A 99 ANS.

The first Sports Experts ad (October 67).

in merchandise. It was a modest but promising start.

Camping equipment accounted for a large part of these sales. Claude Beaulieu therefore decided to go to Europe and buy directly. While in France, in 1968, he discovered that the La Hutte stores had adopted a formula similar to the one he wanted to apply at Sports Experts. La Hutte's senior management provided him with invaluable information on their corporate structure and allowed him to contact their own suppliers. As a result, Sports Experts was able to attain the desired sales results much sooner then anticipated.

In 1970, Sports Experts was supplying thirty stores. The time had come to relocate. A former IGA store on Lévesque Blvd. in Laval, which had been bought for $70,000, served as the new headquarters and warehouse centre. The company had 10 employees by then.

In 1973 Sports Experts joined the international buying group Intersport as the Canadian representative with the recommendation and support of La Hutte, a founding member of the Group. This event was a turning point in the company's history.

Founded in 1968 by 10 buying groups from France, Germany, Norway, Switzerland, Austria, Sweden, Belgium, Denmark, Italy and the Netherlands, Intersport had become the world's largest distributor of sportswear and equipment. Finland and Canada then joined the founding group, followed by Spain, Great Britain, Japan and the United States. In 1986, there were more than 3,500 Intersport boutiques throughout the world. Their retail sales totalled just under $2.4 billion.[3]

Through Sports Experts, Canada was the first non-European country to join Intersport and to benefit from its purchasing power and many services. In those early days of Sports Experts, this arrangement was no small achievement for Claude Beaulieu[4] and his buying group.

Sports Experts can rely on Intersport for sensibly priced, top-of-the-line sporting goods, as well as activewear, which currently represents 50 percent of sales. Not so long ago, activewear could be purchased primarily in department stores, while sports shops concentrated on sports equipment. Here again, Sports Experts broke new retail ground.

In 1977, Sports Experts relocated once again. The brand new distribution centre, built alongside Highway 440 in Laval, stood on a vast 600,000-square-foot lot so the facilities could be expanded if necessary.[5]

At the time, 100 stores already operated under the Sports Experts banner, although each one also displayed its owner's name.

To understand the workings of Sports Experts, it is useful to know that Sports Experts is a private company owned by a maximum fifty shareholders. The company primarily supplies its own shareholders, but it also does business with member buyers.

Despite efforts which had achieved outstanding results, Claude Beaulieu had difficulty convincing the members of Sports Experts to reinvest in the distribution company. Merchants preferred to open a second or third store rather than increasing their investment in the group. Most were more concerned with expanding their own business than with what went on at central office, whose problems were neither a priority nor a day-to-day concern. This attitude may be understandable, but it hindered the development projects originating from head office and caused serious financing and liquidity problems.

In 1980, wholesale sales of Sports Experts reached $30 million. But Claude Beaulieu still had to make periodic tours of the stores to collect the amounts due from merchants who neglected to pay within the prescribed time limit. In slow seasons, unforeseen expenses and all manner of excuses were used to put off paying for merchandise that had long been paid for by Sports Experts from lines of credit that were becoming more and more difficult to negotiate. Imports accounted for the lion's share of the profits; therefore it was vital to meet payment within due dates to remain on good terms with suppliers and Intersport.

To expand, Sports Experts was in serious need of capital. There were other problems too.

For example, it was essential to obtain strategic locations in shopping centres. In general, these sites were held by large companies whose leases served as guarantees in the development of the shopping centre. In the race for the best sites, Sports Experts was up against Arlington and Podium, two competitors who were gearing up for battle.

The word that Sports Experts was experiencing growing pains must have got around. One day someone claiming to represent Provigo asked Claude Beaulieu whether the company was for sale. After several enquiries, Claude Beaulieu learned from Jean-Claude Merizzi that the person had nothing to do with Provigo. He also learned that Provigo was still looking to diversify, and a move into a promising and fast-growing sector, such as sporting goods and leisure wear, was definitely a possibility.

Jean-Claude Merizzi and Claude Beaulieu both felt that Provigo and Sports Experts would make a good pair. With its skills, experience,

Claude Beaulieu (in the centre) with founding members of Sports Experts...

... and his closest associates (1987).

knowledge of real estate and financial and human resources, Provigo could certainly revitalize the company.

Provigo Takes Over

After a preliminary study, Jean-Claude Merizzi reviewed the prospect of acquiring Sports Experts with the Provigo Executive Committee. He stressed the merits and advantages of such a deal. But members of senior management were far from unanimous in their reactions to the proposal and the project was not accepted. Jean-Claude Merizzi then converted Pierre H. Lessard to his view and the proposal was submitted once again to the Executive Committee and Board of Directors. This time, it was accepted. Provigo had decided to acquire all the shares of Sports Experts.

No single person held a significant portion of these shares. Claude Beaulieu himself owned no more than 12 percent. He was entrusted with the delicate task of persuading shareholders to sell their equity to Provigo. He had to take into account not only the financial aspect of the question, but also its human dimension; that is, the proprietary feelings of the shareholders and their sense of belonging to a team. Many of them had the impression of being dispossessed, of losing what they had built from scratch. This understandable emotional reaction prevented them from seeing the positive side of a transaction which would ensure the company's future.

Claude Beaulieu made it clear that Sports Experts, once rid of its financial problems, would benefit from the power and services of a large parent company, while still retaining an appreciable measure of autonomy. Sports Experts would have the support of a solid structure. The introduction of new administrative procedures would rapidly lead to better results and it would be possible to obtain leases for prime locations in the best shopping centres, under the most favourable conditions. In short, the company would have every asset needed to pursue its development and expansion.

Claude Beaulieu managed to dispel every worry. Once all the shareholders were convinced, Provigo acquired Sports Experts. It was now a question of establishing a franchise formula under which all stores would become Sports Experts outlets. A number of member buyers would round out the clientele.

Quebec First

It took two or three years for Sports Experts to find the formula that would not only increase its profitability but also ease expansion. But once the right formula was in place, it was time to move on to other projects.

In Quebec City, Guy Massicotte Sports Inc. dominated the sports equipment market with seven stores. It would have been difficult to open Sports Experts franchises in the region. Rather than trying to muscle in on Guy Massicotte Sports, Sports Experts bought the company. By the end of April 1984, an agreement was concluded: Sports Experts would acquire Guy Massicotte Sports for $2.5 million.

Now that the Quebec market had been captured and Sports Experts had acquired three stores in the Maritimes, the company started to look elsewhere for further expansion prospects. Results were good, everything was going smoothly and the path was clear.

Then the Rest of Canada

At the end of 1984, Provigo announced that an agreement had been signed to merge Sports Experts and Collegiate/Arlington. This amalgamation created the first national chain in the sporting goods business.

The sales network, with 152 stores, covered eight of the ten Canadian provinces. Only Saskatchewan and Newfoundland were missing from the picture. Sports Experts served the greater part of the Quebec market; Collegiate/Arlington had operations in nearly all of Canada's urban areas.

Imasco, which had owned Arlington for eleven years and succeeded in nearly doubling the company's sales, had invested extensively without achieving significant earnings. A year earlier, Imasco had sold Arlington to a Vancouver group which included Joseph Segal, ex-owner of Zellers, who was Chairman of the Board, Norman Paul, who was President, and Maurice Tousson, who acted as Executive Vice-President.[6]

Collegiate/Arlington operated nine stores in Quebec, six of which were in Montreal. Sports Experts had wanted to buy them as early as autumn 1983, but Imasco was looking for a single buyer for the entire network.

In fact, Provigo had thought about buying Collegiate/Arlington at the time of the Dominion purchase in 1980–1981, but Jean-Claude Merizzi's plan had been set aside because the company's every resource had been devoted to the Dominion project.

Later, Provigo tried to acquire the nine stores in Quebec and the four in the Ottawa region. The transaction would probably have succeeded if Imasco had not found a buyer for all its Collegiate/Arlington stores in the person of Joseph Segal and his colleagues. It was from this group that Provigo finally bought Collegiate/Arlington in January 1985.

In reality, Sports Experts and Collegiate/Arlington had merged into a single entity. As of January 27, 1985, Provigo would hold an 80 percent interest in the new company called Sports Experts Inc. According to an income-scale based formula, the seller, which had kept a 20 percent interest in the new company, could either sell his holding or increase it up to 35 percent during the next two years. Instead, it was Provigo which increased its stake to 100 percent as of February 1, 1987.[7]

Up to 1985, Provigo had spent $2 million for Sports Experts and $5.5 million for Collegiate/Arlington. Sports Experts, for its part, had purchased the Massicotte stores in Quebec City for $2.5 million. This investment of $10 million was estimated to be worth three to four times the value.

In 1986, the Sports Experts warehouse on Highway 440 in Laval had to be expanded once again, at a cost of $6 million, to integrate the wholesale activities of Collegiate/Arlington,[8] which had been conducted out of Toronto before the acquisition.

The diversification of Provigo into the sporting goods sector was greeted with enthusiasm by financial analysts. At the time of the merger with Collegiate/Arlington, Martin Kaufman of Nesbitt Thomson Bongard observed: "They want to be the top dogs. They want to dominate the market."[9]

He also pointed out that Provigo's new venture was not a significant departure from its primary vocation to distribute consumer products. As he put it: "Distributing sports products or pharmaceuticals is no more difficult than distributing food; it requires the same expertise, but some sectors are more profitable than others."[10] He was quite right.

Claude Beaulieu, President and Chief Operating Officer of Sports Experts, concisely summed up the situation when he related to *Les Affaires* (March 9, 1985) that after reporting a deficit the first year (1981), following the acquisition by Provigo, the company had recovered its profitability in 1982 and that the third year should see sales increase by 22 percent with a decent profit. He added that Sports Experts expected to maintain an annual growth rate of 20 percent over the next few years.

Claude Beaulieu also insisted that the company did not want to own more than 10 percent of its stores. According to him, franchisees are in a better position to manage their stores and make them profitable. In that way, Sports Experts could concentrate on marketing, merchandising and distribution.

In Quebec, the Sports Experts stores are almost entirely franchised, while most of the stores acquired from Collegiate/Arlington are operated corporately. In Quebec and Ontario at first, then in the western provinces, they will gradually be sold and turned into franchises. Eventually, all stores will operate under the name Sports Experts.

In fact, this is precisely the formula that had made Provigo so successful in the food sector. The company supplies independent merchants with expert services in fields as diverse as financing, human resources, purchasing, advertising, merchandising and new technologies. This support permits the merchant to concentrate his efforts on making a success of his own business. His entrepreneurial and management abilities can only flourish in such an environment.

Encouraging Results

By the end of fiscal 1987–1988, Sports Experts, a wholly-owned subsidiary of Provigo, was active in every region of Canada under the banners Sports Experts, Collegiate and Intersport. Nearly three quarters of the 204 stores were operated by franchisees.

Network sales had risen to $207 million, an increase of 11 percent over the preceding year. At $2.1 million, income had nearly doubled.[11]

Although the restructuring of operations, along with the renovation of certain outlets and the corporate integration undertaken after the Collegiate/Arlington merger increased short-term costs, they also improved productivity in Quebec and Ontario.

Determined to raise the entire national network to the level of productivity achieved by the stores in Eastern Canada, Sports Experts is paying particular attention to its operations west of Toronto.

There was no shortage of obstacles on the path to establishing this network which today enjoys an excellent reputation. Credit for this success must go to Claude Beaulieu and his team.[12] Claude Beaulieu had the good sense to be the first North American to establish an international relation with Intersport. Clearly, Claude Beaulieu is the type of entrepreneur who made, and will continue to make, Provigo a success.

Notes

1. On December 17, 1980, the agreement to acquire Dominion somewhat overshadowed the proposed acquisition of Sports Experts.
2. On the occasion of Sports Experts' 20th anniversary in September 1987, tribute was paid to five founding members who are still active: Alain Goulet, Wilfrid Prud'homme, Marcel Papineau, Gilles Beaulieu and Claude Beaulieu.
3. Since 1976, Intersport head office is located in Bern, Switzerland.
4. Claude Beaulieu was elected Chairman of the Board of Intersport for the term 1988–1990.
5. They were in fact expanded twice subsequently.
6. *The Gazette* (February 5, 1985).
7. Provigo Inc. Annual Report for the year ended January 30, 1988.
8. The official opening took place on September 16, 1987.
9. *The Gazette* (February 5, 1985).
10. *La Presse* (February 6, 1985).
11. Provigo Inc. Annual Report for the year ended January 30, 1988.
12. After a brilliant career with Sports Experts, Claude Beaulieu now acts as an advisor to the company. Since April 1989, Michel Marcotte has been President of Sports Experts.

CHAPTER SIXTEEN

FURTHER DIVERSIFICATION

Every large company has operations that are not strictly consistent with its primary activity but that have developed in response to specific corporate circumstances or needs. Provigo is no exception. Starting in 1980 its annual reports contain a section entitled "Other Operations" which at the time grouped petroleum, real estate and various other sectors. Other Operations accounted for 4 percent of total annual revenue in 1981.[1]

Sales of petroleum products in the 188 Top Valu Gasmarts and Provi-Soir stations totalled 443.3 million litres in 1981.[2]

In real estate, alone or with various co-owners, Provigo owned some 15 million square feet of land in use, over 6.7 million square feet of land held for future development, and nearly 3.7 million square feet in building space. Real estate management was directed by Placements Denault at Provigo, Shoppers City at Loeb and Food Giant at Horne & Pitfield. The real estate division also supplied a range of services and specialized assistance to various company divisions as well as to client retailers. In recent years, it has added engineering services.

Also included under "Other Operations" were cartage companies (Capital City Transport, Lobem Transport and Canadian Western Brokers), printing shops such as Cloverdale Printing in Ottawa and various specialized operations. These companies rendered Provigo and its subsidiaries important services with guaranteed priority and assured quality.

In 1981–1982, Provigo's Other Operations included the results of Sports Experts, which raised this sector's contribution to 6 percent of overall sales.

Although relatively small, Other Operations achieved impressive profit figures: $12.2 million income on sales of $202.8 million. This 6 percent yield compares favourably with the 2.5 percent achieved in Drug Distribution and the 1.8 percent in Food Distribution.

It was precisely such profitability levels that justified subsequent attempts to diversify Provigo's operations. These were always undertaken within the context of a primary commitment to the distribution and sale of food products.

Jean-Claude Merizzi, who had been responsible for developing the Provi-Soir stores since 1973, was appointed to the newly created position of Vice-President, Planning and Business Development, in 1978. This position had been created by head office to facilitate Provigo's monitoring of market developments and opportunities. Jean-Claude Merizzi was entrusted with the planning and implementation of projects in new sectors. In August 1981, he became Vice-President, Development and Expansion, with additional responsibilities covering the real estate sector.

He was constantly on the lookout for diversification opportunities. He investigated potentially valuable acquisitions or the possibility of ownership interests at reasonable cost, and then prepared recommendations for senior management. Among his achievements, Jean-Claude Merizzi prepared and concluded the acquisition of Sports Experts in March 1981 and Collegiate/Arlington in April 1985 as related in the previous chapter. He also negotiated an agreement with La Cour à bois Val Royal Inc. in 1984 to develop and establish home improvement and renovation centres.

The Brico Centres

After several months of studies and negotiations between Jean-Claude Merizzi and Val Royal co-owner Pierre Michaud, an equal partnership agreement was concluded. Val Royal was a long established Montreal based hardware and building material distributor. The new company was Brico Centre (Canada) Inc. Because of its knowledge of the sector and experience in hardware and construction materials, Val Royal was entrusted with managing the individual retail Brico outlets.

The inspiration for the formula derived from the highly popular Home Depot Company in the United States. For Provigo, "this represents a field which has been hardly developed in Quebec and which offers interesting possibilities.''[3]

The first Brico Centre opened in Longueuil on Montreal's South Shore in the spring of 1985. It was a combination warehouse-store with an immense area of 50,000 square feet and some 35,000 products covering the entire range of hardware, construction, do-it-yourself and home improvement needs. The emphasis was on expert advice to help homeowners carry out their own projects. Initial sales were gratifying. The anticipated figure of $10 million was surpassed by $1 million and the initial operating deficit was smaller than expected. The company was confident of profitability by the second year.

In passing, it should be mentioned that this Brico Centre was a counterpoise to the first Maxi superstore, which stood at the opposite end of the shopping centre. The Maxi stores were created by Provigo in response to the entry into the Quebec food sector of the giant Super Carnaval stores.

The second Brico Centre was even larger than the first; whereas the Longueuil store covered 50,000 square feet, the new one had a floor area of 85,000 square feet. Officially opened in April 1986 in Ville LaSalle, in the suburban southwest end of Montreal, the new centre had been set up in a former K-Mart building at a cost of $5 million.

At the inauguration of the LaSalle store, it was announced that five or six new stores would be opened in the Montreal region during the next two years. Expansion would then continue in Quebec City and Ottawa. Renovation and home improvement was a fairly new market in Canada. In Canada, it was estimated at $6 billion a year; in Quebec alone at $1.5 billion. Based on these figures, it would be possible to operate profitably eight Brico Centres in Quebec and twenty or even twenty-five throughout Canada.

In May 1985, Pierre Lortie became President of Provigo. A few months later, he set up a new senior management structure. Jean-Claude Merizzi was appointed Executive Vice-President, President of the Convenience Group, and President of the Development Group. He was still in charge of furthering Provigo's interest in Brico Centre.

Val Royal became a public company in December 1986 under the name Groupe Val Royal Inc. Claude Michaud and Pierre Michaud of Val Royal were appointed Chairman of the Board and President respectively. The company launched a public share issue which brought in $9 million in capital and 3,000 new shareholders.

The first indication that Val Royal was being reshaped along different lines was its acquisition of the 50 percent interest held by Provigo in Brico Centre for $2.25 million. Provigo made a profit in the transaction but it was leaving behind the renovation and home improvement sector even though the experience had been fruitful and the future appeared promising.

The Restaurant Business

The first Hibouf take-out counter in Provi-Soir stores in 1983 was a diversification of sorts as it was Provigo's first experience in the restaurant sector, more precisely, the fast-food business. The name is an imaginative combination of the French word "hibou" for owl — the Provi-Soir trademark — and "bouffe", the French colloquial term for a meal. The menu was simple: sandwiches, pizza, submarines, salads, pastry, fruit and beverages, all in individual portions. Customers could heat their food on the premises in microwave ovens.

An Hibouf fast-food counter.

The Hibouf formula was a hit from the start. Within five years, 173 Provi-Soir stores had a fast-food counter. The experience would eventually benefit Provigo outlets elsewhere in Canada.

In 1984, Provigo made a brief incursion into the traditional restaurant business by acquiring a 60 percent interest in Restaurants Les Prés Canada Ltd. This chain, directed by its founder André Verdier, comprised eight restaurants under franchise in the Montreal area. According to Pierre H. Lessard, President and Chief Operating Officer of Provigo, another ten units were to open that year.[4] These establishments featured a limited menu offering good quality food in an original, cordial atmosphere.

In August 1985, Provigo brought to an end its experience in the restaurant business by reselling its interest to André Verdier. By this time, Provigo had decided to concentrate exclusively on distributing consumer goods and services, a focus which was described as Provigo's specific mission by Pierre Lortie in his first annual message to Provigo shareholders.[5]

Banking Services

Banking, to be sure, was not part of Provigo's mission as elaborated in 1986. Yet the Company had previously acquired an interest in the Montreal City and District Savings Bank in March 1979. At the time, there were few comments on this subject at Provigo. At board meetings, Antoine Turmel would only say that it was a sound investment and a first-class security in the Company's portfolio.[6]

Provigo management had seen the need to diversify its investments and felt that the banking sector could prove interesting. Indeed, it turned out to be a profitable one. The 600,000 shares for which some $6 million were paid in 1979 were sold in June 1986 to The Laurentian Group[7] for over $15 million.

According to the President and Chief Executive Officer, Pierre Lortie, Provigo's decision to divest itself of its interests in the banking sector showed that the company was committed to channelling its assets strictly into sectors related to its primary mission.[8] But Provigo's withdrawal from the banking sector did not mean that it was no longer interested in banking services. In 1985, Provi-Soir outlets were gradually equipped with automatic teller machines, one of the many services a 24-hour outlet can provide 365 days a year. The following year, there were already forty such machines, and by the end of 1987, eighty throughout Quebec and Ontario. As well, twenty Provigo supermarkets offered this service. And the number of automatic teller machines continues to grow from year to year.

24-hour banking at Provi-Soir.

The company took the idea even further by later introducing debit-card payment in some fifty supermarkets.

For Provigo, diversification is not an end in itself. The company is equally adept at divesting as it is at acquiring and investing.[9] Management consistently monitors the situation, keeping an eye out for opportunities. Depending on its corporate goals, the company adjusts, intensifies, moderates and, if need be, lets go.

Notes

1. Provigo Inc. Annual Report for the year ended January 31, 1981.
2. As mentioned earlier, Provi-Soir's gas sales were included in "Other Operations." Its other sales were reported under "Food Operations."
3. Provigo Inc. Annual Report for the year ended January 26, 1985.
4. Provigo Inc. Annual Report for the year ended January 26, 1985.
5. Provigo Inc. Annual Report for the year ended January 25, 1986.
6. In addition to being a good investment, this interest could have helped pave the way for the National Bank of Canada to acquire City and District. But the project was abandoned.

7. It was The Laurentian, rather than the National Bank, which gradually dominated City and District; the latter is now called The Laurentian Bank of Canada. The institutions involved are known in the business world as ''friends'' of Provigo.
8. *La Presse* (June 28, 1986).
9. As in the case of Consumers Distributing (Chapter 21).

CHAPTER SEVENTEEN

THE SOBEYS SHUFFLE THE DECK

During the mid-seventies, in the wake of the company's disastrous foray into the Chicago market, the market price of M. Loeb Limited shares was ridiculously low. As a result, everybody seemed to want a piece of the company. It was generally believed that once its administration was firmly in hand, Loeb would offer tremendous potential and profit opportunities.

Antoine Turmel himself made a move to acquire Loeb in 1975 but the transaction was forestalled because of legal problems. This attempt by Provigo was kept secret.[1]

A few years earlier, George Weston Ltd. had started to buy Loeb shares after Bertram Loeb refused to sell the entire business. In 1974, however, the federal government not only stopped this takeover attempt, but also ordered Weston to divest itself of the shares it had previously acquired. The consensus was that Weston-Loblaw already controlled a substantial share of the food market.[2]

Frank Warnock, who had become President of Loeb in 1975, knew of another potential buyer: the Sobey family from Nova Scotia. The Sobeys were among his top customers when he was with Scott Paper and he had remained on good terms with them. For some time he had been hoping that the Sobeys would eventually control the company. He was convinced that they would be easier to deal with than Bertram Loeb.

The Oshawa Group, which owned various IGA regional franchises, also had an eye on Loeb. Loeb and the Oshawa Group were hardly strangers, since they were the principal shareholders in IGA Canada.

An offer from the Sobeys would be the most likely one to be accepted. They had an important ally at Loeb in the person of its President, Frank Warnock. However, for any transaction to be successful, it was essential to convince the Caisse de dépôt et placement du Québec to sell its Loeb shares to the Sobeys. But the Caisse had other plans.

Pierre Arbour, then a member of the Loeb Board of Directors and the Caisse's senior investment advisor, would later reveal that the Caisse had, three or four years before the 1977 transaction, tried to engineer a voluntary merger between Loeb and Provigo. According to Michel Paris, first assistant director general at the Caisse, such a project had been contemplated as early as 1971.

In 1977, Frank Sobey, the father and chief of the Sobey clan, was still running Sobeys Stores with his sons. He wanted to acquire control of Loeb with the intention of retaining Frank Warnock to run the business. He had prepared a takeover strategy with the help of experts among his acquaintances and with the support of his sons. The Sobeys were poised for action.

After a meeting with Frank Warnock in Ottawa, on Friday June 17, 1977, the decision was taken to offer the Caisse de dépôt et placement $5 a share for its 1,147,400 Loeb shares. A week later, the offer was submitted to Caisse President Marcel Cazavant.

But it was too late. Provigo had already bought the Caisse's shares for $5 a share and was itself preparing an offer to acquire the remaining outstanding shares at the same price.[3] Yet there remained two sizable blocks of Loeb shares that could be pursued by the Sobeys with fair possibilities of success. At the time, Weston owned the largest block of shares. Another significant portion comprised stock owned or controlled by Bertram Loeb. Weston had already declared that selling at a loss was out of the question but they would remain open to an attractive offer. Bertram Loeb, for his part, refused to sell to Provigo at any price.

A Strategy to Foil Provigo

The Sobey family empire had no counterpart in Nova Scotia, perhaps even in all of Canada; it was controlled directly or indirectly by Frank Sobey[4] and his three sons, Bill, David and Donald. It comprised some thirty companies active in food distribution, pharmacies, real estate, securities management and movie theatres.

The company had its start in 1907 when Frank Sobey's father, John William, bought a meat business in Stellarton, Nova Scotia, where the Sobeys still have their headquarters. After a modest business debut, John William, along with his brother Charles, became owner of a butcher shop built by the brothers in 1912. His son Frank eventually introduced grocery products. This small business evolved into Sobeys Stores Ltd. and many other companies that make up the family holding, aptly named Empire Company Ltd.[5]

In 1977, when Frank Sobey first became interested in acquiring Loeb, sales of Sobeys Stores totalled $236.8 million, while those of Loeb were over one billion. But Frank Sobey and family were no less ambitious than Antoine Turmel and his associates. One wanted to expand beyond Nova Scotia and the other beyond Quebec.

Frank Sobey tried his luck with Weston-Loblaw, even though his relations with its management had not exactly been cordial after Weston-Loblaw's attempt to acquire control of Sobeys Stores against the Sobeys' will.[6]

According to analysts, the $5 offer from Provigo was not very generous. The book value of a Loeb share was $6.50. Furthermore, Frank Sobey knew that Weston-Loblaw would not let the Loeb shares go for less than they had cost.

In short, he felt he had a chance to acquire the Weston-Loblaw interest in Loeb.

But when Frank Sobey and his sons went to the Weston offices in Toronto on June 27, their offer of $6.25 or $6.50 for a Loeb share was rejected. As Donald Sobey put it: "The nuts and bolts of it was that in no way were they going to sell to us."

A few days later, Frank Sobey, Donald Sobey and Antoine Turmel met in Montreal to discuss what would happen if the Sobeys made a public offer of $6.50 a share.

Donald Sobey remembers that Antoine Turmel tried to discourage them by stating flatly that such an offer could only serve to increase the cost of Loeb's acquisition for Provigo. Provigo was determined to acquire the shares. For Antoine Turmel, the deal was in the bag. The Sobeys left with the distinct impression that an agreement between Provigo and Weston-Loblaw already existed.

Donald Sobey also remembers that his father was quite impressed with Antoine Turmel, whom he called "a real businessman and manager." Donald was equally impressed and ultimately suggested that the Sobeys should buy Provigo.

During this period the Sobeys continued to discuss various possibilities with Bertram Loeb. All were contingent on the acquisition of the Weston block of shares.

On July 13, Provigo acquired Weston-Loblaw's shares in Loeb. With no hope left in that direction, the Sobey abandoned the idea of acquiring Loeb and turned their attention to Provigo itself. They had decided to chip away at the company that had beaten them to Loeb. According to them, if Antoine Turmel and his team had done well without Loeb, they would certainly do better with it.

Why Not Buy Provigo?

During the summer of 1977, the Sobeys sold their 37 percent interest in National Sea Products.[7] The proceeds from this $10 million sale were used to buy Provigo shares.

Later, Antoine Turmel would say that after the acquisition of Loeb by Provigo, everybody sold his Provigo shares to take advantage of the increased market price except the Sobeys and Turmel himself, who were buying in.

The Sobey family's ownership of Provigo stock increased rapidly. At the beginning of September, they made a major acquisition in the form of 260,000 shares at $14 apiece. They now owned 12.7 percent of the outstanding shares.[8]

The rumour that the Sobeys were trying to take over Provigo began to circulate. The Sobey family, however, assured Antoine Turmel that they were only looking for a solid investment. But Turmel was not taking any chances; he made sure that control of Provigo would remain in the hands of its directors, friendly financial institutions, the Caisse de dépôt et placement and Soquia,[9] an agency sponsored by the Quebec government to support development in the agri-food industry.

For a while, the Sobeys eased up on their purchases of shares. Nonetheless, their total holding continued to mount, rising slowly but surely to the level held by the Caisse de dépôt et placement.

Bertram Loeb's Shares

Provigo owned 80 percent of the shares in Loeb, but Bertram Loeb had sworn that his shares would never go to Provigo, no matter how much he was offered. His attempt to have the transaction declared illegal under the pretext that it would pave the way for a monopoly failed; as did his initiative to have Loeb resume quarterly dividends that had been discontinued by its new Board chaired by Antoine Turmel because of the company's poor cash flow situation. So Bertram Loeb decided to sell his shares to the Sobeys.

Frank Sobey had come up with the idea of buying Bertram Loeb's shares. He felt that they would one day be quite valuable; in other words, they could ultimately be sold to Provigo. He knew that sooner or later Provigo would be willing to pay a high price to obtain all Loeb shares as a way of eliminating the minority shareholders, especially if they were not entirely friendly, and run the company in its own way. It was no secret in business circles that Provigo insisted that its subsidiaries should be wholly-owned.

In July 1978, the Sobeys approached Bertram Loeb with an offer for his shares in Loeb. The private transaction was concluded after a modicum of bargaining. The Sobeys paid $7 for each of Bertram Loeb's 550,000 shares. This was $1.1 million more than he would have obtained by selling to Provigo. Bertram Loeb would later say that he was pleased to have sold his shares to the Sobeys and to have helped them eventually increase their interest in Provigo.

No sooner were Bertram Loeb's shares sold to the Sobeys than Antoine Turmel attempted to buy them. Provigo offered $8 a share. For the Sobeys, the deal would have netted a profit of $550,000 in a few short weeks. But they were not interested in a cash sale, as the profit would be taxed. They asked instead for Provigo shares in exchange for their Loeb holdings.

This suggested exchange of shares was initially rejected by Provigo but would later be accepted after a decision of the Ontario Securities Commission in the Sobeys' favour.

What To Do About Loeb's Minority Shareholders?

In the summer of 1978, Antoine Turmel decided that the time had come to buy the Loeb stock owned by minority shareholders. He asked

Claude E. Leduc, legal advisor and secretary of Provigo, to find a way to arrange the purchase. Claude E. Leduc was quite familiar with the details of the situation.[10]

The transaction would take place through Loebex, created by Provigo with the ultimate objective of merging. Within this arrangement, minority shareholders would receive preferred shares redeemable within fifteen days in exchange for their Loeb common shares. At the same time, Provigo would redeem the minority shares in Horne & Pitfield Foods.[11]

Loeb had owned 85.5 percent of the outstanding common shares of Horne & Pitfield Foods since 1973. Once the project was approved by the Boards of Directors of Loeb and Horne & Pitfield, it took three or four trips to Edmonton to settle the Horne & Pitfield transaction and, on November 1, 1978, the shareholders approved the merger. In exchange for their shares, they received preferred shares redeemable for $15.50 each. The merger went through on November 4. All preferred shares were redeemed almost immediately, and Horne & Pitfield became a wholly-owned subsidiary of Loeb and, subsequently, of Provigo.

Trouble at Loeb

Matters were not so easily arranged with Loeb's minority shareholders.

As planned, Provigo transferred its Loeb shares into Loebex. But not all minority shareholders followed suit. The Sobeys, holding 555,500 shares through Empire Company, managed to obtain an injunction to cancel the shareholders' meeting scheduled for November 3, 1978, to ratify the Loeb and Loebex merger. At the same time, they took their case to the Ontario Securities Commission. They also had the support of Blanche Loeb, who still owned 35,000 Loeb shares.

The Sobeys asked the Commission to apply its rule that a transaction specifically relating to minority shareholders could not be effected without the prior approval of the majority of the minority shareholders involved. With their 11.7 percent of the Loeb shares, the Sobeys constituted the majority of minority shareholders, who held some 19.7 percent of the shares.

The hearing was held on October 23, 1978. The Sobeys claimed that Provigo was trying to oust them from Loeb without paying a fair price. For their part, the Provigo lawyers maintained that the Sobeys' real intention was to use their Loeb shares to increase their interest in Provigo, an interest that had already reached 19 percent. Provigo offered $8 a share, even though the market price had peaked at $7.50 in September and Nesbitt Thomson Securities had appraised a share at $6.75. The argument was advanced that, since the Sobeys had paid Bertram Loeb $7 a share, the price offered was reasonable and fair.

The Ontario Securities Commission ruled in favour of the Sobeys. Frank and Donald Sobey lost no time contacting Antoine Turmel to let him know they were ready to make a deal. In the wake of his defeat, Antoine Turmel took a while to come round to their point of view.

He eventually realized, however, that holding a grudge against the Sobeys was not the way to go about securing all the Loeb shares. Shortly before Christmas, he called Donald Sobey to suggest an exchange of Provigo shares for the Loeb shares owned by the Sobeys. This was exactly the deal that they wanted.

On April 24, 1979, a press release announced the anticipated merger between Loeb and Loebex. The minority shareholders would receive one common share of Provigo in exchange for two common shares of Loeb, or the equivalent of $12.50 per share.[12]

A special meeting of Loeb shareholders held June 14 approved the agreement. The transaction can be succinctly summarized: "As of June 16, 1979, the Company (Provigo) acquired all of the outstanding common shares not already held by it (19.7 percent) of M. Loeb, Limited (Loeb) in consideration of the issue of 458,601 common shares of Provigo, being an equivalent cash consideration of $11,465,000. Immediately prior to this transaction, Loeb had redeemed all of its outstanding preferred shares. As a result of these transactions, Loeb became a wholly-owned subsidiary of Provigo. The increase in Provigo's interest in Loeb has been accounted for as a purchase and the excess of cost over the book value of the corresponding minority interest at the date of acquisition amounting to $2,732,000 was added to goodwill."[13]

As a result of the exchange of shares, some 1,800 Loeb shareholders were paid considerably more than the $5 they had been offered in 1977. Not surprisingly, many of those who had accepted the earlier offer were sorely disappointed.

But the most disappointed participant was undoubtedly Antoine Turmel, who had to deliver the 277,750 Provigo shares to the Sobeys. With over a million shares or 24.5 percent of Provigo's stock now in their possession, the Sobeys had become a more important shareholder than the Caisse de dépôt et placement. They were now a power to be reckoned with.

The Caisse de dépôt et placement, seeing its role of principal shareholder threatened, was beginning to worry. Meanwhile, Antoine Turmel was doing everything in his power to keep Provigo's control in the hands of Quebeckers. Perhaps the Sobeys had other ideas?

Notes

1. Dean Walker in *Executive* (September 1980).
2. Weston owned 837,005 Loeb shares or approximately 18.3 percent of the outstanding common shares.
3. See Chapters 9 and 18.
4. The company is now run by the three Sobey sons.
5. Actually, the company owes its name to a fire-damaged movie house in New Glasgow that Frank bought in 1945 and turned it into a cash-and-carry grocery store.
6. Weston eventually had to settle for 40 percent of the common shares. Despite this considerable investment, Weston was probably kept at arm's length and never played an active role in the management of the Sobeys' company.
7. National Sea Products had once been the largest fishery and fish processing plant on the Eastern Seaboard but its profits had fallen considerably.
8. *The Gazette* (September 7, 1977).
9. And, unofficially, the Quebec government — see Chapter 18.
10. Claude E. Leduc has been Provigo's legal advisor since the early days and company secretary since 1974.
11. This procedure, known as a "going private" transaction, was common at the time. A similar transaction had been arranged in the case of National Drug (see Chapter 12).
12. The quoted market price of Provigo shares was $25 at the time.
13. Provigo Annual Report for the year ended January 26, 1980.

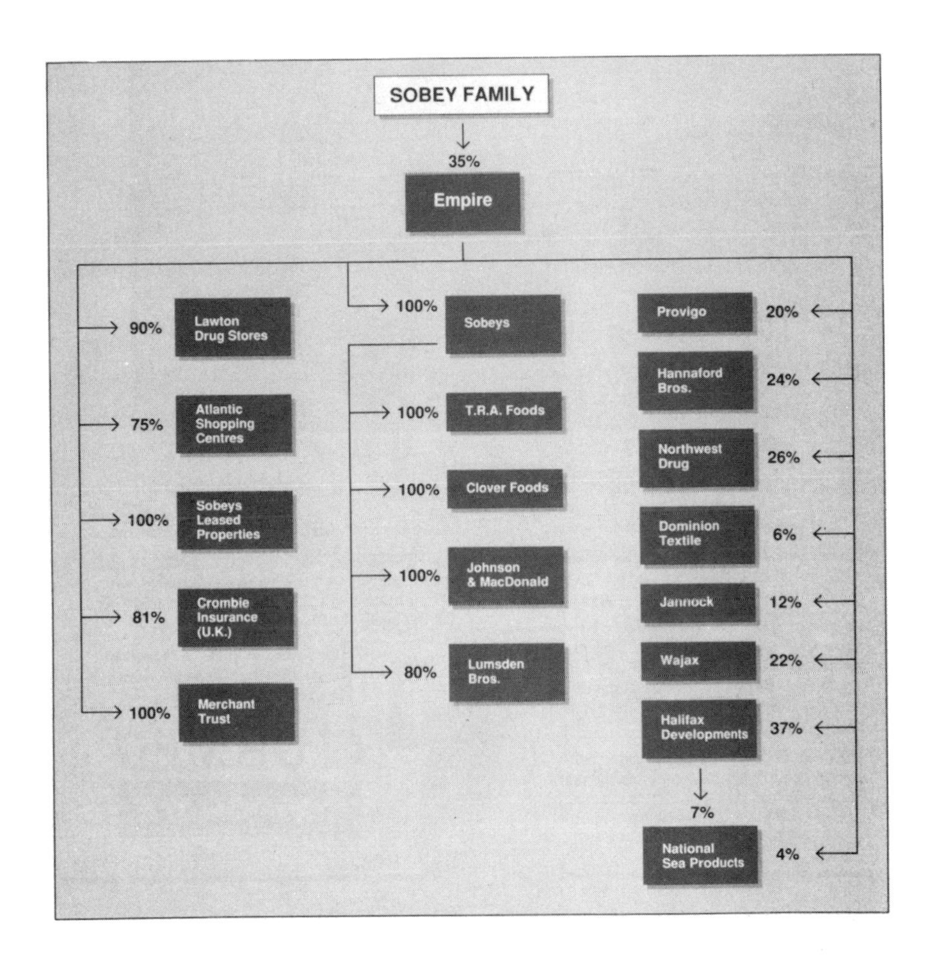

The Sobeys' empire. (Source: *Financial Post 500,* 1988 edition)

CHAPTER EIGHTEEN

THE CAISSE DE DÉPÔT ET PLACEMENT: AN IMPORTANT PARTNER

It would be impossible to recount the history of Provigo in any depth without touching on the role played by the Caisse de dépôt et placement du Québec. From the early days of the Provigo pioneers, through the important Loeb acquisition, to the emergence of the powerful Sobey family on the Board, the Caisse has been at the centre of Provigo's development. It is no exaggeration to claim that the Caisse has been a principal actor in shaping the company's future.

Created on July 15, 1965, the Caisse de dépôt et placement began building an investment portfolio on March 1, 1967. From the outset, this portfolio contained shares of the Provigo founding companies.

Couvrette & Provost made its first appearance on the list of authorized purchases around May 1967, followed by Denault about a month later, then Lamontagne in the fall. In short order, the Caisse had acquired an interest of approximately 10 percent in each of the three companies. This was the limit the Caisse had set for itself at the time, although it was then legally empowered to hold up to 30 percent of a company's outstanding shares, as it is today.

Needless to say, the Caisse management regularly met with

Antoine Turmel, René Provost and Jean-Louis Lamontagne to follow the progress of the three companies and to discuss the various initiatives sponsored by the companies. They also assessed future acquisitions and, without doubt, the possibility of a three-sided merger among the companies.

According to any realistic merger proposal, the Caisse, further to an exchange of shares between Couvrette & Provost, Denault and Lamontagne, would obtain nearly 25 percent of the new company's common shares. So with a potentially substantial holding in the new company, it was clear that the Caisse would have to give the merger its blessing. In fact, it did play a central role in the discussions that led to the formation of Provigo.

Principal Shareholder

In the official document containing the offers submitted to the shareholders of Denault and to those of Lamontagne by Couvrette & Provost on May 23, 1969, the Caisse is the only name to appear on the mandatory list of persons and institutions directly or indirectly holding 10 percent or more of the new company's outstanding shares. As of May 5, 1969, the Caisse was, in fact, the principal shareholder. It held 25 percent of the shares, while the Provigo executive officers and members of the Board owned 20.5 percent.[1]

For several years, the Caisse was Provigo's principal shareholder, while officers and management continued to be important shareholders.

In July 1971, when Provigo published its first prospectus for debentures, the Caisse held 21.1 percent of the common shares, while officers and directors held 29.3 percent. Together, they controlled 50.4 percent of the shares, a little over the absolute majority.[2]

In October 1975, the Caisse increased its interest to 23.95 percent. The officers and directors reduced theirs to 16.8 percent. At that point, the two groups were alone in each controlling over 10 percent of the shares.[3]

Two years later, a special general meeting of the shareholders was called for October 1977 to authorize an increase in capital stock through the creation of two million preferred shares. Half of these shares were issued partly to pay for Provigo's acquisition of 80 percent of the outstanding shares of Loeb. Other significant changes were taking place as well.

The list of those directly or indirectly holding over 10 percent of Provigo's common shares indicated that the Caisse was still the largest shareholder with 22.8 percent of the shares. Antoine Turmel held a 10 percent interest. But there was a newcomer, Sobeys Stores Ltd. and Empire Co. which were controlled by the Sobey family and its subsidiaries. The Sobeys already held a 17.2 percent interest in Provigo stock.[4]

The Rise of the Sobey Family

Antoine Turmel's success in acquiring control of Loeb in the summer of 1977 had caused a mixture of frustration and admiration in the Sobeys. While they themselves had been ready and willing to acquire M. Loeb, the family was impressed by Antoine Turmel's astuteness in turning the situation to Provigo's advantage. They determined to increase their holdings in Provigo after the acquisition.

While several people were selling their Provigo shares to cash in on their increased value since the Loeb deal, the Sobeys kept buying. For instance, they acquired a block of shares held by Sun Life for $14 each ($1.50 above the quoted price), as well as other blocks sold by the Bell Canada and Air Canada pension plan portfolio. The Sobey family's massive buying was in fact pushing up the value of Provigo shares.

Antoine Turmel would later say: "The Sobeys looked at what the acquisition of Loeb would do to Provigo. They were very smart. I have to give them credit for this. They, and I, were the only ones who bought Provigo stock at the time."[5]

However, the Sobeys' increasing interest made Turmel uneasy. He suspected them of planning a takeover, even though they claimed a sound investment was their only objective.

In his reply to questions about a possible takeover attempt, Antoine Turmel was clear: "In part due to the support of a few friendly financial institutions, control rests firmly in the hands of management."[6]

René Provost, Vice-Chairman of the Board and Director of Corporate Affairs, added: "One of management's current tasks is to look closely into these transactions to determine who the sellers and buyers of our shares are."

The situation remained more or less unchanged over the next two years, with management controlling some 20 percent of the shares and the Caisse remaining the dominant shareholder.[7] But at the meeting of May 21, 1980, it turned out that the Sobeys had assumed the dominant position with the block of 277,750 Provigo shares obtained in June 1979. These had been acquired in exchange for their minority shares in Loeb, which they had purchased earlier from Bertram Loeb himself. The Sobeys now controlled 1,057,182 Provigo shares, or 22.3 percent of all outstanding shares, while the Caisse de dépôt et placement held 851,700 shares, or 19.7 percent.[8]

Soquia to the Rescue

In 1979, the Quebec government was on the alert for any foreign takeovers of Quebec companies. It had already intervened in the case of Crédit Foncier. In those days, it worried that Provigo faced a similar threat.

The majority of Quebec ministers felt the same way, particularly Bernard Landry, Rodrigue Tremblay and Jean Garon, who kept a close watch on the economic and the agri-food sector. Antoine Turmel was also monitoring the situation.

In the Quebec cabinet, various hypotheses concerning the Provigo situation were formulated and discussed with the President of the Caisse, Marcel Cazavant. But the Caisse was not in a position, at that point, to buy more shares. The Société québécoise d'initiatives agro-alimentaires — commonly referred to as Soquia — then entered the picture as a possible important shareholder in Provigo. This role was a first for Soquia, which was later to acquire partnerships in other companies such as Culinar and J.E. Landry.

Soquia had neither the resources nor the experience needed to make this kind of investment. But help was readily available. The required financial resources were granted by the cabinet and the expertise was supplied by the Caisse de dépôt et placement, which not only knew Provigo but was also familiar with the securities market in all its complexity.

In the fall of 1979, Marcel Cazavant discreetly purchased approximately 6 percent of Provigo's outstanding shares on behalf of Soquia. These shares were placed in a numbered account in trust. Soquia had become a major ally.[9]

With all the shares held by the Caisse, Soquia, a few institutions well disposed towards Provigo, and the Company's senior executives, an absolute majority was guaranteed at all times. But this reassuring situation was not to prevail.

There was little change until 1982. At the May 26, 1981 general meeting, the shareholders approved a four-for-one common stock split and an increase in the Company's authorized capital. On July 21, 1981, two million common shares were issued.

The new issue of two million shares diluted the Sobey's holding, which dropped to slightly over 21 percent. Provigo management asked stockbrokers to distribute the new issue among small shareholders. According to Antoine Turmel, institutions should refrain from buying shares sold in blocks of 25 to 1,000. With the advantages of the Parizeau stock savings plan, he felt that small Quebec investors could end up with a sizable portion of the issue.

Needing money for other purposes, the Sobeys did not buy any of the new shares. In fact, in January 1982, they were preparing their first public offering of common shares in their holding company, Empire Company Ltd.

An Alliance Between the Caisse and the Sobeys

On the one hand, the Sobeys were seeking additional funds; on the other, the Caisse de dépôt et placement had plenty of liquidity. And the Sobeys were pragmatic people.

On January 5, 1982, Donald Sobey went to Montreal to talk finances with the current president of the Caisse, Jean Campeau. He suggested that the Caisse buy shares in the family's holding company, Empire.

Donald's father, Frank Sobey, hated the thought of any government intrusion in private enterprise but, as a pragmatist, he was resigned to this new reality. "It's bad when government gets into these things, but there they are. You can't fight city hall," was his comment.

Donald Sobey soon realized that Campeau wanted to buy the portion of the Provigo shares held by the Sobeys to keep control of the company firmly in the hands of Quebeckers.

According to Donald Sobey, it was Jean Campeau who alluded to the Sobeys' frustration at not being invited to sit on the Provigo Board of Directors. Jean Campeau was even more displeased with the Caisse's meager representation at Provigo, restricted at the time to André Marier, President of Soquia.

Generally satisfied with Antoine Turmel's administration, the Sobeys had requested membership on the Provigo board on several occasions. They were not unduly insistent, but as their interest in Provigo's capital stock grew, so did their hopes of a seat on the board. The invitation never came.

Together, the Sobeys and the Caisse owned over 40 percent of Provigo's common shares. The reason Antoine Turmel refused to increase the Caisse's representation on the Company's Board was to avoid any confusion caused by a perceived government intrusion into Provigo's affairs.

As for the Sobeys, Provigo management regarded them as competitors. In Provigo's view, their large-scale operations in the food business (Sobeys Stores in the Maritimes and Lumsden Brothers in Ontario) and in the pharmaceutical sector (in the Maritimes and Alberta) created a conflict of interest.

Between the Caisse, whose request to have its representation increased had been rejected by Antoine Turmel, and the Sobeys, who were also frustrated in their attempts to gain board representation, the ground was paved for an alliance. Both groups believed that with so much money invested in a company, it was essential to monitor its growth closely, just as it was important to participate, as a member of the Board, in the establishment of general policies.

The Caisse and the Sobeys held similar views on Provigo shares and on forming a voting trust to obtain positions as directors from Antoine Turmel.

The Sobeys owned four million Provigo common shares. They were ready to sell a portion of them, at a premium, to the Caisse, which would act as their banker. They also demanded that they be guaranteed the option to repurchase the shares within the following nine years.[10]

On March 12, 1982, the Caisse bought 1,444,427 Provigo common shares from the Sobeys for $15,888,697 or $11 per share. The quoted price was approximately $10 at the time. It had climbed to $16.50 by summer 1981, at the time of the issue of two million new shares, only to drop afterwards. With these shares, the Caisse's interest reached the 30 percent regulatory ceiling. The Sobeys holdings dropped to 13 percent.

The transaction was intensively discussed in all the newspapers, which hinted at a secret agreement between the Caisse and the Sobeys.

In an interview,[11] Antoine Turmel was adamant that he was not about to let the government run Provigo while he was in charge. He termed the agreement, which had not been made public, "undesirable."

Turmel went on to say that he disapproved of the way the Caisse had acted. The fact that it had upped its interest from 22 percent to 30 percent was in itself a positive development but he took a dim view of the agreement with the Sobeys, according to which the Caisse obtained voting rights for their 13 percent holding in Provigo. As a result, the Caisse now virtually controlled Provigo with 43 percent of the votes. He deplored the fact that, for all its fine talk about businesses run by francophones, the Caisse had joined hands with an English-Canadian firm to control Provigo.

Turmel admitted that in doing so the Caisse had demonstrated its confidence in Provigo management. But he pointed out that Provigo had never been subjected to pressures from a major shareholder before.

While he would not go as far as to say that the Caisse was likely to exert pressure, he made it clear that he had always ensured that Provigo not be controlled by a majority shareholder and that he had taken measures to prevent the Sobeys from influencing Provigo even though the Sobey family was an important shareholder. They were, after all, in the same business and could find themselves in a potential conflict of interest on Provigo's board. He had no objection, he said, to the Caisse owning between 20 percent and 30 percent of Provigo. But control was another matter.

A Few Facts About the Caisse-Sobey Agreement

The details of the agreement between the Caisse and the Sobey family were never made public. Whatever Antoine Turmel knew of the arrangement he had learned from the President of the Caisse himself, Jean Campeau. Once the deal was concluded, Donald Sobey had felt it better to let the Caisse break the news to Antoine Turmel. With his predecessor, Marcel Cazavant, who had remained a special advisor to the Caisse, Jean Campeau arrived at Antoine Turmel's office late in the afternoon of Friday March 12, 1982, while preparations were under way for Provigo's annual meeting.

It seems that the agreement provided for a voting trust between the Caisse and the Sobeys. Moreover, the Sobeys' interest in Provigo would be frozen until 1991 and was not to exceed 21 percent of the outstanding shares. Furthermore they agreed to demand five representatives on Provigo's Board of Directors — three from the Caisse and two from the Sobey family. As well, one of the Caisse representatives would be appointed to the Board's Executive Committee.

In certain circles, a connection was made between this joint demand of the Caisse and the Sobeys to be represented on the Board and the problems encountered by Provigo after the acquisition of the Dominion supermarkets. Perhaps the Caisse and the Sobeys were unhappy with the acquisition and the high costs of integration. But Donald Sobey strongly denied in a later interview that there was any such connection; had he been a member of the Board at the time, he would have approved the purchase. The acquisition was, in his view, a good idea and had strengthened the Sobeys' confidence in Provigo.

Antoine Turmel must have been less than pleased at the thought of the May 25, 1982 annual meeting; a bylaw to increase the number of directors would have to be approved to satisfy the demands of the Caisse and the Sobeys.[12]

There were other items to be submitted to the shareholders as well. These included the Company's intention to continue operating under Section I A of the Companies Act, which allowed for a more flexible corporate procedure and set no limits on the number of common shares the company was authorized to issue, as well as a proposed bylaw which would raise from 65 to 68 the age limit for the position of director. Without this approval, Antoine Turmel himself would have become ineligible to sit on Provigo's Board.

The Caisse insisted on scrutinizing every item that would be submitted at the shareholders' meeting, including, of course, the new candidates for the Board. Jean Faubert, Portfolio Manager, Stock Investment, and Carmand Normand, Assistant General Manager of the Caisse de dépôt et placement du Québec, were proposed as the two additional representatives of the Caisse; David F. Sobey, Deputy Chairman of the Board and Chief Executive Officer of Sobeys Stores, and Donald R. Sobey, President of Empire Company, represented the Sobey family.

The Caisse's representative on the Board, André Marier, President of the Société québécoise d'initiatives agro-alimentaires (Soquia), was again on the list of candidates. He was subsequently elected to the Executive Committee.

The Only Constant Is Change

The agreement between the Caisse and the Sobeys had not settled all irritants. Despite the presence of their candidates on the Board and Executive Committee, the Sobeys had difficulty in learning more about the company's operations from Antoine Turmel, even though he was the official link between them and the company. All the other members of Provigo management, including the President and Chief Operating Officer, Pierre H. Lessard, had little contact with the Caisse or the Sobeys. Tradition, and no doubt common sense, dictated that this was the role of the Chief Executive Officer.

The Caisse did not hold on to its 30 percent interest for long. From 30 percent in May 1982 it dropped to 29.6 percent in May 1983, 26.7 percent in May 1984, 26.37 percent in May 1985, 21.86 percent in May 1986 and

INVESTISSEMENTS EN ACTIONS ET EN OBLIGATIONS D'ENTREPRISES

au 31 décembre 1987
(valeur de réalisation – en millions de dollars)

	Désignation	Actions – Nombre	Actions – Montant	Valeurs convertibles
Abitibi-Price Inc.	ordinaires	1 083 548	29,3	
	bons de souscription	57 713	0,3	
Air Products and Chemicals, Inc.		107 200	5,7	
Alcan Aluminium Limitée		6 867 726	238,7	
Altamira Capital Corporation	ordinaires	12 940	0,4	
	privilégiées	501 900	5,0	
American Barrick, Société extractive		2 051 100	55,4	
American Home Products Corporation		55 500	5,2	
American International Group, Inc.		80 700	6,3	
Artopex International Inc.[1]		978 854	7,0	
Asamera Inc.		1 608 469	13,9	
Atlantic Richfield Company		65 000	5,9	
Auberges des Gouverneurs Inc.[1]	ordinaires	1 417 654	3,6	
	actions de participation	2 206 889	5,6	
Auto Point Inc.[1]		1 686 798	2,1	
Avcorp Inc., Industries				7.5
		140 100	0,7	
B.A.T. Industries		508 333	5,5	
BCE Inc.[2]		14 993 533	556,7	
B.S.N. – Gervais Danone		48 900	5,2	
Banque Canadienne Impériale de Commerce		4 699 216	91,6	
Banque de Montréal	ordinaires	6 333 771	166,2	
Peerless Limitée, Les Tapis				
Pepsico, Inc.		129 000	5,6	
Philip Morris Companies Inc.		84 400	9,4	
Place Desjardins Inc.				
Placer Dome Inc.		7 358 614	144,4	
Power Corporation du Canada	subalternes			
	à droit de vote	5 969 911	85,1	
Power Corporation financière[1]		10 493 600	149,5	
Provigo inc.[1]		9 431 600	80,2	38.8
Québec-Téléphone		1 282 804	16,7	
Ranger Oil Limited		1 843 017	9,0	
Reitmans (Canada) Limitée	ordinaires	14 900	0,3	
	classe A	711 720	12,8	
Rio Algom Limitée		968 023	18,9	
Royal Dutch Petroleum Company		48 350	7,1	
Sceptre Resources Limited[1,2]				14.9
	ordinaires	10 706 100	29,1	

The Caisse de dépôt's investment in Provigo

10.46 percent in May 1987.[13,14]

Meanwhile, the Sobeys' interest was rising from 13 percent to 14.2 percent, to 15.4 percent, to 16.56 percent, remained at 16.54 percent for a year and in May 1987 rose to 19.6 percent.

By then the Caisse had sold a portion of its shares to Unigesco, which now owned 20.04 percent of the shares. It seems that after playing a key role in Provigo's history until 1986, the Caisse de dépôt et placement was gradually backing away from its relation with Provigo. Now that the company's future was securely in the hands of Quebeckers, it could safely relinquish its leadership position to a reliable company, in this case Unigesco, under the direction of Bertin Nadeau.[15]

Notes

1. Offers by Couvrette & Provost Ltée to holders of all Denault and Lamontagne shares. See Chapter 5 for details.
2. Prospectus for new Provigo Inc. Serial Debentures maturing between 1974 and 1981 and Sinking Fund Debentures maturing on July 15, 1991.
3. Prospectus for a new issue of Sinking Fund Debentures maturing November 1, 1995.
4. Information sent to shareholders along with the notice of a special general meeting to be held on October 20, 1977.
5. From a ''conversation'' between Antoine Turmel and Dean Walker in *Executive* (September 1980).
6. *The Gazette* (September 24, 1977).
7. Information circular sent to shareholders along with the notices of annual general meetings to be held May 24, 1978 and May 23, 1979.
8. Information circular sent to Provigo shareholders along with the notice of a general special meeting to be held on May 21, 1980.
9. According to its 1985–1986 Annual Report, between November 1979 and March 1982, Soquia invested some $12 million, representing 7.5 percent of the Provigo Inc. capital. In subsequent years, this portion declined to 6.24 percent under the combined effect of new issues from the Company and the sale of a small block of shares by Soquia. Soquia resold its shares to Unigesco in March 1986 for $48.4 million and made a substantial profit, which ultimately ended in the Quebec government coffers.
10. The Sobeys repurchased their shares before the nine years expired. *Les Affaires* (March 20, 1982) referred to an option to repurchase the shares in blocks of 240,737. The option could be exercised between March 1985 and February 1991.
11. *Les Affaires* (May 8, 1982).
12. Taking into account the seat left vacant after the resignation of Frank M. Warnock, Loeb's President, the number of directors increased from 15 to 18 to make room for four new members.
13. Information circulars sent to shareholders along with the notices of annual general meetings for 1982, 1983, 1984, 1985, 1986 and 1987.

14. In 1985 Provigo effected from the Caisse a 10-year loan of $20 million through the issuance of promissory notes with an interest of 6 percent per year, convertible into common shares. An amount of 4,480,000 common shares is reserved to provide for the conversion right attached to these convertible promissory notes which are exercisable at a price of $4.48 per share until June 1989 and $4.93 per share thereafter until June 1994.
15. See Chapters 19 and 20.

CHAPTER NINETEEN

PROVIGO'S SECOND CHAIRMAN

For Provigo 1984–1985 was a remarkable year. In fact, it was the best year in Provigo's history to date. Revenues exceeded $4 billion for the first time. Income grew by 52 percent. Return on equity reached 22 percent. But it was also the end of an era. Antoine Turmel was on the verge of retiring as Chief Executive Officer. At the Annual Meeting held May 27, 1985, he could truly say that his mission had been accomplished. Over the years he had seen his small business merge with Lamontagne and Couvrette & Provost, and expand its base of operations outside Quebec to become one of the largest distribution companies in North America.

Turmel could step down with an easy mind and hand over the reins to his most trusted associate, Pierre H. Lessard, who had been President and Chief Operating Officer of Provigo since 1976 and was considered by almost everyone to be his rightful successor.

But this was not to be. Pierre H. Lessard would not succeed Antoine Turmel.

Pierre H. Lessard

Pierre H. Lessard was 25, with a recent MBA from Harvard, when, in 1967, Antoine Turmel offered him a job with Denault in Sherbrooke. A career in a large company was more in keeping with Pierre H. Lessard's plans. But he was won over by Antoine Turmel's positive attitude and determined ambition to expand his company, and by the advice of a former Université Laval professor, Marcel Bélanger, who was then a member of the Denault Board of Directors and who would become a Provigo director in 1969.[1]

Pierre H. Lessard began his career as assistant to the President of Denault. He then assumed the responsibilities of Controller and Treasurer. His first mandate was to establish an annual operational plan with a budget system organized around profit centres that would give each employee a share of responsibilities. This approach was far from common practice at the time.

In this capacity, he become acquainted with everyone in the organization and, above all, with every aspect of a food wholesaler's operations. Despite some suspicion in certain quarters, his earnestness and skills won him the confidence of colleagues who were older and had a wider experience of the food business. He soon distinguished himself by the quality of his work, his team spirit and his loyalty.

He contributed to the financial analysis preliminary to the 1969 merger that established Provigo and the following year he became Controller of the new company. By the age of 28, he had already acquired valuable business experience. Indeed, in the spring of 1971, he was entrusted with added responsibilities and became Vice-President, Finance and Administration, while retaining the position of Treasurer. His duties covered not only accounting, auditing and financing, but also included human resource development, and the supervision of major transactions and real estate development. He discharged all his mandates with great skill and earned the respect of every member of senior and middle management.

In September 1976, Pierre H. Lessard became a member of the Board of Directors and succeeded René Provost as President and Chief Operating Officer of Provigo. H. Paul Gobeil, his assistant, advanced to the position of Vice-President, Finance and Administration, and Treasurer.

In less than ten years, Pierre H. Lessard, who had been reluctant to work for Antoine Turmel's small Sherbrooke-based company, had become President and Chief Operating Officer of a company with sales of over half a billion dollars.

The following year, with the purchase of Loeb, Provigo had exceeded the billion mark in sales and acquired a national, even North American, stature. Pierre H. Lessard was appointed to the boards of directors and

Pierre H. Lessard, Vice-President (1971-76), President and Chief Operating Officer of Provigo from 1976 to 1985.

executive committees of Provigo's major subsidiaries, Loeb, Horne & Pitfield, National Drug and Market Wholesale.

The acquisition of Loeb had caused Provigo a number of problems. Loeb was twice Provigo's size with operations outside Quebec and outside the food business. It was Pierre H. Lessard who successfully coordinated the integration of Loeb and its subsidiaries with the Provigo group of companies.

Pierre H. Lessard also participated in all other acquisitions, consolidations, and integrations needed to further Provigo's growth. He was particularly attentive to real estate development, projects related to expansion, the Company's cash flow position and human resources management. He shared power with Antoine Turmel who, despite a committed willingness to delegate authority, retained for himself those roles which best typified Provigo in the eyes of the business community. No doubt Antoine Turmel's closest associate was deeply convinced that "there is no limit to what a man can do or where he can go if he doesn't mind who gets the credit."[2] In short, Pierre H. Lessard was a team player.

When Antoine Turmel decided to retire, Pierre H. Lessard had been working with him for 18 years. He was his closest colleague and had been Chief Operating Officer for a decade. He was the logical choice as his successor.

A Surprise Announcement

April 23, 1985, to the surprise of everybody, a short press release issued by Provigo announced that the Board of Directors had submitted the names of Pierre Lortie and Bertin Nadeau as candidates for the positions of Provigo directors. The elections were to be held at the May 27 Shareholders' Annual General Meeting.

Annoyed by these surprise developments, Antoine Turmel decided not to seek a new mandate. His reaction was understandable. Pierre Lortie was then President of The Montreal Exchange, but he had announced to his colleagues, that very morning of April 23, that he would step down a few weeks later.

It was a foregone conclusion among journalists and business watchers that Pierre Lortie would succeed Antoine Turmel.[3] At 38, Pierre Lortie was leaving the Exchange covered in glory. The Provigo offer had come unsolicited with prospects of numerous challenges that he could not easily turn down. "I find it quite an honor to join such a great corporation."[4]

According to Jacques Ménard, Chairman of the Exchange's Board of Governors, Pierre Lortie had advised the board several weeks in advance that he was negotiating with Provigo.[5] Apparently, after the Provigo communiqué was released, Pierre Lortie did confirm to the Board that he was stepping down as President of the Exchange. In a comment to *Le Devoir* on April 24, 1985, he declared that he had reached, and in some cases exceeded, the goals he had set for himself when he was appointed President four years earlier.

The Gazette reported a cautiously worded statement from Jacques Lesage, Vice-President of Human Resources and Public Affairs at Provigo. In further elaborations to the press, he observed that it would have been normal for Antoine Turmel, who was 67 years old, to retire at 65, but he had been asked to continue as Chairman of Provigo for another two years. Jacques Lesage, however, could not confirm that Pierre Lortie would be appointed to succeed Antoine Turmel. He added that, to his knowledge, Pierre H. Lessard, would once again be proposed as a candidate to a director's position and would remain President and Chief Operating Officer of Provigo.

The French press reported that Antoine Turmel was retiring after leading Provigo since its inception and throughout its subsequent period of sustained growth, and that he had sold most of his shares over the previous two years.[6]

During this period newspapers mentioned on several occasions that Antoine Turmel, who had accumulated a vast number of shares over the years, had been gradually selling his Provigo holdings. At the end of September 1977, he owned 10 percent of Provigo's stock;[7] as of April 30, 1984, he controlled, directly or indirectly, 1,091,154 shares or 5.6 percent of the outstanding shares.[8] *Finance* reported on February 18, 1985 that he had sold some 565,000 shares in the last twelve months. Subsequently, he continued to sell significant portions of his Provigo holdings. Most were sold in private transactions through the Caisse.[9]

Certain analysts wondered why Antoine Turmel was selling his shares in such large quantities. Had Turmel's confidence in Provigo's future been shaken? They even went so far as to hint that the sales amounted to a vote of non-confidence in his possible successor, Pierre H. Lessard.

Provigo spokesman Jacques Lesage put these fears to rest. As reported in *Finance* (February 18, 1985), he indicated that if Mr. Turmel had been 50 years old and if all the senior executives had been getting rid of their shares, there might be cause for worry. But since he was close to retirement age, it was entirely normal for him to consider diversifying his assets. Whatever the particular reason for selling, it was certainly his business.

To add to the rumour mill, Pierre H. Lessard had worked with financier Paul Vien in the fall of 1984 on a transaction to hold jointly 63.5 percent of the votes of Télé-Capitale, a network of television stations in Quebec City and Sherbrooke.[10]

Prior to the May 27, 1985 Annual Meeting, the newspapers had much to speculate about: Antoine Turmel's retirement and the presumed succession by Pierre H. Lessard; the impending accession of Pierre Lortie to the Provigo Board of Directors and his resignation from the Exchange; Pierre Lortie as head of Provigo and the possibility of a Lortie-Lessard team. Never in Provigo's history had an Annual Meeting so much uncertainty to resolve.

A New Generation of Entrepreneurs

In an article published in *La Presse* (April 27, 1985), Pierre Lortie observed that Provigo had become a powerful symbol of success both in Quebec and throughout Canada. He went on to say that the Provigo management team was exceptional and that he looked forward to working with this second generation of entrepreneurs whose task was to give new impetus to an already formidable machine. This declaration echoed previous informal remarks of Jean Campeau and Donald Sobey.

La Presse commented that it was one of the first times in Quebec that a large and important home-grown company was experiencing a change of generation among its leaders. The two principal contenders were Provigo's Pierre Lessard and Pierre Lortie, who were 43 and 38 respectively. In the end, Pierre Lortie would head a management team which, according to Provigo's inside people, had had its feathers badly ruffled during the selection process. For them, Pierre Lessard was the man for the job. "For us, the choice was Pierre Lessard. We've all worked well together, with excellent results."[11] Indeed, Pierre Lessard's impressive results from 1976 to 1985[12] spoke for themselves.

Senior management had even anticipated the appointment of Pierre H. Lessard. According to them, when Pierre H. Lessard succeeded Antoine Turmel, it would be H. Paul Gobeil who would replace Pierre H. Lessard as President and Chief Operating Officer.

Far from Unanimity

Shortly before the annual meeting, journalists began to speculate that Antoine Turmel would not attend. They had discovered, as well, that Pierre H. Lessard had taken a two-week vacation to mull things over.

On May 5, 1985, *Le Devoir* reported that the selection of Pierre Lortie had hardly been to everyone's liking and that the Provigo directors' meeting held April 23 to choose the slate of nominees for directors of the food giant had occasioned a fierce battle between the supporters of Pierre Lortie, President of The Montreal Exchange, and those of Pierre Lessard, President and Chief Operating Officer of Provigo. In fact, this meeting had been scheduled to deal with matters left pending after the previous day's meeting was adjourned due to overheated discussions between the two camps. Antoine Turmel's successor would not be approved unanimously.

The Candidates

Early in May, Claude E. Leduc, Secretary of Provigo, called the Annual General Meeting of the shareholders for May 27 to study the directors' report and elect the new Board of Directors.

The notice was accompanied by the usual information, indicating that on April 30, the Caisse owned 26.37 percent of the outstanding shares and the Sobeys 16.56 percent.[13]

Shareholders were to elect 14 directors rather than 16, as they had the previous year. The list of candidates read as follows (*designates a new candidate):

Marcel Bélanger	President, Gagnon et Bélanger Inc. (management consultants)
Jacques Desmeules	Vice-President of the Executive Committee and Managing Partner (Quebec), Groupe Raymond, Chabot, Martin, Paré & Cie (chartered accountants)
Jean Faubert	Vice-President, Lapierre & Associés (investment consultants)
H. Paul Gobeil	Executive Vice-President, Provigo Inc.; and President and Chief Operating Officer, Loeb Inc. (food distributor)

David A. Golden	Chairman of the Board, Telesat Canada (telecommunications)
Jean-Louis Lamontagne	Executive Vice-President, Provigo Inc.
Pierre H. Lessard	President and Chief Operating Officer, Provigo Inc.
*Pierre Lortie	President and Chief Executive Officer, The Montreal Exchange
*Bertin F. Nadeau	Chairman of the Board, President and Chief Executive Officer, Unigesco Inc. (holding company)
Carmand Normand	Consultant
René Provost	Vice-Chairman of the Board, Provigo Inc.
Guy Saint-Germain	President and Chief Executive Officer, The Commerce Group Insurance Company (insurance)
David F. Sobey	Deputy Chairman and Chief Executive Officer, Sobeys Stores Limited (food distributor)
Donald R. Sobey	President, Empire Company Limited (holding company)

The list introduced two new figures, Pierre Lortie and Bertin Nadeau. The latter represented the Caisse, which had asked him to offer his candidacy.[14]

Among Provigo's senior executives, three former members of the Board had refused to stand as candidates. Antoine Turmel had handed in his resignation on May 2, to take effect May 20, 1985. At their own request, Carl R. Goslovich, President of Market Wholesale and Kenneth W. Quinn, President of Horne & Pitfield, had declined to seek re-election, as had Norman W. Robertson, Executive Vice-President and Chief Operating Officer of Atco Ltd., who, since May 1980, had been sitting on the Provigo Board to represent the shareholders residing in Western Canada.

Pierre Lortie at the Helm of Provigo

The May 27, 1985 Annual Meeting went smoothly despite the shadow that Antoine Turmel's absence cast over the proceedings and the evident tension felt by Pierre H. Lessard. René Provost, Vice-Chairman of the Board, chaired the meeting in place of Antoine Turmel.

The list of directors was presented by Guy Desmarais, President of Geoffrion Leclerc. Then Jean-Guy Lambert, the authorized representative

Pierre Lortie, Chairman of the Board, President and Chief Executive Officer since 1985.

of the Caisse de dépôt, immediately moved that the nominations be closed.

Since the directors on the list were all eligible, they were proclaimed elected. As is the custom, the Board of Directors met within minutes of the General Meeting. Not surprisingly, Pierre Lortie was elected Chairman of the Board and Chief Executive Officer.

Following the Annual Meeting Pierre Lortie had his first press conference as Chairman of Provigo. He praised the qualities of Pierre H. Lessard, stressing that there had never been any conflict and that there was no reason why he should resign. He added that initial meetings between the two pointed to the possibility of forming a remarkable team. He concluded by saying that Pierre H. Lessard had attributes essential and crucial to the company's success and hoped that he would stay with the Company for as long as possible.

Pierre H. Lessard, for his part, was obviously disappointed and announced that he had to assess the situation before deciding what course his own career would take. He told journalists that although he was acquainted with Pierre Lortie he could not say what style the new management would adopt. Time would tell whether he could work with him as closely as he had with Antoine Turmel. He added that his immediate priority was to ensure that the change in management would be as smooth and orderly as possible.

Prior to the directors' meeting on April 22, Antoine Turmel had not officially outlined to the Board his recommendations with regard to a successor. In the opinion of many, at the peak of his powers, he could have held out against the Caisse and the Sobeys. On the verge of retirement, he obviously had far fewer assets in hand.

Meanwhile, the role played by Pierre H. Lessard during Antoine Turmel's chairmanship had not given him a chance to prove his worth to the principal shareholders. At Provigo, it had been Antoine Turmel who dealt with the President of the Caisse, Jean Campeau, and the Sobey brothers. Pierre H. Lessard kept a low profile. Some might say that this approach indicated a lack of openness or willingness to communicate on his part and it might have even led some to believe that he was little involved in formulating Provigo's plans and objectives. However, all those who worked with him have clearly stated that he was extremely competent and had a clear vision of the Company's direction.

In fact, if Pierre H. Lessard was not always at ease with outsiders when it came to discussing such matters as Provigo's plans, orientations, policies, strategies and objectives, he simply may have felt that he did not have the required authority. As chief executive officer, it was normal for Antoine Turmel to be the company's principal spokesman. As long as Turmel was in charge, Pierre H. Lessard showed himself to be loyal and mindful of his position in Provigo's management hierarchy.

Not Everyone Was Surprised

Some people were not surprised by the newspaper headlines that started to appear on April 24, 1985. The secret agreement[15] between the Caisse and the Sobeys apparently provided, among other things, for a choice of chairman of the board and chief executive officer in the joint voting convention. The current principal shareholders readily admit this feature of the entente. The succession of Antoine Turmel was their first opportunity to exercise the power conferred by the agreement. Not surprisingly, Jean Campeau and Donald Sobey had begun to take an active interest in the choice of successor long before the meeting of the board to prepare the list of potential candidates.

In fact, during a meeting between Jean Campeau and Antoine Turmel a year earlier, it had been agreed that he would remain in his position for another year. But in the fall of 1984, the question was raised once again. The Caisse and the Sobeys were eager to know more about the views of Pierre H. Lessard on Provigo's management and future plans in order to decide whether he was the right man to head the company. Antoine Turmel suggested that Jean Campeau meet Pierre H. Lessard to discuss the matter directly with him.

So, accompanied by Donald Sobey, Jean Campeau went to Pierre H. Lessard to find out what strategic course the latter intended to follow should he succeed Antoine Turmel, the nature of his development plan for the next five years, the direction expansion would take, etc.

Donald Sobey and Jean Campeau both knew the man and considered him brilliant. They appreciated his excellent work as President and Chief Operating Officer. But they were looking for a second Antoine Turmel. They wanted to see an entrepreneur rather than an administrator or manager at the head of Provigo. They maintained that Provigo needed another powerful driving force to expand its markets further and faster.

Donald Sobey summed up his feelings in saying that Pierre H. Lessard was excellent under Antoine Turmel but that he could never replace him. According to Donald Sobey, Antoine Turmel could have encouraged

Pierre Lessard to assert himself more. Others declared that he should have given him a chance to demonstrate his capacities and potential earlier.

In any event, Pierre H. Lessard had not scored many points with the major shareholders during the integration of the Dominion supermarkets, even though they had approved the acquisition. He was quietly reproached with having supported Richard Constantineau, the man in charge of the Dominion project. Period after period, year in and year out, the results of the Dominion deal had been disastrous and the losses considerable.[16]

For all these reasons, the principal shareholders decided to look elsewhere for a successor to Antoine Turmel. They hoped that Pierre H. Lessard would stay on as President and Chief Operating Officer, a position for which everybody agreed he was ideally suited. Early in 1985, four or five interesting possibilities had surfaced. In February, Jean Campeau and Donald Sobey interviewed several candidates. Pierre Lortie was among them.

Who Is Pierre Lortie?

Since becoming President and Chief Executive Officer of The Montreal Exchange in 1981, Pierre Lortie had made quite a reputation for himself. He had managed to breathe new life into an institution that had been losing ground to the Toronto Stock Exchange year after year and had even dropped to third place in volume behind the Vancouver Stock Exchange.

Pierre Lortie can be credited with countless innovations which increased the number and variety of products and securities traded on the exchange, raised the volume of transactions and, more importantly, made the general public aware of that organization's important economic role. His capable leadership and the Quebec Stock Savings Plan ushered in a new period of growth for The Montreal Exchange.

Even the President of the Toronto Stock Exchange once said about Pierre Lortie, "he doesn't wait for things to happen, he makes them happen." In 1985, Lortie looked somewhat older than his 38 years because of his silver hair. But his vigour and dynamism gave little hint of the extraordinary energy he had expended during an extremely active career.

A graduate engineer from Université Laval, at 23 he was executive assistant to Raymond Garneau, who was then Minister of Finance and President of the Quebec government Treasury Board. He held that position from 1970 to 1972. He then returned to his studies and in 1974 obtained a diploma in applied economic science from the Institut d'administration et de gestion at Université de Louvain (Belgium) and an MBA with honors from the Chicago University Graduate School of Business.

That same year, The Montreal Exchange offered him the position of Director, Development, then, in 1975–1976, that of Vice-President, Development. The following year, he left the Exchange to become President of A. Prud'homme & Fils. After four years as senior partner with Secor Inc. (1977–1981), he returned to the Exchange, this time as President, rather than taking the helm of a large Montreal daily newspaper. He had accepted the chairmanship of the Chambre de Commerce de Montréal and felt he could not reconcile this role with that of a publisher, at least not during the first year.

In 1981–1982, at 34, he was the youngest person to be elected President of the Chambre de Commerce. He would go on to become a member of the Economic Council of Canada and the Comité sur les relations université-industries of the Natural Sciences and Engineering Research Council of Canada.

Pierre Lortie had no specific career plan in mind. He was a leader rather than a follower. He would not have left his position at The Exchange for anything less than the opportunity to lead a national company, either immediately or in the near future.

Jean Campeau, President of the Caisse de dépôt et placement, had asked a mutual friend to find out Lortie's reaction to the possible offer of an interesting position. Pierre Lortie, who had reached his goal of being President of The Exchange, declared himself ready to consider any serious offer. A month later, he learned that the position in question was at Provigo.

He then met with Jean Campeau, who already knew him well, and Donald Sobey, on whom he had made a strong impression at a Halifax meeting of the Economic Council of Canada. Donald Sobey called him an outstanding candidate and declared that Pierre Lortie was at the top of his list to succeed Antoine Turmel.

Finally, in early March 1985, the position of Chief Executive Officer of Provigo was offered to this outsider who knew little about the food business rather than the man who had made a career of it and who many already thought of as the successor to Antoine Turmel.

The Successor

Certain to become Chairman of the Board and Chief Executive Officer of

Provigo, Pierre Lortie handed in his resignation as President of the Exchange the same day the list of new directors was submitted to the Provigo Board of Directors.

Since mid-March, Antoine Turmel and Pierre H. Lessard had been aware of the intentions of the principal shareholders and the feelings of certain outside directors. In response, a few directors and members of senior management met repeatedly to develop a strategy capable of countering the actions of the principal shareholders or, at the very least, amending the proposal they were to submit at the April 22 meeting. This meeting, as mentioned earlier, would give rise to clashes between the supporters of Antoine Turmel and Pierre H. Lessard and those who sided with Pierre Lortie.

René Provost formulated two alternative proposals:

1. Antoine Turmel would remain Chairman of the Board for one year and Pierre H. Lessard would take up the duties of Chief Executive Officer. After one year, his performance could be assessed.
2. The status quo would be maintained at the May 1985 Annual Meeting; candidates for the position of Chief Executive Officer would be sought and assessed by a selection committee which would present its report in September 1985.

Antoine Turmel and Pierre H. Lessard supported either approach, as did the in-house members of the Board.

Then the cat came out of the bag — Donald Sobey declared that Pierre Lortie had already been approached and hired. The principal shareholders had solidified the support they needed in case of a vote at the Annual Meeting and nothing would make them change their minds at the meeting of the Board. In case of systematic obstruction by dissident board members, they were even ready to call a special general meeting of the shareholders. The Caisse and the Sobeys could lose the battle but not the war.

As reported in the newspapers, the ensuing discussion was stormy and emotional. Votes were divided equally at first between those in the Antoine Turmel faction, who favoured Pierre H. Lessard, and those, such as the Caisse and the Sobeys, who wanted Pierre Lortie.

At the April 22 meeting, Turmel cast the deciding vote in favour of Pierre H. Lessard. The lengthy and acrimonious discussions that followed led to the adjournment of the meeting to the following day at the request of Carmand Normand, a representative of the Caisse. Finally, on the 23rd,

Pierre Lortie obtained the majority of the Board's votes, even though all executive members of Provigo and its subsidiaries were still in support of Pierre H. Lessard.

Some directors wanted the issue decided by the shareholders at the upcoming general meeting. Meantime, a certain lobbying continued in favour of Pierre H. Lessard. It met with little success and, in the end, the idea of bringing the matter before the shareholders was abandoned. What certainly added to the confusion was the fact that Pierre H. Lessard agreed to be one of the representatives authorized to cast proxy votes at the Annual Meeting.

In any case, recourse to the general meeting would undoubtedly have done nothing more than bring the behind-the-scenes disagreement and quarrelling out into the open. The Caisse and the Sobeys had made sure they would obtain a solid majority in this shareholders meeting, even though they hoped the matter would not be brought to a general vote. In their firm determination to have Pierre Lortie elected, they had even agreed on his tenure and even his remuneration, regardless of the views held by the Board of Directors or management. They had left nothing to chance.

The Caisse and its allies were well aware that they could count on a majority at the general meeting, since they had made sure that a large number of favourable proxies had been filed. Sure enough, 71.6 percent of the shareholders attending the meeting or voting by proxy pronounced themselves in favour of the proposed list. This proportion was significantly higher than usual.

A Tribute to Antoine Turmel

The day after this memorable general meeting, all the newspapers commented on the accession of Pierre Lortie to the chairmanship of the Provigo board, the disappointment of Pierre H. Lessard and the absence of Antoine Turmel, who had resigned a few days earlier. In the annual report, Turmel had written a Chairman's message that contained no hint of his impending departure. He left no last words.

His former colleagues, particularly René Provost, Vice-Chairman of the Board, took it upon themselves to pay him tribute at the Annual Meeting. When René Provost spoke of the key role played by Antoine Turmel in the creation and phenomenal success of Provigo, underscoring the man's unquestioned leadership qualities, the shareholders rose to their feet and applauded.

Antoine Turmel, Chairman of the Board and Chief Executive Officer from 1969 to 1985.

Antoine Turmel had long before prepared a text that he was to deliver himself at the general meeting when he would transfer management of Provigo to Pierre H. Lessard. No one else could read it in his place. But the man who since 1969 had ruled with such a sure hand the company that had become a symbol of success in Quebec and Canada was unable to make this final gesture of handing over the reins of power to someone chosen by him. His speech was never delivered.

At Board meetings, Antoine Turmel was used to making proposals that brooked no compromise. He could have, at the end of 1984 or beginning of 1985, put his cards on the table when it came to the question of his successor and proposed Pierre H. Lessard. But he had chosen not to. Everyone knew that he was leaving, but he remained sole master on board to the last.

As for Pierre Lortie, he refused to comment on the resignation of Antoine Turmel. In *Le Devoir* (May 28, 1985), he was quoted as saying that he had inherited in Provigo a remarkable company that represented both sentimental and symbolic value for the success of Quebeckers in the business world.

He was ready to work with Pierre H. Lessard, for whom he had nothing but praise, and his top priority was to meet everyone in management as quickly as he could. Furthermore, he had already started doing his homework on Provigo before his official appointment.

According to Pierre Lortie, the new generation, which included Pierre H. Lessard, had a fundamental commitment to the advancement of Provigo. His mandate was clear: Provigo was a company that had to continue growing and it was foolish to think that any person could do it single-handedly. He declared that the focus of the company had to remain on food, but that this emphasis should not preclude diversification into other areas. The experience acquired in food distribution could be useful in related businesses, even though different products might be involved.

The Perfect Team

In everyone's eyes, including Pierre Lortie's, the Lortie-Lessard team was perfect. Pierre H. Lessard refused, however, to make a long-term commitment. In *La Presse* (May 28, 1985), he declared that his priority was to smooth the Turmel-Lortie transition on behalf of the shareholders and senior management. Decisions concerning his own career would have to wait. He emphasized that things were proceeding according to plan and that life had to go on.

Rumour had it that Pierre H. Lessard was on the verge of announcing his departure. *Finance* (June 3, 1985) stated that many observers were expecting Pierre H. Lessard to leave Provigo before long and that there were rumours of his departure to Métro-Richelieu or to Télé-Capitale, where he was one of the principal shareholders with 15.9 percent of the voting rights. The article also suggested that, in the event of Lessard's departure, the Executive Vice-President, Paul Gobeil, might very well also hand in his resignation. Paul Gobeil, who had worked closely with Pierre H. Lessard for several years, had accomplished excellent work at Provigo and at Loeb as President and Chief Operating Officer.

His career with the Company can be traced back to the days of Denault where he was external auditor before the 1969 merger. His long friendship and fruitful collaboration with Pierre H. Lessard also goes back to those days. He then became Vice-President (Finance and Administration), Treasurer and Assistant Secretary from 1976 to 1981, and Vice-President (Finance) from 1981 to 1984. In 1983, he became Executive Vice-President and in 1985, President and Chief Operating Officer of Provigo Distribution.

From 1981 to 1985, he was also President and Chief Operating Officer of Loeb Inc. and Loeb Corporation. There he accomplished remarkable work, returning the company to a sound footing, imparting new confidence to the team in place and ensuring the profitability of the operations. During that period, he acceded to the position of Vice-Chairman of the Board of IGA Canada Ltd. In May 1983, he was invited to sit on the Provigo Board of Directors.

When, in August 1985, Provigo acquired a major share in Consumers Distributing, Paul Gobeil became a member of the Board, of the Executive Committee, and of the Audit Committee of that company.

Paul Gobeil expected to be appointed President and Chief Operating Officer of Provigo, but the choice of Pierre Lortie as Chairman had forestalled that promotion. As the man who was probably closer to Pierre H. Lessard than anyone else, Paul Gobeil had been badly shaken by the events surrounding the succession. For a while, he was incapable of concentrating on his work. Like many others, he made no attempt to hide his sympathies. He found it hard to accept that Pierre H. Lessard had not been given the opportunity to show his mettle as Chief Executive Officer.

A few months later, everyone went his separate way. Pierre H. Lessard became Vice-Chairman of the Board with Télé-Capitale Inc., in which he was already a principal shareholder.[18] H. Paul Gobeil was elected Member of the National Assembly for the riding of Verdun in December 1985, and became Minister responsible for Administration and President of the Treasury Board.[19]

Paul Gobeil would no doubt have played a key role in Provigo's future. He was Pierre H. Lessard's most trusted collaborator and together the two had few equals. With his departure, Provigo lost a highly dedicated and competent man who later channelled all his energies and resources into politics.

It was with deep regret that Pierre Lortie accepted the resignations of Pierre Lessard and Paul Gobeil. Both had contributed in major ways to the success of Provigo.

Notes

1. Marcel Bélanger retired from the Board on December 31, 1987.
2. These words appear on a plaque in his office.
3. The next morning, a headline in *Le Devoir* proclaimed that Lortie was leaving the Exchange to replace Turmel at Provigo and *The Globe and Mail* announced: "Lortie to take over as head of Provigo." Similar comments appeared in *The Gazette* and *La Presse*.
4. *The Gazette* (April 24, 1985)
5. It was not, in fact, Provigo that was negotiating with Pierre Lortie, but two of its largest shareholders.
6. *La Presse* (April 24, 1985).
7. Information circular in the notice of a special general meeting of the shareholders held October 20, 1977.
8. Information circular in the notice of the annual and special general meeting of the shareholders held May 28, 1984.
9. In April 1985, according to the shareholders' record, he had sold all but 35,400 of his shares.
10. *Finance* (March 4, 1985).
11. *The Gazette* (April 30, 1985).
12. See Appendix I.
13. The principal shareholders could count on the support of the Société québécoise d'initiatives agro-alimentaires (Soquia) and other organizations, to ensure the majority of votes.
14. It should be kept in mind that Bertin Nadeau did not own any Provigo stock at the time.
15. See Chapter 18.
16. See Chapter 14.
18. Since March 1988, he has been President and Chief Executive Officer of Aeterna-Life Insurance Co.
19. Since June 1988, he has been Minister of International Affairs and Foreign Trade.

CHAPTER TWENTY

UNIGESCO GRABS THE REINS

Before the succession saga, the Caisse de dépôt et placement du Québec had decided to relinquish the role of principal shareholder in Provigo — a role it had played ever since the days of Couvrette & Provost, Denault and Lamontagne. The Caisse had not particularly appreciated the controversy surrounding the succession proceedings. As soon as that problem was settled, the Caisse started a well planned retreat from the front lines of Provigo's affairs.

On the morning of July 26, 1985, the press reported Unigesco's purchase of 500,000 Provigo shares from the Caisse with an option to purchase 1.5 million additional shares. Observers were puzzled. Unigesco and Bertin Nadeau, its President, were known in Quebec financial circles, but nobody could figure out what was happening. However, there was already rumour of a takeover of Provigo by Unigesco with the blessing of the Caisse; the purchase option which he was expected to exercise would increase his holdings to 10 percent.[1]

Bertin Nadeau spent $12 million to acquire these 500,000 shares. To procure the funds needed to achieve the 10 percent level, Unigesco would have to raise an additional $35 million.

Le Devoir (July 26, 1985) reported that Bertin Nadeau's plans went even further. By his own admission, the operation would only be complete when he had acquired a sufficiently high interest to exercise a dominant influence over Provigo, a company he had once referred to as one of the most exciting in Canada.

The article added that Unigesco wanted to secure an interest of at least 20 percent in the capital stock to consolidate its position. Bertin Nadeau underscored that it was indeed an ambitious project for a company the size of Unigesco but, he added, it could be accomplished by proceeding one step at a time.

Because Unigesco had bought its shares without paying a premium over the market price, it was possible for Bertin Nadeau to operate privately. He had paid $24 a share, compared with the quoted market price of $24.75.

Provigo and Pierre Lortie were not unfamiliar to Bertin Nadeau. He had sat on the Board of The Montreal Exchange during Pierre Lortie's tenure as President and had recently been appointed to the Provigo Board of Directors at the suggestion of the Caisse. Although he had not participated in the selection of Pierre Lortie as Chief Executive Officer of Provigo, he was aware of it and fully agreed with his appointment.

Moreover, according to *Le Devoir,* the new Chief Executive Officer supported Unigesco's plan to become an important Provigo shareholder. Bertin Nadeau declared that Pierre Lortie was aware of Unigesco's plans and had given his assurance that he would not oppose it in any way. On the contrary, he had been strongly in favour of the move, said Nadeau.

The announcement that Unigesco had bought 500,000 Provigo shares and, above all, the news that Bertin Nadeau intended to control the company took everyone by surprise. Outsiders had no idea that the Caisse de dépôt et placement was looking to sell a portion of its Provigo shares and, even if they had known, they would probably not have suspected Unigesco of preparing such a brilliant coup.

After all, in 1985 Provigo was a giant with sales figures far exceeding four billion dollars. By contrast, Unigesco had revenues of slightly less than $16 million. Moreover, Unigesco had no holdings in Provigo and to achieve his goals Bertin Nadeau would have to acquire over 4 million shares (or 8 million after the October 1985 stock split). Such an acquisition would require approximately $130 million.

From Professor to Tycoon

Bertin Nadeau, who was 46 years old in 1985, is a fascinating figure. The son of a furniture manufacturer from Saint-François-de-Madawaska in

New Brunswick, he studied at the École des Hautes Études Commerciales in Montreal, where he later lectured.

Everything he taught about business management he had first put into practice in the family business as its President and General Manager. In 1976, he quit teaching, borrowed a million dollars and bought Casavant Frères Ltée of Saint-Hyacinthe. His goal was to steer the company towards the manufacture of top-of-the-line furniture for home and office, at a time when it was exclusively producing organs and church furniture. In 1978, his keen business sense earned him an invitation to sit on the Board of Directors of Unigesco, a company initially created by a group of young, innovative university graduates intent on founding a life insurance company. That company, the Unique, had in fact been established in 1967.

Bertin Nadeau viewed Unigesco as a potential source of capital for other business ventures. In 1982, he acquired 22 percent of the business, sufficient to give him effective control. Today, Casavant owns 60 percent of Unigesco's stock.

After selling the Unique and its subsidiaries for $10.5 million in 1982, Bertin Nadeau developed a strategy to invest in other concerns. This time, his goal was for Unigesco to take over certain companies. He was looking for interesting business opportunities in non-cyclical sectors that would not be threatened by foreign competition. In addition, the targeted companies had to be leaders in their field, occupy sizable market niches, be well managed and long established.

In rapid succession, Unigesco acquired Breuvages Kiri Ltée, a soft drink producer, in 1983, and two years later a competitor called Maxi. He integrated these two companies' operations with the result that Kiri has become one of the largest independent bottlers of soft drinks in Quebec. In 1984, Nadeau managed to repeat the success by buying, on the same day, London House and National House, two competitors which were the largest Quebec suppliers of coffee for hotels and restaurants. The new company, which eventually became Aliments Excelco Inc., continued to expand by buying several related businesses, primarily in coffee distribution in Quebec, Ontario and elsewhere. It has since become the largest roaster and distributor of coffee for the Quebec institutional market.

But further acquisitions required money. Bertin Nadeau approached Geoffrion Leclerc to propose a new share issue which would raise some $9 million. On December 18, 1984, during a conversation with Guy Desmarais, President of Geoffrion Leclerc, at the closing of the share issue, Bertin Nadeau learned that the Caisse was interested in selling part of its Provigo block of shares and was looking for someone to take over as principal shareholder.

Guy Desmarais advised Bertin Nadeau to think the matter over. Nadeau's immediate reaction was that it was far too big a transaction for him. Nonetheless, before leaving for his vacation he put Provigo's annual report in his suitcase. Even though he already knew a great deal about Provigo, he was impressed by what he read. The scope of the company's operations came as a surprise. Of course, he had heard about the imminent departure of Antoine Turmel as Chief Executive Officer. He could sense that an element of risk was involved, but at the same time it was a major opportunity. In those days, Pierre Lortie had not yet been mentioned as a potential successor to Antoine Turmel.

It was one thing to be interested in Provigo; another to take it over. Even Bertin Nadeau had doubts. But in January 1985 he met with Jean Campeau, the President of the Caisse. Campeau knew and respected Bertin Nadeau, who had represented the Caisse on the Board of Directors of the Société d'investissement Desjardins (SID) for five years.

On this occasion, Bertin Nadeau asked whether the Caisse would agree to finance Unigesco's acquisition of a block of Provigo shares. Jean Campeau replied that the Caisse would be willing to sell him shares, but that any financing was out of the question. Two or three other meetings failed to change that decision. Besides, as Jean Campeau was preoccupied at the time with the Antoine Turmel succession, the discussion had to be deferred.

At the Provigo Annual Meeting of May 27, 1985, Nadeau was elected to the Board of Directors of the Company, and then to the Executive Committee. Along with Pierre Lortie, he was one of the candidates proposed by the Caisse. Although he was well acquainted with Provigo's succession problem, he had no influence in the final choice for chairman nor in the manoeuvering that occurred during this difficult period.[2]

500,000 Shares to Begin

After the annual general meeting, Bertin Nadeau resumed his attempts to acquire part of the Caisse's holding in Provigo. Intense discussions began in June 1985 and, on July 24, Unigesco announced that it had bought 500,000 Provigo shares for $12 million and obtained an option on a further 1.5 million shares held by the Caisse. Unigesco had two years to exercise the option. Bertin Nadeau had also obtained a right of first refusal on another block of shares held by the Caisse. Reciprocally, the Caisse had a right of first refusal on the shares owned by Unigesco. Bertin Nadeau wanted the agreement between the Caisse and the Sobeys to be maintained, since it effectively ensured that control of Provigo would rest with the major shareholders.

Bertin Nadeau's ultimate plan was for Unigesco, the Sobeys and the Caisse to assume the role of principal shareholder. Unigesco would become the dominant figure in this controlling group. In his view, the role of principal shareholder was to monitor the growth of the company, exercise a firm influence on its course and management, participate in the choice of the chief executive officer and determine such matters as financial structure and dividend policy. The object was not to interfere in daily management and operations but to oversee the quality and performance of the management team, follow the company's progress and, of course, assess its results.

Most of all, Bertin Nadeau wanted the Sobeys to support his view of the role played by the principal shareholder, along with his position that Unigesco should be the leader among the major shareholders. He felt that Provigo should continue to belong to Quebeckers first. Today that conviction has become reality.

From 2.5 percent to 20 percent

Bertin Nadeau could not act alone to achieve his plan to become the dominant shareholder in Provigo. He required significant financial support. But at the mere mention of Provigo's name every door opened before him. Along with the announcement of the first acquisition, he asserted in *La Presse* (July 26, 1985) that Unigesco wanted to triple its size by the fall, through private investments and a share issue of $40 million, eligible for the Quebec Stock Savings Plan, which would raise the Company's capital to $60 million.

He also revealed that negotiations were under way with other major shareholders, including the Caisse and the Sobeys, for the purpose of forming a Provigo holding group which he would head. He added that the Sobey brothers approved the Caisse's support of Unigesco and that his company was willing to work with them.

With 2.5 percent of the shares, Unigesco already ranked third or fourth among shareholders. By joining forces with the National Bank, The

Laurentian Group and a few others, Bertin Nadeau was able to strengthen his position in the Provigo holding group.

From the start, Bertin Nadeau explained that Unigesco was not interested in Provigo simply as an investment. It wished "to be in a position to exert a major influence on the company's orientation and management."[3] In a series of transactions Unigesco was able to accomplish its goal and announce on March 27, 1986 that the company had increased its interest to over 20 percent and could account for its investment on an equity basis.[4]

The shares acquired since July 1985 had cost $133.4 million or $15.88 per share on average. By March 29, 1986, the end of Unigesco's fiscal period, Provigo shares were worth $19.25. The investment was already worth $161.7 million.

With 20 percent of the shares, Bertin Nadeau now held a larger interest in Provigo than the Sobeys or the Caisse. He had started from scratch and displayed considerable financial ingenuity. The details merit a closer look.

The National Bank of Canada had already sold 50,000 Provigo shares to Unigesco, increasing its stake from 2.5 percent to 2.75 percent in Provigo's capital stock. In return, the National Bank had received from Unigesco a number of units enabling it to acquire shares of Casavant.[5] Today, Casavant is a holding company which has no interest in organs and office furniture. It controls Unigesco and, in turn, is 60 percent owned by Bertin Nadeau.

Unigesco prepared a $35-million issue of subordinate Class B shares, eligible for the 1985 Quebec Stock Savings Plan, which would enable Unigesco to acquire the Provigo shares on which it held an option from the Caisse. At the time, The Laurentian Group joined forces with Casavant to control Unigesco through the holding company Univantage.[6]

Through an exchange of units, once again, Unigesco acquired 120,000 shares of Provigo owned by Laurentian. Together with another block of 127,500 shares acquired under the agreement with the Caisse, Unigesco now owned 4 percent of the Provigo shares.

All these transactions followed Bertin Nadeau's careful plan to acquire a dominant stake in Provigo. But then Provigo decided to issue shares also eligible for the 1985 QSSP; such an increase in the number of Provigo's outstanding shares would certainly add to the cost of the 20 percent of the common stock that Bertin Nadeau wanted to purchase.

When asked by journalists about a possible conflict of interest because of his presence on the Provigo Board of Directors, Bertin Nadeau replied that if the share issue was beneficial for Provigo and promoted the company's future expansion, Unigesco would have no objection to such a decision since it enhanced Provigo's value as an investment.[7]

Meanwhile, the issue of Unigesco shares in the fall of 1985 was so successful that it was increased to $50 million from $35 million. In the end the issue raised $60 million toward the acquisition of Provigo shares.

In November 1985, Unigesco acquired a further $37.8 million worth of other Provigo shares held by the Caisse. The relative positions of the principal shareholders began to change. The Caisse, which was divesting in favour of Nadeau, dropped to third rank with 11.2 percent of the capital stock, behind Unigesco, whose interest had risen to 11.6 percent. The Sobeys were still on top with 20.2 percent.

Observers felt that the 6.7 percent held by the Société québécoise d'initiative agro-alimentaire (Soquia) would probably go as well to Unigesco.[8] At the Unigesco general meeting of December 19, 1985, Bertin Nadeau declared that the Company still had some $17 million in liquid assets and that the exercise of outstanding warrants should bring in some $35 million over the next two years. As well, the company's borrowing power was virtually intact.

He added that from a financial standpoint Unigesco's investment had already paid off. The average cost of its Provigo shares had been $13 after the November 1985, two-for-one share split, while the market fixed the current value at over $15. This appreciable capital gain was not, however, reflected in the company's financial statement.[9]

At the same meeting, new directors were elected to the Board of Unigesco. Pierre Lortie of Provigo, Claude Castonguay and Jacques Drouin of The Laurentian Group, and Jean-René Halde[10] of the Centre d'image et de son Atlantique Ltée joined others who represented organizations such as Le Fonds F.I.C. and La Solidarité. Guy Desmarais, President of Geoffrion Leclerc, was also a member of the Board.

Unigesco Moves Ahead of the Sobeys

On March 27, 1986, two days before the end of Unigesco's six-month fiscal period, Bertin Nadeau announced new share purchases in Provigo that made Unigesco the company's principal shareholder. Among the final blocks acquired were the 2.6 million Provigo shares held by Soquia, which were bought for $48.4 million or $18.50 a share. Concluded on March 16,

1986, the transaction was the culmination of negotiations initiated in the fall of 1985. Along the way, the Company had also acquired 200,000 shares held by Hydro-Québec.

Finally, on March 27, through two private transactions, Unigesco added to its portfolio 1.45 million Provigo shares purchased at a cost of slightly over $27.5 million.[11]

In eight months, Bertin Nadeau had built his interest in Provigo to over 20 percent. He began with no holdings and had spent $133.4 million to outdistance, by a few tenths of a percentage point, the stake held by the Sobeys.[12] A member of the Provigo Board of Directors, Bertin Nadeau also became Chairman of the Executive Committee and a member of the Human Resources Committee. True to his word, which he gave when he set out to become Provigo's principal shareholder, he follows the company's progress closely without interfering in everyday management. Pierre Lortie has his entire confidence.

Since then, Unigesco has signed an agreement with the Sobeys concerning the voting trust of Provigo shares. The two groups wanted to strengthen their position within the Company. To do so, they launched, in June 1988, a takeover bid to buy 8,535,000 shares of Provigo at $10.75 each (following a two-for-one split in June 1987). The offer was well received and the goal was attained. The Caisse, for its part, has retained a major block of shares. By the end of June 1988, the three principal shareholders owned 63 percent of Provigo's capital stock: Unigesco 26 percent, the Sobeys 25 percent and the Caisse de dépôt 12 percent.

Under the agreement, Unigesco is the leader of the group. At all times it maintains a 1 percent edge over the Sobeys with regard to the total number of outstanding common shares held by the two groups. Bertin Nadeau achieved what he set out to do.

Bertin Nadeau, Chairman of the Board,
President and Chief Executive Officer of
Unigesco, and its group of companies.

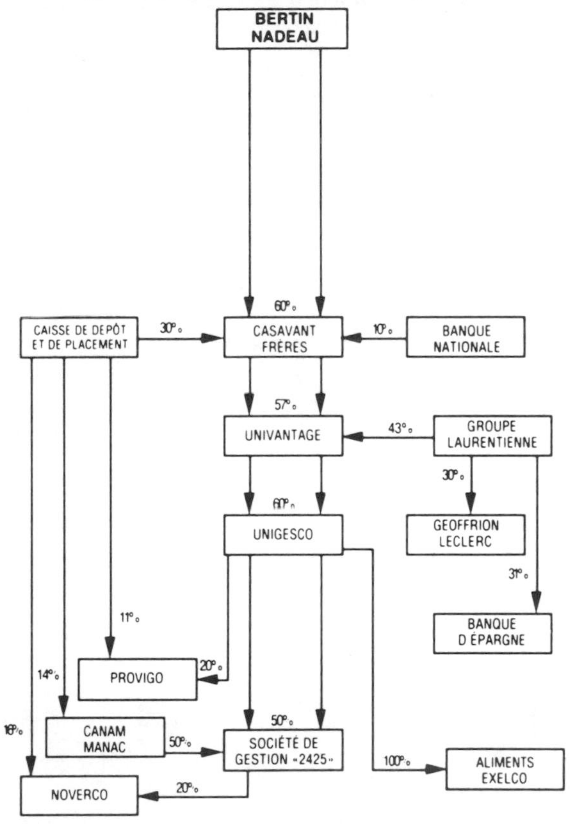

As of August 31, 1987 (*Actualités*, October 1987)

Notes

1. *La Presse* (July 26, 1985).
2. See Chapter 19.
3. Unigesco 1985–1986 Annual Report.
4. Ibid.
5. *Le Devoir* (August 22, 1985) reported this transaction in which the National Bank of Canada received 238,005 Unigesco units in exchange for 50,000 Provigo shares. Each unit equalled one Class A share with ten voting rights and half a purchase warrant. A full purchase warrant entitled the holder to one multiple-vote share for $5.50 before December 1987.
6. *Le Devoir* (August 23, 1985). The chart at the end of the chapter illustrates the connections between the various holding companies established by Bertin Nadeau.
7. *Les Affaires* (September 7, 1985).
8. *The Gazette* (November 30, 1985).
9. *Le Devoir* (December 20, 1985).
10. Jean-René Halde was a Director of Provigo from September 1985 to March 1987.
11. Unigesco Annual Report for the period ended March 29, 1986.
12. According to the information sent to Provigo's shareholders along with the notice of a general meeting to be held on May 25, 1988, 158897 Canada Inc., a wholly-owned subsidiary of Unigesco Inc., held 20.6 percent of Provigo's shares. The Sobeys owned 19.6 percent and the Caisse 11.7 percent.

CHAPTER TWENTY-ONE

CONSUMERS DISTRIBUTING: A NEW ADVENTURE

During the eighties Provigo had become the market leader in distribution and sales of food products, pharmaceutical and health care products, and sporting goods. It was also a major player in the convenience stores sector and an important distributor of petroleum products. But the company was still seeking to broaden the scope of its activities and penetrate other sectors of consumer goods distribution.

At the time Provigo had not really made a dent in the semi-durable goods market. To be sure, in the larger supermarkets, depending on the occasion or season, a fairly wide range of such products was available. But the selection was limited and the sales volume insufficient to earn the company a substantial place in this market.

All Provigo competitors were basically working along these lines. Some, however, went further than others. The Loblaw superstores had a strong selection of semi-durable goods, while the Steinberg ''M'' stores, Bonimarts and Tower Stores of the Oshawa Wholesale Group, dealt completely in semi-durables. According to Pierre Lortie, if Provigo allowed itself to be outdistanced in this sector, it would become more vulnerable, since profit margins on such goods were higher.

But why emulate others when there existed the opportunity to operate a different type of business? A significant block of shares in Consumers

Distributing was available. By acquiring a major interest in this specialist in catalogue showroom sales, Provigo could branch out into a highly desirable retail sector. The acquisition of Consumers Distributing in the summer of 1985 was Pierre Lortie's first major transaction. He had been with Provigo for barely a month.

A False Start

Jack Stupp, the founding President of Consumers Distributing, was so keen on this transaction that he announced it before it was even finalized.

Jack Stupp, founder of Consumers Distributing, and a pioneer in the catalogue showroom business.

A press release issued by Consumers Distributing on June 20, 1985, declared that Provigo had agreed to pay $30.4 million to acquire 33.6 percent of the voting shares held by Jack Stupp and his family. The news of the deal was refuted by a second release, issued minutes later by Provigo, which asserted that there was no agreement. It seemed that Pierre Lortie's first transaction had not come off.

Pierre Lortie explained that the error was due to a misunderstanding at Consumers Distributing. On the verge of being signed, the agreement was to be announced jointly by both parties, but the Provigo Board of Directors, at the June 19, 1985 meeting, had decided that they needed more information and further details on Consumers' operations before coming to a final decision. Provigo also found the asking price too high in view of problems in the American operations.

In a statement to the press, Pierre Lortie declared that Jack Stupp had been informed that Provigo could not proceed with the transaction for the time being. But because of a mixup at Consumers, the press release prepared beforehand to announce the transaction had been issued.

He added that Provigo had been on the verge of concluding the transaction because it offered obvious advantages. But there were still problems on the American side and the final decision would have to wait.

In these remarks Pierre Lortie alluded to Consumers Distributing's extensive losses in the United States. In fact, on total corporate sales of over one billion dollars in 1984–1985, U.S. sales represented more than $450 million. Losses on the American side amounted to $6 million and the profit situation was in fact deteriorating. The previous year, American sales had totalled $369.6 million with losses of $903,000.

Pierre Lortie would later say that the initial terms of the deal were unacceptable at the outset of discussions. In the Western U.S., losses were considerable, while in the East the company was just scraping by. In short, Provigo would be paying too much for a company that was not entirely sound.

The premature announcement triggered unenthusiastic comments from financial analysts. Martin Kaufman of Nesbitt Bongard Thomson observed that there didn't seem to be any synergy resulting from the deal and that Consumers hadn't performed impressively in recent years. George Hartman of Brown Baldwin Nisker thought that the asking price of $8.50 was somewhat high; the market price was about $2 lower and Consumers had just reported a first quarter loss of $2.37 million.[1]

A Second Attempt

Despite its evident problems and weaknesses, Consumers Distributing did achieve a billion dollars in sales in a growing sector and seemed an attractive prospect. It was by far the largest catalogue showroom retailer in Canada. For example, it ranked first in sales of toys and watches, second in sales of small household appliances and third in jewellery. It was not exactly a lame duck.

A month later, the apprehensions voiced by the Provigo Board of Directors had been satisfied, and at its July 18 meeting the Board obtained the requested information on Consumers' financial statements and overall operating situation. Best of all, the asking price had dropped from $8.50 to $7 a share. That clinched the deal. On July 20, 1985 the press announced the transaction.

Provigo would buy 19.5 percent of Consumers Distributing's shares, with 45.5 percent of the voting rights, for a total of $32 million. Provigo was paying $7 per share at a time when the market price of Class A shares was $6.625 and that of Class B shares $6.25. Almost all of these shares were previously in the hands of Jack Stupp and his family.

Provigo management was pleased with the transaction. The price certainly was better and Pierre Lortie was reassured that a new management team would help turn the U.S. operations around.

This time, the analysts' opinions were divided.[2] David Schulman of Geoffrion Leclerc likened Consumers' profit situation to a roller coaster ride and concluded that the company wouldn't do that much for Provigo's earnings.

Barry Gruman of First Marathon Securities Ltd. found that it was an excellent move for Provigo and that Consumers fit in nicely with Provigo's efforts to diversify. It should be noted that Marathon Securities was acting on behalf of Jack Stupp in the sale of Consumer's shares.

The market's reaction seemed positive — Provigo's quoted share price rose rapidly, closing at $25 on July 22, an increase of $2.75 in two days.

Control of Consumers Short of the Objective

Provigo held just under 20 percent of the shares. As a result it was not obliged to make the same offer to all shareholders. Nevertheless, a few weeks later Provigo presented a bid, valid until August 26, to acquire the rest of Consumers Distributing's shares at $7 a share, the same price that had been paid to Jack Stupp.[3] The object was to end up with 62 percent of the existing shares or 50 percent of diluted shares.

On August 26, when the general offer to all shareholders expired, Provigo was considerably short of its goal to attain 62 percent of the shares. It had managed to buy only 135,298 Class A shares and 434,900 Class B shares. The market clearly wanted more than the $7.00 paid by Provigo for the control block. In fact, Consumers' shares were consistently trading in excess of $7.00 during the whole period the bid was outstanding.

The company had only succeeded in obtaining 21.7 percent of the outstanding shares with 46.1 percent of the voting rights.

It seems that the shareholders were holding onto their shares, hoping that the price would increase because of Provigo's positive influence on Consumers' operations. There was also speculation that Provigo would, at a later date, want to acquire a larger stake in the company. Any attempt to increase the current holding, however, was out of the question; the offer would have had to be raised and, at the time, such a move seemed unwarranted.

Pierre Lortie indicated that even though Provigo would have preferred to acquire a greater number of Consumers Distributing shares, management was satisfied with the ongoing situation, since Provigo had gained effective control of the company.

The new regime was much in evidence at the general shareholders' meeting of August 1985. Seven of the thirteen members elected to the Consumers Distributing Board of Directors came from Provigo.[4] At the meeting, Michael Haberman, who had become President and Chief Operating Officer on June 29, 1985, the day of the premature announcement, explained how Consumers Distribution would collaborate with Provigo. For instance, Consumers might try placing catalogue counters in the Provigo stores. The merchandise would not be on the premises but orders could be taken and prompt delivery guaranteed. In his opinion this approach could bring in sales of $300 to $400 million within three to four years. Moreover, continued Haberman, why not try pooling purchases? For example, if Consumers Distributing and Sports Experts teamed up to buy bicycles, the two could become the biggest distributor of bicycles in Canada.

Despite these projects, some people wondered whether Provigo and Consumers Distributing would be more successful together than each had been on its own.[5] Len Kubas, a marketing consultant from Toronto, pointed out that catalogue sales were facing fierce competition from retailers who slashed prices. However, allied with Provigo the company might become enormously successful and benefit from a certain synergical effect. But, he added, the market is changing and Consumers might well be subjected to new pressures.

Speculating about the future, Pierre Lortie himself foresaw the emergence of combination stores offering traditional food products and a wide variety of semi-durable items with a good profit margin. But what if there were not enough space for all these products in the 2,100 stores operated by Provigo? Not to worry, said Pierre Lortie, catalogue sales counters would be set up, and Provigo would invent what he called "micro-combos." There is no doubt that Pierre Lortie saw a unique opportunity in Consumers.[6]

Year One

Since Consumers Distributing remained a public company listed on the Toronto Stock Exchange, the company continued to publish its own annual reports. However, a note in Provigo's 1985–1986 Annual Report gives a summary of Consumers' financial position as at February 1, 1986, along with its operating results after Provigo had acquired an ownership interest in July 1985.

Consumers Distributing's sales since the acquisition had totalled $520.9 million and net income, $1.3 million. With the amortization related to the purchase price, Provigo's share of net income was negative — the deficit amounted to $100,000.

Consumers Distributing's results for 1985 had been severely affected by the poor performance of the American operation. As well, the company had experienced major difficulties in setting up a new computerized sorting system at its Toronto distribution centre. In fact, during the critical fall period, when merchandise had to be shipped to stores for the coming holidays, the system performed poorly. As a result, there developed a major shortage of merchandise in Consumers outlets, with millions of dollars in lost sales. The episode was disastrous for Consumers' image. It would take a great deal of time and effort to regain the confidence of dissatisfied customers everywhere.

In the United States, the situation was even worse than anticipated and still deteriorating. Drastic action was required. One approach was to discontinue operations in the Western United States and rationalize operations on the East Coast. A provision of $26 million was established to cover the expenses related to the abandonment of activities in the Western United States area. In 1986–1987, Consumers Distributing therefore had to settle its problems on the American side.

Consumers Distributing was also planning to expand its network of twenty Toyville stores. Their main source of revenue was toys, but they also sold a variety of other products for infants and children. Together, Toyville and Consumers Distributing served one third of the Canadian toy market.

Consumers Distributing no longer has sales of over $1 billion, as it did in 1984–1985. The lesson has been learned — concentrating on sales is fine, but profits have to be made. There was every indication that once the problems were successfully resolved, profits will follow. In 1986–1987, net income had already gone up to $5.6 million, much better than the $3.6 million deficit of 1985–1986. But it was a long way from the $13.2 million income of 1984–1985.

There was still much to be done.

The Origins of Consumers

In some ways, Consumers' history parallels Provigo's. Like Provigo and its constituent companies, Consumers Distributing is the result of an entrepreneur's imagination and efforts. Jack Stupp began to build his business in extremely modest circumstances during the 1950s. At the age of 15, he left school and worked as a door-to-door salesman, offering his customers kitchen utensils, encyclopedias and magazines. He learned much about human nature, sales techniques and the working world during those days.

He eventually decided to open a small store (1,100 square feet) in his own basement to sell the products of some of the manufacturers he dealt with. To launch his business, he raised the necessary $1,000 by selling his own furniture.

Unable to make a decent living from such a small venture, he had the idea of putting together a small catalogue with pictures and advertising flyers from the manufacturers. The catalogue consisted of twelve black and white pages stapled together and offered at bargain prices, products which Jack Stupp had bought wholesale. *Consumers Health Cookware* was born.

Eventually, the catalogue grew thicker and listed not only kitchen utensils but also tableware and small home appliances. Jack Stupp then hired his own salesmen. Since business was going well, operations were relocated on Eglington Avenue in Toronto. Jack Stupp's first employee, Dave Dawson, still works for the company as supervisor in the Toronto showroom.

Jack Stupp went on the road to promote his company and take orders that he phoned in to Dave Dawson who, after collecting the merchandise from different suppliers, routed the goods through Jack Stupp to his various customers.

Jack Stupp made the round of companies, showing his catalogue to managers, who bought items as gifts for their employees or clients.

But he soon discovered that the employees themselves were interested in the items he offered at discount prices. He also realized that his business was changing; more and more, his customers were the consumers themselves; his role consisted of distribution. The two aspects of the operations were combined in the company's name. Consumers Distributing Limited, which was incorporated in December 1956, later operated in Quebec as Distribution aux Consommateurs.

The company relocated once again and opened its first showroom in a warehouse on Castlefield Avenue in Toronto. People working in the neighbourhood would come in to browse through the catalogue and buy directly on the premises during their lunch break or at the end of their workday.

Early in 1958, Jack Stupp published a new, 32 page catalogue. Since his capital was limited, he managed to obtain extended terms from his suppliers that enabled him to pay for the merchandise when it was sold. The printer was paid as money came in over the course of the year. The business grew steadily and in 1960 Consumers Distributing opened its first real retail outlet on Castlefield Avenue, where it is still in operation.

In 1967, the first colour catalogue came out and six outlets opened in Ontario. There were problems, however. Jack Stupp realized that consumers were reluctant to buy merchandise made by unknown manufacturers, sight unseen, even at discount prices. They wanted to be sure that they were buying quality products. They preferred popular brand names. But at the time it was difficult to sell brand-name products at discount prices. Many manufacturers restricted the distribution of their products to a limited number of retailers who sold only at the suggested retail price.

The Magic of Rebate

All the same, Jack Stupp toured the wholesale distributors to try and obtain known products for his retail outlets. But no one was willing to sell him the merchandise he needed to make his business grow. His luck was no better with manufacturers; they refused to have their products sold at prices undercutting other retailers. But he continued to buy their merchandise, even though it was difficult to move, since he had to sell at the same price as everyone else.

The following year, without consulting manufacturers, Jack Stupp began to offer brand name products in his catalogue, including Sunbeam, GE and other well known appliances at a 10 percent rebate on the suggested retail price. Sales were so good, and the manufacturers so pleasantly surprised by the results, that in less than two years they agreed to sell to Consumers Distributing regardless of its discount pricing policy.

In 1968, Jack Stupp opened five more stores and, a year later, he decided to launch a series of smaller stores designed to meet specific local needs.

On November 22, 1968, Consumers Distributing became a public company and its shares were listed on the Toronto Stock Exchange.

Expansion

In December 1970, the company formed a partnership with The Oshawa Wholesale Ltd. to operate stores outside Ontario. Each partner owned 50 percent of the newly formed Consumers Distributing Company (National) Ltd. The name Distribution aux Consommateurs was registered for future Quebec operations.

The partnership with Oshawa lasted eight years. On January 27, 1978, the company paid $8 million to redeem the 50 percent interest of The Oshawa Group, which received $5 million in cash and 600,000 Consumers Distributing shares. On July 29, all the Canadian operations were merged into a single company, Consumers Distributing Company Ltd.

Consumers, however, was not the only company to use the catalogue showroom formula. In Quebec, for example, the Cardinal Distributors Ltd., chain of catalogue sales outlets owned by Steinberg, was already established. On February 5, 1979, Consumers Distributing purchased the assets of Cardinal for $22.5 million, five of it in cash.

In 1984 the company acquired a 50 percent interest in Manufacturer's Jewellery Showroom Ltd., which operated retail outlets in Toronto. But the price of jewellery had to be considerably reduced when gold prices fell. Losses were substantial. Seeing that business was taking a turn for the worse, Manufacturer's Jewellery filed for bankruptcy on March 22, 1985. Consumers, its 50 percent partner, lost $800,000 in this venture.

The story of Consumers in the United States is rather more complex. An initial partnership with The May Department Stores Company in August 1972 enabled it to operate Consumers Distributing outlets in the U.S. In May 1975, The May Department Stores acquired the 50 percent owned by Consumers to become sole owner. The purchasing agreement stipulated that the Canadian company had to provide technical services and advice for five years.

But on August 26, 1978, the tables were turned. Consumers once again took control of the American stores. The May Department Stores received 1.6 million shares of Consumers in return for the total assets of the American operation, which then consisted of some 70 stores. In 1983 The May Department Stores sold all the shares it held in Consumers to Jack Stupp and his family.

Fast Approaching the Billion

By 1985 Consumers Distributing had repatriated all its operations in the United States and Canada. Jack Stupp and his family controlled the company.

Progress had been extraordinarily rapid. Sales soared from $344.2 million in 1979 to over $1 billion for the year ended February 2, 1985. There were now 212 outlets in Canada compared with 169 six years earlier. In the United States, the number of outlets had risen from 70 to 160 during this period.

But it takes more than sales and growth to make operations profitable. With sales of less than $345 million, Consumers' net income for 1978–1979 had reached $12.14 million, compared with net income of $12.1 million in 1985 on sales of over $1 billion. Over this period sales had tripled but income was slightly lower, and a long way from the 1983–1984 income level, which had exceeded $16 million.

Consumers Distributing was the only survivor among the 36 companies of this type that operated in Canada in 1956 when Jack Stupp was starting his business. But problems with its American West Coast operations had reduced some of its momentum. Consumers' operations were far more profitable in Canada, where the company was growing steadily. In 1983–1984, for example, with sales of $576 million in Canada, net operating income totalled $17.5 million, whereas in the United States Consumers suffered a loss of $4.6 million on sales of $451 million.

Such was the company's position when Provigo acquired 46.1 percent of Consumers' voting rights for $36.2 million in 1985.

When it eliminated its American West Coast activities early in 1986, Consumers closed 73 stores with a loss of some $200 million in sales. Thus, despite progress elsewhere, company sales for 1985–1986 were $876.6 million or $150 million below the previous year's total.

Recovering from the Downturn

In 1986–1987, Provigo slightly increased its interest in Consumers Distributing. From 21.7 percent, Provigo's holding rose to 23.4 percent of the shares, but the voting rights dropped slightly, from 46.1 percent to 45.9 percent. The company was still autonomous and administered separately.

Consumers' situation was improving, thanks to the measures taken by Provigo. Even though the West Coast operations had been discontinued, sales jumped from $876.6 million to $933.4 million, and earnings from a loss of $3.5 million to a profit of $5.6 million.[7,8] Consequently, Provigo's share of Consumers' earnings increased by $800,000 from the previous year's deficit of $100,000.[9] This major turnaround was due to more efficient operations in both Canada and the U.S.

Consumers Distributing was now part of the Group of Specialized Stores operated by Provigo. The company was under the responsibility of Henri A. Roy, Executive Vice-President at Provigo, who was given the task of making far-reaching changes within a short time.[10]

Consumers Distributing was on the verge of a major turning point. Its mission was to become a leader in the distribution and sale of semi-durable consumer goods by offering the best possible value. The long-range plan is to convert the network of retail outlets into a system of franchised stores. The latest technology would be combined with the considerable experience acquired by Provigo in other distributional areas to ensure greater efficiency of operations and better service to customers in the showrooms.

In the future, Consumers Distributing will penetrate the most remote regions and secondary markets through agents, set up a telephone-order department and offer delivery services in major urban areas. Changes are already taking place. For example, 120 Provigo outlets in Quebec now offer a catalogue sales and order service, and the number of such agencies is rapidly increasing. Sales from such agent outlets now represent about 12 percent of total sales in Quebec. It is now possible for customers to order by telephone and, in Toronto and Montreal, to have the merchandise delivered.

At the June 1987 Annual Meeting, Henri A. Roy announced that Consumers' corporate financial objective was to achieve a 15 percent return on investment within three years. This was no small challenge, particularly when one considers that the return was 5 percent at the time.

The strategies adopted may produce the desired results. However, it is clear that in a relatively short time much has been accomplished and Provigo has met many challenges.

All or Nothing

From the outset, Provigo wanted to acquire complete control of Consumers Distributing.

In August 1985, an attempt to acquire the rest of the company's shares had fallen short of its objective. Provigo tried again in October 1987, by means of a purchase bid, to acquire all the outstanding shares at the price of $5.50. This time, the attempt was successful.

On November 6, 1987, Consumers Distributing became the exclusive property of Provigo. To raise its interest from 23.5 percent to 100 percent, Provigo had spent $120.3 million in cash. In total, Consumers Distributing had cost $166,155,000.

In 1987–1988, Consumers Distributing achieved sales of $1.01 billion and income of $11.4 million. However, for the period extending from the acquisition to January 30, 1988, the end of the fiscal year, the consolidated results of Provigo indicate sales of $401 million and income of $15.1 million for Consumers Distributing.[11] As it turned out for this particular fiscal year Provigo was able to report, to its advantage, Consumers' most active and most profitable sales period.

Even though it had given up its West Coast stores, the American division of Consumers Distributing was still underperforming. Now sole master on board, Provigo settled the situation once and for all. Under Henri A. Roy as Chairman of the Board and Chief Executive Officer, the company was first divided into three autonomous sectors. Catalogue sales operations in Canada were entrusted to Maurice Tousson. His U.S. counterpart was Stanley Seiden, a man with considerable experience in this area. Fred Delsey remained General Manager of the Toyville stores. On March 3, 1988, Provigo concluded an agreement to sell its 87 U.S. Consumers outlets to Semi-Tech Microelectronics (Far East) Ltd., a Hong Kong company, for a net price of approximately $60.5 million U.S.

Thereafter, all Canadian operations of Consumers Distributing and Toyville were grouped and headed by Maurice Tousson, who became President and Chief Operating Officer.

The sale of the American operation was a smart move. It strengthened Provigo's financial structure and restored flexibility to its development plans. Among other benefits, it included a cooperation agreement between Provigo and the buyer, which will make it easier to import merchandise from China and the Far East. "Provigo stands to gain from a close working and financial association with an organization that is ideally positioned in the economy of the People's Republic of China.''[12] Such value-adding partnerships are part of Provigo's strategy for continued profitability and growth.

With Provigo's expertise in franchising, merchandising and technological innovation, there is no question that Consumers Distributing now has all it needs to become a successful enterprise.

A modern Consumers Distributing outlet.

Notes

1. *The Gazette* (June 21, 1985).
2. *The Gazette* (July 20, 1985).
3. *The Gazette* (August 10, 1985).
4. The Provigo representatives were Jacques Desmeules, Jean-Louis Lamontagne, Pierre Lortie, Jean-Claude Merizzi, Kenneth W. Quinn, Henri A. Roy, who succeeded H.P. Gobeil, and David F. Sobey.
5. *The Gazette* (August 31, 1985).
6. *Ibid*.

7. The elimination of the 3 percent inventory tax allowance in the 1986 Federal Budget had an impact of $4.2 million on the on-going profitability of Consumers.
8. Consumers Distributing Annual Report for the year ended January 31, 1987.
9. Provigo Annual Report for the year ended January 31, 1987.
10. Henri A. Roy succeeded Michael Haberman as President, while Maurice Tousson became Executive Vice-President.
11. Provigo Annual Report for the year ended January 30, 1988.
12. Provigo Annual Report for the year ended January 30, 1988.

CHAPTER TWENTY-TWO

A STRUCTURE FOR THE FUTURE

When Pierre Lortie became Provigo's chairman in May 1985, the company had been going from strength to strength. Moreover, it had all the financial and human resources needed to maintain its dominant position in its traditional markets. In short, Pierre Lortie's challenge was to develop Provigo's presence outside the province of Quebec.

Pierre Lortie was not the kind of man to settle for being a big fish in a small pond. In his view, the Quiet Revolution had given francophones the means of competing with anglophones on an equal footing, not only in Quebec but elsewhere in Canada and throughout the world. It was up to the new generation of business people, he would say, who had grown up and thrived in this new environment to preserve and develop the momentum begun by their predecessors.

Pierre Lortie spent his first two months at Provigo visiting every last subsidiary, operating company and corporate facility. He also met the management team of each of the Provigo group of companies. He was attentive and took abundant notes. Some members of the Board claimed that there were no major problems at Provigo. But studies that he had commissioned before assuming his duties indicated that Provigo's retail food operations in Quebec were experiencing certain difficulties, particularly in terms of image.

In Quebec City, Provigo — like Steinberg and Métro — had been humbled by Super Carnaval, which in January 1983 opened its first store in Beauport in an ex-Provigo supermarket. Fierce competition from Super Carnaval was making life tough for everyone in the retail food business throughout the province.[1] In addition, the integration of several former Dominion supermarkets in the Montreal area continued to cause problems.

The picture was not entirely bleak but certain corrective measures were necessary to secure a successful future for Provigo in the retail food sector.

For example, Provigo's senior executive officers in Montreal were also directing the affairs of the Quebec operations. As a result, the management of the other subsidiaries outside Quebec often felt that aspects of their operations were not given sufficient attention. Pierre Lortie saw that simply because Provigo senior management knew the Quebec market so well, it did not follow that more attention should be paid to the establishment of a Maxi in Trois-Rivières than to what was happening in Alberta or California. As well, the problems caused by the takeover of the Dominion stores had left the other subsidiaries with the impression that they were subsidizing, to a certain extent, the incompetence and poor administration of the Quebec retail sector.

Based on his initial observations about Provigo, its recent performance and future possibilities, Pierre Lortie proceeded to draft an initial report to take stock of Provigo's situation.

The report was not intended to criticize or evaluate past achievements. Rather the report would be a comprehensive guide to Provigo's future; it would suggest a redesigned corporate structure to reflect the recent evolution of the company's activities and propose several concrete changes to implement the new structure.

Pierre Lortie submitted a preliminary version of the report to Provigo's senior management team. The text was discussed extensively and revised several times. In the interest of sound management, it was vital for Pierre Lortie to win the confidence and loyalty of his people, especially since his arrival had not been without controversy. He wanted to be sure that those concerned would have their say.

The text was eventually adopted by senior management and ratified by the Board of Directors. It was the result of extensive consultation and served as a step-by-step guide to building a sound structure for the future.

Provigo's Five Groups

The main goal of the proposed structure was to turn a Quebec company with outside investments and activities into a truly Canadian company. In the longer term, Provigo should be able to attain the status of a North American, and even an international, company without modifying its structure to any significant degree.

According to the proposal, subsidiaries, which had little in common apart from belonging to Provigo, would be grouped as operations in similar industry sectors.[2]

Provigo's head office would act as the entire company's head office, to be directed and administered by a small corporate group responsible for the principal functions and administrative guidelines. All subsidiaries known as operating companies would be granted greater autonomy, without losing sight of the Provigo Group's objectives, policies and controls.

Over and above these corporate legal entities, Provigo would be restructured to include five homogeneous groups corresponding to sectors of operations dictated by the market or geography. There would be the Food Group, the Health and Pharmaceutical Group, the Convenience Group, the Development Group and the USA Group.

During the months that followed the implementation of this ''structure for the future,'' Pierre Lortie applied a few final touches that made it more realistic and more efficient. Some groups were transformed into new companies and Provigo Distribution acquired its own head office. But in all important regards this new structure established towards the end of 1985 exists today.

1. Food Group

The Food Group initially comprised Provigo Distribution in Quebec, Loeb in Ontario, and Horne & Pitfield in Alberta. Its objective is to establish and maintain a dominant presence in the various wholesale and retail food sectors throughout Canada. In July 1987, Dellixo Inc., a newly formed company active in food services, was added to the Group.[3]

The Group ranks first in food products distribution in Quebec, second in Canada, and is continually strengthening its dominant position.

2. Health and Pharmaceutical Group

Made up at first of National Drug with its subsidiaries and also

Georges Painchaud (formerly a division of Loeb in Quebec), the Health and Pharmaceutical Group is now known as Medis Health and Pharmaceutical Services Inc. The Group's mandate is to establish and maintain throughout Canada a dominant presence in various sectors of health and pharmaceutical products distribution.

3. Convenience Group

The Convenience Group, now incorporated under the name C Corp., is a national group that comprises various Provigo convenience store networks patterned on the successful Provi-Soir outlets in Quebec. Each network has its specific personality based on market conditions, circumstances, needs and particularities of each province or region.

C Corp. operates three divisions: the Quebec Division, which is made up of the Provi-Soir outlets; the Ontario Division, with the Winks convenience stores, Pinto stores and Top Valu service stations; and the Western Division, which integrated the Alberta network of Red Rooster stores in 1988 when it took over this responsibility from Horne & Pitfield.

4. Development Group

The Development Group was later given the more appropriate name of Specialty Retailing Group. It explores new segments of the distribution market so that Provigo can branch out into fast-growing or promising sectors, and provides management and development support for distribution companies that for one reason or another cannot be grouped into an autonomous entity.

The Development Group includes Sports Experts and Consumers Distributing. The first is a wholly-owned integrated subsidiary of Provigo and the second was an affiliated company until it became a wholly-owned subsidiary on November 6, 1987. Through these companies acquired over the past few years, Provigo has established itself in the specialty retailing sector.

5. USA Group

The USA Group became Provigo Corp., which now comprises two operating units: Market Wholesale Grocery in California and Tidewater Wholesale in Virginia. By forming this specific group, Provigo indicated its intention to capture a significant share of the American market. According to Pierre Lortie: "Given the diversity and scope of the distribution sector in the United States, reinforcing Provigo's presence in the U.S. is a long term development and expansion priority.''[4]

Today Provigo Corp. concentrates exclusively on food distribution and generates annual sales of $800 million.

Complete Commitment

While Provigo's new corporate structure did not affect day-to-day operations, key roles,with their attendant responsibilities,took on new meaning for officers and senior management. The new structure required a new style of management, new values and new attitudes.

Because of the constituent companies' responsibilities and autonomy, it was vital for communications between the operating companies, the various groups, and head office to become more direct and more frequent. Pierre Lortie spared no effort to make sure everyone knew what was expected. Once the structure was approved, he made another round of the organization. This time, he met not only with the decision-makers, but also with middle managers and supervisors. He also assumed direct responsibility, at least for the present, for the largest group of all, the Food Group.

In keeping with the proposed structure, each of the other groups had direct access to head office through a senior executive. A Provigo Executive Vice-President such as Jean-Claude Merizzi, for instance, was responsible for Sports Experts and C Corp., while Henri A. Roy, also an Executive Vice-President, was responsible for Medis, Provigo Corp. and Consumers Distributing.

Henri A. Roy, who joined Provigo in the fall of 1985, was no stranger to Pierre Lortie. They had both worked for the then Minister of Finance and President of the Treasury Board, Raymond Garneau. Like Pierre Lortie, he is an engineer by profession. He studied at McGill University and has an MBA from Harvard Business School. He also studied Administration at the International Management Institute of Geneva.

Henri A. Roy acquired experience in commercial banking with the Bank of Montreal. From 1977 to 1985, he worked with the Standard Oil group of companies in various senior financial capacities. Before joining Provigo in 1985, Henri A. Roy was posted to the corporate offices in Cleveland as Director responsible for Finance and Investments.

The senior management team would include the following corporate officers.

David R. Friesen, C.M.A. was Vice-President in charge of Control and Corporate Services.[5] His career with the company goes back to National Drug Limited, in Winnipeg. After holding various positions in accounting and information systems, he was appointed Vice-President, Finance and Planning, and Treasurer at National Drug's head offices in Montreal. He has been working at Provigo's head office since 1980.[6]

In June 1988, Yvon Marcoux, a lawyer, became Senior Vice-President, Administration. Human Resources, Technology and Communications also fall under his responsibility. Before joining Provigo, Yvon Marcoux had experience in banking and with the Quebec government. From 1970 to 1978 he worked for the Quebec government, first with the Treasury Board and then with the Ministry of Municipal Affairs. After holding various senior management positions in the banking sector, Yvon Marcoux was Chairman and Chief Executive Officer of the Société générale de financement du Québec from 1986 to 1988.

In June 1986 Paul Biron became Vice-President, Technology and Information Systems. Prior to joining Provigo, he was with IBM (Canada) for twelve years in management positions, particularly associated with the distribution industry.

Richard G. Sutton joined Provigo as Treasurer in June 1986 and oversees all the company's funding requirements. Previously, he spent eight years with the Chemical Bank (New York) and has gained extensive experience in corporate finance and real estate both in Canada and the U.S.

The People in Charge of the Operating Companies

The object of the new corporate structure was to emphasize the role played by Provigo's operating companies in a more rational, sectorial context. Under the proposal they retained significant autonomy and their senior management were important figures in the Provigo hierarchy.

Yvan Bussières is President and Chief Operating Officer at the head of Provigo Distribution. In many ways, Provigo Distribution is the original Provigo of the 1970s multiplied many times. The company's principal activity is wholesale and retail food distribution throughout Quebec, as it has been since 1969.

At Loeb, William "Bill" Kipp, after a successful career with the company, has been President and Chief Operating Officer since 1985, when he succeeded H. Paul Gobeil. Loeb is a major food distributor in Ontario with dominant market positions in Ottawa, London and Sudbury.

Wayne A. Wagner, who had been Vice-President, Wholesale, became President and Chief Operating Officer at Horne & Pitfield Foods in June 1987, when Kenneth W. Quinn retired. Edmonton based Horne & Pitfield is an important food distributor in Alberta with operations in northern British Columbia and the Yukon.

In the fall of 1988, David R. Friesen became President and Chief Operating Officer of Medis Pharmaceutical and Health Services. He replaced William H. Brown, who had succeeded Gordon J. Odell in 1986.

One of the early builders of Provi-Soir, Claude Perreault, became President and Chief Operating Officer of the new company, C Corp. inc. Claude Perreault had been the top man at Provi-Soir for several years.

At Sports Experts, Claude Beaulieu, one of the founders of the company, was Chairman, while Michel Marcotte became President and Chief Operating Officer early in 1989.

The most recent acquisition, Consumers Distributing Company Limited, is now headed by Maurice Tousson as President and Chief Operating Officer.

On the American side, Keith H. Thye succeeded Carl R. Goslovich as President and Chief Operating Officer of Market Wholesale Grocery in September 1987. Neil Larson is General Manager of Tidewater Wholesale.

Provigo used to operate a sector which served the restaurant, hotel and institutional trade. That sector has resurfaced as Dellixo. Reynald Gagné is President and Chief Operating Officer of this company created in 1987.

Finally, in 1987, Provigo appointed Jonathan Goldbloom as President of Phone Market, which offers home-shopping supermarket services. Customers can phone in their grocery orders and have them delivered the following day. The system is being tested in the Toronto region.

A Focused Direction

To determine a structure for the future, Pierre Lortie needed to project the direction in which he would steer the company.

From an in-depth study of all of Provigo's operations he knew that they shared a remarkable number of characteristics. Together these operations provided a framework within which the company must develop. Nonetheless, his report emphasized that the company was in fact diversified. The nature of this diversification was special in that it resulted from the expansion of the company's markets or range of products via the application of

Provigo's acquired techniques and talents. This, he argued, formed the basis of Provigo's unique character.

In essence, Provigo was and must remain a distributor of goods and services in both wholesale and retail. Its mission is to offer consumers a large selection of products, quality at the best possible prices; in short, the best value.

As for diversification, Pierre Lortie agreed with Antoine Turmel that Provigo must remain active in distribution while diversifying its activities and widening the geographic scope of its operating base.

But he deemed it inadvisable to stray from Provigo's central mission. In his own words: "Provigo is an outstanding entrepreneurial success. With such a record, it is tempting to fall for the myth that superior performance can be transplanted to any other sector. Our traditions, values, management skills, knowledge and expertise, all relate to the distribution of consumer goods and services. There is a strong consensus throughout the company that our success has come from focusing our efforts on the things we do best. This demonstrates the sharing of deep values, ones we can and should build upon. The new definition of Provigo builds on these strengths: *a leading North American distributor of consumer goods at the wholesale and retail levels*.

"This mission statement establishes strong guidelines for our corporate decision making by eliminating ambiguity about Provigo's nature, its activities and its direction for the future. This clarity of purpose is most valuable not only for Provigo's management teams, but also for current and potential stakeholders in the Company. Our corporate mission also embodies many challenges. North America is our primary trading territory. This implies increased geographical diversification and a shift in the centre of gravity of the corporation. Also, as a leader, we must innovate, anticipate customer needs, adapt to rapidly changing market environments and produce superior performance consistently."[7]

The importance of Pierre Lortie's first analysis of the direction and development of Provigo cannot be overemphasized. The corporate structure that was established in 1985 is in place today and three years later Provigo's statement of purpose continues to inform the company's every activity. "Our mission has become a leitmotiv within the organization. It serves to focus expansion as well as day-to-day management decisions."[8]

The statement of Provigo's mission is a general call to action for its nine operating companies. Each company has its own goals and is given a clear mandate within the directives of the corporate mission. As we have seen, this decentralized structure was designed by Pierre Lortie to encourage each operating company to adopt distinctive strategies and action plans required by its particular situation and position in the marketplace. It is clear that this approach relies heavily on the initiative, creativity and decision-making capabilities of all members of the Provigo team. Pierre Lortie's structure for the future is more than an organization chart: it points the way to future successes via the talent and efforts of the complete Provigo team.

Notes

1. At the time Super Carnaval was a subsidiary of Burnac Investment of Toronto which, ironically, was directed by Michel Robin, an ex-Dominion man that Provigo had let go. In May 1987 the Super Carnaval stores were acquired by Métro, a Montreal-based food distributor.
2. The subsidiaries remained but their role was to be more sharply focused on their primary operations.
3. See Chapter 23.
4. Provigo's Annual Report for the year ended January 31, 1987.
5. In November 1988 David R. Friesen was appointed President and Chief Operating Officer of Medis.
6. Germain P. Lecours, C.A., succeeded David R. Friesen in January 1989, and subsequently was appointed Senior Vice-President, Finance and Control, and Chief Financial Officer.
7. Pierre Lortie's first annual message to Provigo shareholders in the Annual Report for the year ended January 25, 1986.
8. Provigo's Annual Report for the year ended January 30, 1988.

CHAPTER TWENTY-THREE

NEW DIRECTIONS FOR THE QUEBEC FOOD GROUP

The structure of a company may often reveal more about its history and development than about its ability to deal with future opportunities. Provigo is no exception. During the summer of 1985 Pierre Lortie dealt quickly with one organizational anomaly in the Provigo group of companies by creating Provigo Distribution Inc.

The problem was at the heart of the transformation of Provigo from a Quebec food distribution company to a North American distributor of goods at the wholesale and retail levels. Even though the Provigo operating companies enjoyed a large degree of autonomy, the company's core operation in the distribution and retail sales of food in Quebec was supervised by Provigo head office.

Provigo Québec, as it was then known, may have been the largest company in the Provigo group, but it did not even have a senior management group or a head office of its own. It was still directed by several of the early pioneers and its top management was more or less the same as that at Provigo Inc.

Under the new structure established by Pierre Lortie, Provigo Distribution became a distinct entity completely independent of the Company's headquarters in September 1985. Paul Gobeil, Executive Vice-President at Provigo, was selected as the first President of Provigo

Distribution. Shortly after, however, he opted for a career in politics. Yvan Bussières,[1] an engineer and MBA, succeeded him.

In a sense, Provigo Distribution is the original Provigo, the Provigo that predates the acquisition of Loeb, the Provigo that operates exclusively in Quebec and strictly in the food business. Yvan Bussières and his immediate colleagues had for the most part been with the company since 1969 or since the days immediately following the merger of the founding companies. Provigo Distribution is the core of the company. Here the top men are Yvon Deschênes, one of the Senior Vice-Presidents, in charge of the distribution centres, or the wholesale side of the business;[2] as well as Guy Lessard and Gérard Tremblay, both Senior Vice-Presidents responsible for the Provigo supermarkets, i.e., the retail business, the former for the western region and the latter for the eastern region of Quebec.[3]

The other senior members of the team were all part of the founding companies; today they are in charge of specialty retail stores such as Maxi, in such fields as finance and administration, human resources, technology and logistics, procurement, information systems, engineering, communications, and legal affairs.[4]

Yvan Bussières and his team designed and applied a new management strategy with new methods. The results were soon apparent. Several acquisitions enabled Provigo Distribution to expand its market and add to the range of its products.

1. Approvisionnements Atlantique

Provigo had long been a presence in nearly every corner of Quebec, save for the Gaspé Peninsula. With the purchase of Approvisionnements Atlantique in November 1985, Provigo Distribution became the owner of a food wholesaler serving the Gaspé Peninsula, Matapédia valley and the northern part of New Brunswick.[5] The cost of the acquisition was $2.9 million.

The company belonged to André Beaulieu, who owned and operated eight retail stores. Approvisionnements Atlantique also served stores under such diverse banners as Marino, Servi-Mat, Servi-Pro, Servi-Plus and Servi-Express.

The transaction enabled Provigo to establish its banners — Axep, Jovi and Proprio — throughout the region. The Matapédia Distribution Centre was also better located than the one in Quebec City to serve affiliated stores in the Mont-Joli/Matane region of Quebec.

The most recent distribution centre, built in Matapedia in 1988.

At the time of the acquisition, Approvisionnements Atlantique had sales of approximately $30 million. But the 40,000-square-foot warehouse could accommodate sales of $50 million, a target which was seen as readily attainable. This optimism turned out to be more than justified since, less than 18 months later, a new warehouse had to be built. The new building would include the offices and distribution centres for grocery products and produce.[6]

2. Alphonse Allard

In the fall of that year, Provigo Distribution decided to resume a service that had been abandoned twelve years earlier. The decision was prompted by a market study that showed institutional food services as an extremely promising sector.

Alphonse Allard Inc., directed by the Allard brothers, Gilles and Pierre, was the largest produce and frozen products wholesaler in the Quebec City region institutional market. The company had a sterling reputation and its clientele of hotels, restaurants, institutions, cafeterias and convenience stores in Quebec City and the outlying areas was well established. Its acquisition would enable Provigo Distribution to recapture this particular segment of the market.

The transaction and installation of new equipment cost $1.3 million. Provigo also retained the services of the Allard brothers, who had acquired considerable experience and reputation in the field.

By acquiring a company which already served 25 percent of the institutional market in the Quebec City region, Provigo managed to increase its penetration of that market. The entire range of other food products was added to produce and frozen products. In the food sector alone, the Quebec City region institutional market is estimated at $113 million, and Provigo has every intention of achieving a dominant presence.

3. Waldman

The purchase of Poissonnerie Waldman in January 1986 gave Provigo direct access to the fresh fish and seafood market. The experience acquired in this sector would result in savings and, above all, a reliable supply of fresh fish and seafood for the Provigo network.

In recent years, the sale of fresh fish has developed significantly in Quebec. Until the acquisition, Provigo lacked the means and knowledge needed to take full advantage of this promising market. Waldman appeared to hold the answer. Waldman had been a family run business since 1924. The Roy Street retail outlet is a Montreal institution with an international reputation.

At the time of the purchase by Provigo, the company had sales of $26 million, 60 percent from wholesaling and 40 percent from retailing. Despite its national and even international reputation, about 90 percent of its sales were in the Montreal region for lack of a proper distribution network which, of course, Provigo could organize.

Provigo bought all of Waldman's assets for $4.2 million. In fact, the company was more interested in the wholesale operations, and procurement abilities which could be developed to serve retailers as well as the restaurant and institutional sector throughout the province. Provigo sold Waldman's retail division in December 1988.

Towards Dellixo

With the acquisition of Alphonse Allard and Waldman, Provigo began to serve hotels, hospitals, cafeterias and the entire spectrum of restaurants

— an institutional market which it had virtually ignored for over a decade.

Food services had been a specialty of Couvrette & Provost, gradually abandoned after the retirement, in 1973, of Roland Provost, who was Vice-President of the institutional division. In 1976 the business was taken over by the regular wholesale operations and subsequently disappeared.

Management may have had other priorities at the time, but the move was now regarded as a mistake and Provigo was intent on making a go of it this time.

It would have been unwise to continue neglecting the food services industry, which represents a total retail market of $20 billion in Canada. Moreover, it is growing two or three times as fast as the in-store retail market. This rapid growth can be attributed to a number of social changes, such as a steady increase in the number of people eating out in hotels, restaurants and fast-food outlets.

It is also a market supplied by numerous small and medium-sized specialized companies, each serving its own region. When Provigo decided to re-enter this market, Quebec did not have a true leader in this field.

Not counting beverages, tobacco and confectionery, the food services wholesale business represents a market of $5.4 billion in Canada. Aware of these enormous possibilities, Provigo planned to control a one-billion share of this market within five years and developed an acquisition and consolidation strategy to play a dominant role in Quebec and eventually in Canada.

Provigo already served the produce and frozen products market in Quebec City, with Alphonse Allard, and the fresh fish and seafood market in Montreal, with Waldman. The next three acquisitions — Groupe Landry, Pêcheries St-Laurent and Bronstein Frères (Québec) — would enable Provigo Distribution to expand its territory and the range of its products.

First Step: Groupe Landry

In 1986, Groupe Landry was the largest food services business in Quebec, with 5 percent of the market and sales of some $75 million. Founded in 1927 by Joseph-Eustache Landry, Groupe Landry was among the pioneers in food services in Quebec. It distributed its products in the commercial sectors (hotels and restaurants), as well as in the institutional sector (hospitals, government agencies, cafeterias). Its headquarters were in Montreal but it had sales offices in Montreal, Quebec City, Sherbrooke, Saint-Hyacinthe and Trois-Rivières. Under the direction of Raoul Landry, the son of the founder, it grew to be the biggest wholesaler in the field, and a perfect acquisition target for Provigo.

The purchase of Groupe Landry in December 1986 represented a giant step towards recapturing the institutional market in Quebec. Provigo not only acquired the largest distributor of food services in the province but as well the invaluable experience of Raoul Landry, who later became part of senior management at Dellixo.

Les Pêcheries St-Laurent: Fish and Seafood

After Waldman, Provigo set it sights on Pêcheries St-Laurent. Established in Quebec City since 1960, Pêcheries St-Laurent was a family business which had opened an outlet in Montreal in January 1986.

It derived 80 percent of its sales from its Quebec City distribution centre, which served not only the Quebec City area but also the lower St-Lawrence, North Shore, Saguenay/Lac-Saint-Jean and Beauce regions. Sales to retailers accounted for 55 percent of all Pêcheries St-Laurent sales; the rest came from distribution to institutions, hotels and restaurants.

It was a dynamic, fast growing company, with sales that had risen from $3.4 million in 1982 to $24 million in 1986. Provigo once again was acquiring a promising business, complete with knowledgeable personnel.

And Bronstein Frères Makes Three

Bronstein Frères ranked second among food services providers in Quebec. With sales of approximately $32 million, it was Landry's biggest competitor. Bronstein served some 2,000 clients throughout Quebec from a distribution centre located in LaSalle in south-west Montreal. Among them were some of the province's best-known restaurant chains. Bronstein Frères had been acquired in 1963 by Albert Bernstein and his partners, Mark Bernstein and Ron Moore, who sold it to Provigo in February 1987.

Bronstein Frères was highly attentive to customer service. It had set up an integrated information system to process orders, update inventory and provide clients and suppliers with statistical data. This unique system was seen as an excellent marketing tool which could also be useful to the other Provigo subsidiaries in the food services sector, particularly Groupe Landry.

15 percent of the Market in Less than a Year

With the purchase of five establishments in the institutional sector, Provigo had already achieved sales of $200 million in a year, or approximately 15 percent of the wholesale food services market in Quebec.

The official takeover of Groupe Landry occurred in 1987. PSA Distribution[7] (Provigo, Services Alimentaires Distribution) was created to oversee the activities of these five establishments. Reynald Gagné,[8] who had participated in the transactions, was appointed Vice-President of PSA.

Thoroughly acquainted with the food business, Reynald Gagné had participated in every phase of Provigo's history and had played a key role in Provigo's development in Quebec. His goal was to make PSA a leader in its field.

Shortly after it was created, PSA Distribution already ranked third or fourth in Canada, and fourteenth in North America. In Quebec, PSA was the only supplier to offer restaurants and the institutional sector the entire range of food products from groceries, produce and frozen products to meat and fresh fish. It was determined to take full advantage of this unique position and the many services it could offer. The Quebec base would serve as a solid starting point to compete for a significant share of the flourishing and dynamic food services market in Canada.

Number One in Food Services

PSA became Dellixo Inc. on May 26, 1987. Reynald Gagné was appointed President and Chief Operating Officer in July.

Dellixo had a promising start. Thanks to its constituent companies, it was already a leader in its field. Four subsequent acquisitions solidified its dominant position in the Quebec market.

Groupex, a Montreal company acquired on July 4, 1987, specialized in the distribution of such products as paper cups, plates and kitchen utensils as well as basic baking and pastry-making products.

Acquired in October 1987, Groupe Spence distributed grocery products, frozen products and meats, primarily in the Lac Saint-Jean, Saguenay and Quebec City regions, from two centres, one in Chicoutimi and one in Saint-Félicien. The purchase of Groupe Spence also involved the purchase of its subsidiary, Alcide Gagnon Co., specialists in meat and delicatessen products.

Distributions A. Robitaille Inc. had served the Eastern Townships since 1960, supplying a complete range of grocery products, refrigerated foods and frozen products. The company was acquired by Dellixo in October 1987.

In May 1988, a ninth acquisition further strengthened Dellixo's position. Distribution Jean Pigeon Inc., located in Rimouski, served some 1,200 clients along a territory stretching from Sainte-Anne-de-la-Pocatière to Gaspé, which also included the northern part of New Brunswick.

With close to 700 employees, Dellixo today supplies some 12,000 clients. With the backing of Provigo's considerable resources, it has created a brand new and unique range of professional client services centred on technology. From a single access point Dellixo can meet all the requirements of restaurants, cafeterias, catering services, hotels and institutions.

Provigo Distribution: Flexibility and Strength

One advantage of the stucture for the future adopted by Provigo is that a group or subgroup can arrange an acquisition or redefine its orientation without impeding the growth of the other groups. Thus, while Dellixo was created, Provigo Distribution was able to build or renovate warehouses, pursue the rapid development and deployment of its information systems, promote its new banner Proprio (which already consisted of over 290 convenience stores in August 1988), launch its *Circulaire* (a weekly informational newspaper distributed to 2,350,000 homes), open 120 Consumers Distributing counters in supermarkets, increase the number of automatic teller machines, experiment with the debit card in its food stores, renovate, modernize or franchise its corporate stores, add six new Héritage outlets to the existing seven, open two new Maxi stores (raising their number to seven) and create a new concept and orientation for the Octofruit stores.[9]

In August 1986, Provigo Distribution acquired Octofruit, a company well established in the Montreal area as a specialist in the distribution of fruit and vegetables.

Octofruit operated a wholesale business located in Laval, on the outskirts of Montreal. It supplied 17 specialty retail stores, 15 of which were franchises. Octofruit was the largest and best organized chain of its type in Quebec with sales of approximately $15 million.

A specialized Provigo banner.

Jean-Claude Gravel, who owned a produce wholesale company, created Octofruit in 1976 as a way to operate a retail business as well. The first store opened in 1977. Three years later, Jean-Claude Gravel restructured the company to accommodate franchises. Octofruit then started growing at a more rapid pace and eventually became a model of its kind. When Provigo first approached Octofruit, it was not for sale but persistence won in the end. It was an opportunity too good to miss.

By adding an additional $15 million in sales to its wholesale produce business, Provigo had become the largest distributor of fruit and vegetables in Quebec.

Today, more and more consumers insist on buying fresh products, and Octofruit's vast selection fits the bill. The Octofruit stores introduced a great many exotic products that are now available in most Provigo supermarkets.

Specialized Banners

Provigo Distribution is more than the sum of its parts. The group itself consist of several entities within a decentralized management structure.

With sales figures of $2.4 billion in 1988, Provigo Distribution was a leader among the companies that make up the Provigo Group.

Provigo Distribution alone accounted for some 6,000 full-time and part-time employees, 14 distribution centres, 30 cash-and-carry warehouses and 1,038 retail stores under eight different banners.[10]

Stores are placed under a particular banner on the basis of their sales potential and target clientele, and offer specific customer services.

Both the Héritage and Maxi outlets are discount superstores. Almost all are owned by Provigo. The Héritage stores, each with a surface area of 20-30,000 square feet, are discount stores that offer 3 to 5 thousand national brand products. The Maxi stores, which are twice as large as the Héritage outlets, belong to the second generation of superstores. These giant supermarkets offer, in a word, everything. National brand products are available, as well as a wide variety of bulk items, and there is particular emphasis on bakery goods, dairy products, meat, fresh produce and fresh fish. Maxi is Provigo's answer to other superstore competitors.

Provigo's superstores.

But even the smallest retailer should not be underestimated as a potential competitor. Together the banners must cover the entire range of food retailing.

In April 1988, Provigo Distribution launched Intermarché, a new type of establishment that borrows elements from both the corner grocery store and the supermarket. It features short aisles set up in a zigzag pattern and offers a regular selection of fresh products and personalized service. Intermarché stores have a surface area of 5,000 to 8,000 square feet and are operated by independent merchants, some of whom are recruited from among the competition or come from the Provigo, Axep or Jovi groups.

Provigo's most recent entry into a promising sector.

Spearheading Provigo's Success

Provigo has effectively exploited the benefits of large-scale economies to reduce costs and increase efficiency. Yet this is only one aspect of Provigo's success. There is a second dimension that relies upon the strength of individual entrepreneurship attuned to the needs of markets in constant evolution. This combination of distributional efficiencies with retailing entrepreneurship has been termed the Provigo formula, the value-adding partnership.[11]

The Provigo formula encompasses every aspect of the company's operations, combining the strength of a major distributor with the flexibility and initiative of some 2,000 merchant-entrepreneurs. Daily experience shows that this partnership is mutually beneficial. Provigo was quick to realize that the owner of a store who is attentive to his customers is more successful than a centralized organization. This insight prompted the company to adopt a franchise or affiliation policy that is also used by other groups of grocers and which has successfully challenged the powerful chains that once dominated the market.[12]

Merchants know that they can count on Provigo — no effort is spared to provide them with all the support they need to run a successful business. To be part of Provigo is to benefit from more than a centralized purchasing system and efficient distribution, and much more than a continually updated advertising of the most imaginative sort. Provigo Distribution, as well as the other operating companies, has also set up assistance and support programs that cover the entire spectrum of its merchants' requirements.

Provigo did not become number one in Quebec by chance, much less by improvisation. When one looks back on the development of its retail operations, it is easy to see that boldness has been the driving force behind Provigo's success.

The company introduced a network of diversified businesses that have made it stand out from the competition and in most cases outperform it. It was the first to offer grocers a selection of banners designed to serve the various segments of the market, from superstores to convenience stores, and one of the first to put the experience acquired in food distribution to work in various other fields.

As a wholesaler, Provigo had distinguished itself through its efficiency and performance. But senior management was and still is well aware that the success of a wholesaler rests on the success of its associated retailers, and that the success of the latter is based directly on their ability to provide better service than the competition. Provigo has always focused equally on satisfying the retailers and the consumers.

In any retail business consumer satisfaction is the prime consideration. This is why it is vital for Provigo to choose independent merchants wisely, and to establish a mutually beneficial working relationship.

The merchant must have good managerial skills and trust his distributor; the distributor repays this trust by granting the selected merchant a franchise with extensive support services. Success is the result of realistic planning of the wholesaler's and the merchant's needs, on-target evaluation of consumer trends, efficient coordination of a large work force, together with entrepreneurs such as the Provigo retailers, who are determined to be and to remain the best.

With all its assets, Provigo Distribution will no doubt continue to be the uncontested head of the Provigo group of companies, one of Quebec's most remarkable home-grown achievements.

Table II
Development of Provigo from 1970 to 1988
Acquisitions and Formation of Companies

Provigo

J.V. Halle (Provi-Fruit)
Quebec City and Montreal

Aubaines Alimentaires
Trois-Rivières

Jato - Quebec City

The Bay Stores (food)
North Shore

Dionne
Montreal

Dominion Stores
Montreal and Quebec City

Provigo Distribution Inc.
Province of Quebec

Approvisionnement
Atlantique Matapédia

Octofruit
Laval

Provi-Soir
Montreal

C Corp. Montréal
(Canada)

Provi-Viande
Laval

Sports Experts
Montreal

Guy Massicotte
Quebec City

Arlington/Collegiate
Toronto

Sports Experts Inc.
Montreal (Canada)

Consumers Distributing
Toronto

Alphonse Allard
Quebec City

Waldman
Montreal

Groupe Landry
Montreal

Pêcheries St-Laurent
Quebec City

Bronstein
Montreal

Groupex
Montreal

Groupe Spence
St-Félicien

Distributions A Robitaille
Ange Gardien

Distributions Jean Pigeon
Rimouski

Dellixo
Montreal

M. Loeb, Limited
Ottawa

Loeb Inc.
Ottawa

A.L. Raymond
Ottawa

Horne & Pitfield
Edmonton

Market Wholesale
California

Petrini Supermarkets

Lucky Stores and Alpha
Beta Supermarkets

Loeb Corp.
USA

Tidewater Wholesale
Virginia

National Drug
Montreal

Medis
Montreal

Notes

1. An engineer with Canadian Pacific at first, Yvan Bussières has been with Provigo since 1974. He began as manager in the real estate sector. In 1977, he was promoted Director then Vice-President of that department. In 1981, he was given the responsibility of the entire administration and treasury sector, and became Vice-President, Finance and Administration, as well as Treasurer. He was fully acquainted with all facets of the food business.
2. He was previously General Manager of Provigo's Montreal Division. Yvon Deschênes retired early in 1988. Vice-President Jean-Louis Poirier succeeded him.
3. Gérard Tremblay retired early in 1988. Guy Lessard is currently Executive Vice-President of the Provigo supermarkets.
4. This team of vice-presidents consisted of: Alain Beaulieu, Jacques Bouvrette, Jean-Claude Desrochers, Gérard Dubé, Jacques Langlois, Jean-Paul Laperrière, Michel Larue, Jacques Mercier, Jean-Louis Poirier, Gérald A. Ponton, Yves Provencher, Claude A. Savard and André Sicotte.
5. Approvisionnements Atlantique served a 150-mile-radius area around Matapédia, which included Maria, New Richmond, Amqui, Mont-Joli, Campbellton, Bathurst, Petit Rocher, Saint-Quentin, Shippagan, Caraquet, Tracadie, etc. This territory encompassed the northern part of New Brunswick up to Edmunston.
6. This 100,000-square-foot building, built on property covering 300,000 square feet, is advantageously located in Matapédia itself. It has been in operation since May 1988.
7. PSA was a temporary name, later replaced by the more original Dellixo. Dellixo is a subsidiary of Provigo Inc. and an autonomous company.
8. Reynald Gagné's career at Provigo stretches back nearly three decades, if we include his years of service with Rioux Pettigrew, a Quebec City wholesaler acquired by Lamontagne and integrated with Provigo in 1969. He was Controller, then General Manager of the Quebec Division.
9. While remaining a specialist in fruit and vegetables, Octofruit offers related products such as nuts and dried fruit, coffee, cheese and dairy products, deli meats and baked goods.
10. These eight banners are Provigo, Axep, Jovi, Proprio, Intermarché, Octofruit, Héritage and Maxi.
11. Provigo's Annual Report for the year ended January 30, 1988.
12. The market share of independent grocers in Quebec dropped to 57.5 percent in 1976, only to rise again to 69.5 percent in 1988 while the chains were losing ground. This gain of 12 percentage points in 12 years manifests an outstanding performance which continues to this day. (Source: *Canadian Grocer*).

CHAPTER TWENTY-FOUR

A WINNING ORGANIZATION

Provigo had been a winner throughout its history. As the company and its market environment evolved, changes were necessary to invigorate its entrepreneurial spirit and to sharpen its competitive edge. But Provigo could always face the future with optimism, even confidence. By hard work and ingenuity the Provigo pioneers had built a solid foundation for continued success. And in taking bold but calculated risks they have made the company what it is today.

In 1985, Provigo could already boast the best performance among the top five distribution companies in the Canadian food industry. Despite these outstanding achievements, Antoine Turmel had not forgotten that in 1970 and 1975 his five-year plans had been received with skepticism by financial analysts in Montreal and Toronto.

This skepticism seemed to persist, even though Provigo had surpassed every objective. As Antoine Turmel has insisted, Provigo had to work harder than other companies to obtain fair recognition and to acquire a certain status on the financial markets.

For Antoine Turmel what counted most was the bottom line — the best possible return on investment for the shareholders who trusted Provigo. That was the objective of the first merger, and of all the acquisitions that followed.

But no matter how essential, the quest for profit has not been the sole reason behind Provigo's success. What makes the company a winning organization is its strong, competent team of people recruited over the years as Provigo developed and assumed new challenges.

From the start, the company has made it a point to be a good corporate citizen, respect client and employee alike, meet its commitments and, in general, abide by the law and honour the public at large. Antoine Turmel inculcated these fundamental principles of Provigo's corporate culture in all those who worked with him, from senior executives to the rank and file.[1]

In fact, in his speech prepared for the last Annual Meeting, which he would chair as Chairman and Chief Executive Officer, Antoine Turmel returned to these basic principles directing Provigo's philosophy.[2] He first recounted the evolution of the company he had built since the original merger in 1969. Provi-Soir had been developed during the 1970s. Then there had been the acquisition of Loeb and its subsidiaries, the Dominion stores and many other businesses. There followed, with the acquisition of Sports Experts and Collegiate/Arlington, the successful entry into the sporting goods sector. Provigo had become a diversified, solidly established company with sales of over $4.3 billion and net income of $40.3 million. Antoine Turmel concluded: "I wanted to give you an overview of how Provigo became what it is today — a strong company which has struck a fine balance between financial and human resources. But the company is clearly more than the sum of its parts. Over the years, it has developed a culture of its own. This culture is at the root of its vitality. Its prosperity is assured because it is founded on human resources and constant attention to performance. The past successes, no matter how resounding, are but a foretaste of the future. Provigo is impelled by its internal resources to meet new challenges, and the values shared by its employees are a guarantee of excellence in meeting these challenges."

The American Market

What are the new challenges, the new horizons attracting the attention of this winning organization under the new chairmanship of Pierre Lortie?

Antoine Turmel and Pierre H. Lessard had made it clear that Provigo had designs on the American food distribution sector. Overtures were made and in some cases serious negotiations initiated, but with little success. The prices demanded by American sellers were considered too high.

At the very first shareholders' annual meeting he chaired, on May 26, 1986, Pierre Lortie openly declared his intentions: "We have decided to

Jacques Daigle, a successful Provigo retailer and winner of the Mercure Award (1988) for excellence in the retail business.

define Provigo as a North American leader in the distribution of consumer goods and services at the retail and wholesale levels.''[3]

In 1985–1986, the USA Group, which would later become Provigo Corp., represented only 10 percent of Provigo's total sales. There was room for growth. Pierre Lortie declared that within five years Provigo should do as much business in the United States as it did in Canada. This comment, made at the May 1986 annual meeting, was reported in all the newspapers the next day.

Henri A. Roy, Executive Vice-President and Director of Provigo, as well as Chairman and Chief Executive Officer of the corporate entity grouping the U.S. operations, indicated that a breakthrough in the U.S. market would entail the acquisition of companies with dominant market share, well-organized management and strong potential for growth. He added that within the near future, Provigo's presence in the United States would be as important as it was in Canada. In the summer of 1988, the acquisition of two chains of supermarkets in California was part of this breakthrough.

More than a Temptation, an Obligation

Provigo spent the better part of the summer of 1986 studying the Canadian situation, and came to the conclusion that expansion into the American market was essential if the company was to grow as projected.

On September 19, 1986, Pierre Lortie concluded: ''Canada is a 'small' market which is not growing and Provigo is already a relatively large distributor which wants to pursue a rapid rate of growth. Realistically, we are fast approaching the limits; we are outgrowing the Canadian market. In contrast, the size and diversity of the US marketplace offers over a period of ten years sufficient business opportunities to fulfill our performance objectives.''[4]

He also mentioned that the new Canadian legislation on monopolies would make it much harder for Canadian businesses to effect domestic acquisitions and that any large acquisition would cause delays likely to make such transactions impossible. Even though Provigo's transactions are not intended to create a monopoly, the relative importance of the company makes it a target for possible legal skirmishes on the part of competitors.

Under the circumstances, an opening onto the American market was even more vital. In the context of free trade negotiations between Canada and the United States, the Canadian market can expect vigorous assault from U.S. business. Provigo believes that such turnabout is fair play.

Pierre Lortie is acutely aware that any sortie into the American market is not without risk. Canadian experience in U.S. territory has not always met with the anticipated success. Forward planning and caution are very important. If Provigo intends to have extensive operations in the United States by the early 1990s, now is the time to do the spadework.

In May 1987, at the Annual General Meeting, Pierre Lortie addressed some remarks to those who felt that Provigo was taking too long to enter the American market.

Even if the potential is tremendous, he explained, it is better to go about it systematically than to launch into a program of indiscriminate acquisitions, without regard to the probable impact on the company's financial position.

Several companies had already been targeted for acquisition and some of them had even been approached. But the prices, which were then very high, had to be considered. One also had to take a cue from other Canadian companies that had tried and failed to penetrate the American market. No doubt Pierre Lortie was thinking about the failed attempts of Loeb and Consumers Distributing. He would make the right move, at the right time.

The June 1988 successive acquisition of the 11 Petrini supermarkets,[5] part of a chain with annual sales of U.S. $180 million, and that of the 15 Lucky Stores supermarkets, whose sales were approximately $150 million, were significant steps in the pursuit of this goal. Provigo had no need to rush south of the border in order to meet its U.S. operational objectives. The company was marching to its own tune.

Provigo had planned to list its shares on the New York Stock Exchange towards the end of 1987.[6] But with the repercussions of the October 1987 crash on the securities market and the acquisition of Consumers Distributing, Provigo has deferred this decision until the move is clearly required to facilitate its growth objectives in the United States.

Onward and Upward

Provigo's growth has always been phenomenal. But Pierre Lortie and his team have no intention of resting on the laurels acquired over its first twenty years.

When Pierre Lortie was analyzing Provigo's future prospects in 1986, he drew inspiration from past accomplishments: "It is difficult to predict at which level Provigo's sales and income will stand ten years from now. From our present vantage point, a repeat performance in the next 10 years yields 'big numbers' (i.e., $40 billion in sales or, according to a better measure, $500 million in net income). The performance objectives set for the Company assume that it is possible to maintain the organization on an aggressive growth path."[7]

Provigo obviously has more assets at its disposal today than it did 20 years ago. As in many other companies, the acceleration factor comes into play. Claude Béland, President of the Desjardins Group, put it succinctly when he observed at his group's 1987 general meeting that it had taken the Desjardins Group 60 years to reach its first billion in assets and only six years to clinch the second; thereafter, billion followed billion faster than the years.

Provigo, for its part, is no longer confined to the food sector in Quebec. It has and will continue to expand, and its markets will become even more diversified. Antoine Turmel had already set objectives for Provigo, which continue to be elaborated today. Pierre Lortie has referred to them on several occasions since he joined Provigo. In a statement to the press (May 24, 1986), he declared that even though Provigo's mission had been very clearly formulated by Antoine Turmel, it should always be adapted to meet a changing market environment.

In his first annual message as Chairman, Pierre Lortie formulated the following set of goals and, in an unusual move, even made public Provigo's annual corporate objectives or financial targets.

1. To achieve a return on average equity of 18 percent;
2. To achieve an 18 percent growth rate on earnings per share;
3. To pay out in dividends 30 percent of the previous year's earnings before extraordinary items;
4. To limit total debt to a maximum of 40 percent of total capital.[8]

Pierre Lortie was attentive not only to Provigo's financial results but also to its success in the pursuit of corporate objectives. A very positive image of Provigo emerged in his presentation to financial analysts on November 4 and 6, 1986 in Vancouver and Toronto.

In October of that year, the objective of limiting the debt was attained and the Canadian Bond Rating Service upgraded Provigo's credit rating from B++ to A.

Henri A. Roy, Executive Vice-President, Finance and Planning, placed a great deal of importance on this A rating. To him, it was more than a symbol; it was proof that Provigo had acquired a certain standing on the financial markets.

In May 1987, Provigo could be proud of having reached and even surpassed all its objectives. Pierre Lortie even added two further goals, which he claimed were just as important, albeit more difficult to measure.

The first concerned human resources. Our objective, he stressed, is to ensure that each employee attains his or her full potential, thus enabling Provigo Inc. to develop teams of individuals confident in their own ability to generate and adapt to change; motivated by a commitment to remain in the forefront of the distribution industry by attaining high levels of quality in every aspect of their work within one of the best performing Canadian companies.

Insofar as technology was concerned, the goal was to maximize the benefits stemming from the latest information technologies and the mastery of their applications to the distribution industry, to reinforce the Company's competitiveness and leadership position in the North American market.[9]

Important Goals

To build Provigo's future, Pierre Lortie relies heavily on the company's human resources. When sales figures rise at such a pace that the team in place is not sufficient to manage the growth, both the professional development of Provigo personnel and the recruitment of competent and experienced new talent must be stepped up.

According to Pierre Lortie, future industry developments and technological innovations will pose formidable challenges. Better training has become essential. This can be achieved by focusing efforts on training the personnel in place. It also entails setting up a performance-based compensation system and making greater room for women in the workplace.

In short, the pursuit of excellence in human resources stands out as Pierre Lortie's first condition for a successful future.

But progress in this field requires a complete mastery of technology and information systems to optimize efficiency at every level. Better coordination and cooperation among the various constituents of Provigo and greater cost efficiency are but two examples of the potential benefits of technology.

Pierre Lortie believes that Provigo must be a leader when it comes to the implementation of technology. In his opinion, information management is the one component of a company's communications strategy that is the most difficult for competitors to imitate. Rapid, efficient information flow is an ongoing preoccupation of the company.

The Provigo Creed

Pierre Lortie never misses an opportunity to promote Provigo, not only across Canada but on the international scene as well. In Tokyo, for example, he insisted: "We at Provigo intend to continue to expand and to enter new markets in the distribution of consumer goods at the wholesale and retail levels. Our standards of performance will remain demanding and we will challenge our organization to be among the best in the world. More importantly, we will continue to rely on the strengths of business partnerships whether with local store associates, our employees or our suppliers."[10]

Pierre Lortie has written extensively about Provigo. Provigo is his life; his consuming challenge.

At regular intervals, Pierre Lortie uses the opportunity of board meetings to let everyone in on the latest plans. In December 1986 and December 1987, for instance, he presented the Board with comprehensive 50-page documents that analyzed and assessed every Provigo group and constituent company in specific terms. The orientation was strategic. The focus was on the future of Provigo.

The December 1986 document ends with a statement of the Provigo creed. It is both an affirmation and a commitment. "Provigo aims to be a leading North American distributor of consumer goods. Provigo is a winning organization with high performance standards and a commitment to implement and test aggressive business strategies. Provigo is at once an efficient distributor of consumer goods and a retail support organization serving consumers through retailers. Provigo is committed to innovation and the adoption of technologies to serve its suppliers, retailers and customers. Provigo's successes reflect the efforts of its employees — a team determined to rank consistently among the best-performing Canadian companies."

An International Challenge and Mission

Pierre Lortie has been preparing the way for Provigo's international mission for some time. In August 1986, he spoke to senior management of various corporations about this new direction.[11] In Paris, before the annual general meeting of PERIFEM,[12] in April 1987, he summed up his address in these words: "With the globalization of markets it is necessary to develop new patterns of exchange and cooperation with the European community in general and with France in particular."[13]

A corporate division, Provigo International was created in 1987, without fanfare, to look after export operations. Just as quietly, early in 1988, the company entered into a cooperation agreement under which it provides Sonadis, a major distributor of food products in Senegal, with technical support. This reciprocal agreement will facilitate export and import operations between the two countries.

Provigo has already acquired experience with international purchasing groups. It knows the advantages of such ties. A case in point is Sports Experts, a company through which Provigo holds an interest in IIC, Intersport International Corporation, a Swiss-based association which acts as a buying group for sporting goods stores in Europe and North America.[14]

When it sold the American division of Consumers Distributing in March 1988, Provigo concluded an agreement with Semi-Tech (Far East) and Shenzhen Electronics Group, the largest manufacturer of electronic goods in the People's Republic of China. Under this agreement, Provigo and Semi-Tech will cooperate closely in the development of supply sources in the People's Republic of China.

Provigo's international mission is not at odds with the development of its traditional supply sources in Quebec or Canada.[15] The company vigorously supports a supplier development program which allows new businesses access to its national distribution networks. But, as Pierre Lortie has often emphasized: "A valuable lesson we have learned is that the contacts we build around the world inevitably result in extensive exports of Canadian and Quebec products. In fact, we are opening the door to large international markets for our manufacturers and producers."[16]

Conclusive Evidence

Provigo is a team, more precisely a team of teams which are determined to remain among Canada's best. These are not idle words. Provigo has a track record few companies can match. The details can be found in Appendix I. Growth factors between 1969 and 1988, as shown below, are particularly eloquent.[17] The column on the left shows the current multiplication factor between 1969 and 1988; on the right is the resulting average annual growth rate for the same period.

Sales	35.2	20.6%
Operating income	48.3	22.6%
Income taxes	33.4	20.3%
Net income	41.0	21.6%
Net earnings per common share	28.5	19.3%
Dividends per common share	23.2	18.0%
Assets	44.5	22.1%
Shareholders' equity	34.3	20.5%

There were more than 84.6 million Provigo common shares outstanding when the May 1988 Annual Meeting was called. Unigesco owned 20.6 percent, Empire Company 19.6 percent and the Caisse de dépôt et placement 11.7 percent.[18] The remainder belonged to some 8,000 other shareholders. In June 1988, Unigesco and Empire (Sobeys), following a joint takeover bid, raised their respective holdings to 26 percent (Unigesco) and 25 percent (Empire), while the Caisse held on to its major block of shares.[19]

Ordinary investors had not waited until 1988 to buy Provigo shares. Some of them, as early as 1961, invested in Couvrette & Provost, Denault or Lamontagne. They had placed their trust in small businesses which were among the first in Quebec to share ownership with the public by listing their shares on the Exchange. They were not disappointed.

An investor who had bought 100 shares of Couvrette & Provost in 1961 would now own 80 times that number because of stock splits over the years. His $550 investment would now be worth $86,000 or nearly 157 times more. In addition, he would have received $11,400 in dividends, equivalent to an average annual return of 78 percent. Those who invested in Lamontagne or in Denault in 1961 have been just as successful in their investments.[20]

Few companies can boast such results. They are proof positive of Provigo's vast success and an enticing promise of interesting future returns for investors.

A new team of winners has taken over from the pioneers who built Provigo from the ground up with scant resources, the men who laid the foundations for a company that has never ceased to grow. Today, Provigo can look back proudly over twenty years of entrepreneurial success and ahead to a splendid future.

Notes

1. Provigo was among the first Canadian companies to form an ethics committee reporting to the Board of Directors. Recently, a brochure entitled "The Ethics and Behaviour of the Company — Provigo" has been distributed to all personnel throughout the Provigo network of companies, as well as to its suppliers.
2. As mentioned in Chapter 19 the speech was never delivered. But it remains noteworthy as Antoine Turmel's overview of the company he had directed for 17 years.
3. Pierre Lortie's address to the Provigo shareholders at the May 26, 1986 annual meeting.
4. "Growing in the U.S. market: Temptation or Obligation;" internal Provigo document, fall 1986.
5. See Chapter 11, in particular the section on "Market Wholesale."
6. Pierre Lortie's address to the Annual Meeting (May 26, 1986).
7. "Growth in the U.S. Market", an internal document written by Pierre Lortie (December 9, 1986).
8. Provigo Annual Report for the year ended January 25, 1986.
9. Provigo Annual Report for the year ended January 31, 1987.
10. Pierre Lortie's address to members of the Canadian Chamber of Commerce, in Tokyo (February 4, 1987).
11. "De l'émergence à la consolidation."
12. The acronym stands for PERformance, Investissements, Fiabilité, Économie, Maintenance. PERIFEM is an association that promotes technology in the distribution sector.
13. "Le Canada : une occasion à re-saisir."
14. See Chapter 15.

15. Provigo Distribution alone bought $1.4 billion worth of goods from Quebec suppliers in 1987.
16. Pierre Lortie's address to the Annual Meeting (May 25, 1988).
17. See Appendix II for further details.
18. Information circular to shareholders included in the notice of the Annual General Meeting held May 25, 1988.
19. See Chapter 20.
20. See Appendix IV.

APPENDIX I

FINANCIAL REVIEW 1966–1989

APPENDIX II

GROWTH RATES AND MULTIPLES
... 23 YEARS (1966–1988)
... 20 YEARS (1969–1988)

APPENDIX II
GROWTH OF PROVIGO
(UP TO JANUARY 30, 1988)

		Since 1966[1]		Since 1969[2]	
		Multiples[3]	Growth rate over 23 years (annual basis)	Multiples[4]	Growth rate over 20 years (annual basis)
Sales		53.32	19.81%	35.22	20.62%
Operating income		95.27	23.01%	48.32	22.64%
Income taxes		81.56	22.15%	33.39	20.28%
Income before extraordinary items		84.74	22.36%	41.05	21.59%
Net income		84.74	22.36%	41.05	21.59%
Dividends paid on common shares		46.47	19.06%	33.46	20.29%
Total assets		67.06	21.07%	44.54	22.12%
Shareholders' equity		50.47	19.51%	34.33	20.46%
Earnings per common share					
– before extraordinary items	3.48 x 16[5]	55.65	20.04%		
– net	3.48 x 16[5]	55.65	20.04%		
	1.78 x 16[5]			28.48	19.28%
	1.78 x 16[5]			28.48	19.28%
Dividends per common share	1.93 x 16[5]	30.93	16.88%		
	1.45 x 16[5]			23.20	18.00%

Common shares outstanding at	$24.11 \div 16^5$	1.51	1.89%		
year-end	$23.16 \div 16^5$			1.45%	1.98%
Return on shareholders'					
equity before	1966 @ 1975		16.2%		
extraordinary	1976 @ 1985		22.0%		
items — annual average	1986 @ 1988		20.8%		
	1966 @ 1988 (23 years)		19.3%		
	1969 @ 1978				18.3%
	1979 @ 1988				21.9%
	1969 @ 1988 (20 years)				20.1%

Note : To calculate any of the above multiples, divide the data in the 1988 column of Appendix I by the data in the 1966 (or 1969) column.

1. During those 23 years, Provigo paid $331,626,000 in income taxes alone. During the same period, its shareholders received $96,743,000, or 27% of the governments' income tax revenue from Provigo.
2. During those 20 years, the company paid $328,200,000 in income taxes alone. During the same period, its shareholders received $95,535,000, or 27% of the governments' income tax revenue from Provigo.
3. Growth since 1966.
   Example: 1965-1966 sales must be multiplied by 53.32 to arrive at the 1987-1988 figures.
4. Growth since 1969.
   Example: 1968-1969 sales must be multiplied by 35.22 to arrive at the 1987-1988 figures.
5 Example: 1965-1966 earnings per share must be multiplied by 3.48 to arrive at the 1987-1988 figures. However, to take into account stocks splits on the basis of 4 for 1 in 1981-1982, and 2 for 1 in 1985-1986 and 1987-1988, these results must be multiplied by 16.

APPENDIX III

CANADIAN PRICE INDICES 1961-1988

Appendix III

To appreciate the real value of certain figures over the course of Provigo's history, the Consumers Price Index between 1961 and 1988 must be taken into account. The table below was established on the basis of the changes in this index as computed by Statistics Canada with a reference point of 100 in 1981.

	Price Index (all products)	Price Index (food only)
June 1961	31.6	26.1
June 1969	39.8	33.5
June 1977	67.7	61.7
June 1981	100.0	100.5
June 1982	111.2	109.9
June 1985	131.9	121.4
Jan. 1988	140.8	134.1

Source: Statistics Canada. Consumers Price Index.

The years included in the chart were chosen to reflect significant events in Provigo's history.

1961: The shares of the three pioneer companies — Couvrette & Provost, Denault and Lamontagne — are listed on the Exchange.

1969: The above mentioned companies merge to form Provigo.

1977: Provigo triples its sales volume; operations expand outside Quebec and corporate activities acquire greater scope with the acquisition of Loeb.

1981-82: Provigo completes a major acquisition — the Dominion stores in Quebec. The acquisition of Sports Experts signals a period of diversification.

1985: Pierre Lortie is appointed President and Chief Executive Officer of the company.

1988: Provigo Inc. enters its 20th year.

As the sales figures of Provigo and the founding companies were generated primarily by the food sector from 1961 to 1988, it is more appropriate to use the food sector price index to discount the impact of inflation on Provigo's performance figures. Note that the food price index was lower than the consumer price index for every year except 1981.

To assess results from the vantage point of 1988 — for food products and according to the table and data in Appendices I and II — requires, for example, multiplying the 1961 figures by more than 5 (134.1/26.1); or the 1969 figures by 4 (134.1/33.5); or those of 1981 by 1.23 (134.1/100.5:1.23).

In 1988 dollars, the 1961 sales would have come to $200 million, those of 1969 to $728.9 million and those of 1981 to $3,236.5 million.

APPENDIX IV

GROWTH OF PROVIGO SHARES FROM 1961 TO 1988 AND FROM 1969 TO 1988

Appendix IV

Growth of Provigo shares since 1961 and since 1969

The three companies that originally formed Provigo — Couvrette & Provost, Denault and Lamontagne — became public companies in 1961, when their shares were listed on the Canadian Stock Exchange. A few years later, these shares were listed on the Montreal Exchange and Toronto Stock Exchange.

Let us take the example of a shareholder who made an investment in these companies in 1961 and kept his holding in Provigo until July 1988.

Company	Purchase	Investment
Couvrette & Provost	100 A shares @ $5.50	$550
Denault	50 A shares @ $9.50	$475
Lamontagne	175 A shares @ $6.00	$1,050

Between 1961 and 1969, these shares underwent a number of changes, depending on the company concerned. In 1965, the Couvrette & Provost shares were split on a 5-for-1 basis. In 1967, all outstanding shares were converted into common shares; the original shareholder would then own 500 Couvrette & Provost common shares.

In 1965, the Denault shares were split on a 5-for-1 basis; our shareholder would then own 250 Denault shares. In 1968, the Lamontagne shares were split on a 4-for-1 basis; the original shareholder would then own 700 Lamontagne shares.

In 1969, through a share exchange, the three companies merged to form a new company which would subsequently adopt the name Provigo Inc.

In this share exchange, the Couvrette & Provost shareholders keep the same number of shares, those of Denault receive 2 for 1 and those of Lamontagne 5 for 7.

Thus, in 1969, no matter which of the three companies he invested in, the original shareholder would have 500 Provigo common shares (C & P 500/1 = 500; Denault 250x2 = 500; Lamontagne 700/7x5 = 500).

Between 1970 and 1988, Provigo shares were split on three occasions:

In 1981, on a 4-for-1 basis. The original shareholder now owns 2,000 shares.

In 1985, on a 2-for-1 basis. The same shareholder now owns 4,000 shares.

In 1987, on a 2-for-1 basis. At this point, the original shareholder owns 8,000 shares.

In June 1988, the market value of a Provigo common share was $10.75.[1] The shareholder's investment of $550 in Couvrette & Provost, $475 in Denault or $1,050 in Lamontagne would now be worth $86,000 (8,000 shares at $10.75).

This is a substantial capital gain: $85,525 in the case of Denault; $85,450 in the case of Couvrette & Provost and $84,950 in the case of Lamontagne.

Given the fact that Provigo, like its constituent companies, paid uninterrupted quarterly dividends year after year to all its shareholders, each of our original investors received, between 1961 and 1988, close to $11,550 in dividends, or a yearly average of $430 for shareholders who had invested in Lamontagne. Those who invested in Couvrette & Provost received dividends of $11,400 and Denault shareholders were paid dividends of $11,300.

At this rate, the capital invested in 1961 by a Couvrette & Provost shareholder increased nearly 157 times for an annual return of 78.2 percent.

Since 1969

In the case of a shareholder who, when Provigo was created in May 1969, paid $4,500 for 500 shares of the company at the market price of $9 per common share, the gain was substantial as well.

Between 1970 and 1988, as in the first example, the shares were split on three different occasions, on an overall basis of 16 to 1. This particular shareholder therefore also owns 8,000 Provigo shares. In June 1988, as mentioned above, the market value of a Provigo common share was $10.75.

Thus, 19 years later, our investor is now worth $86,000 (8,000 shares at $10.75). This is a capital gain of $81,500; his investment has increased nineteen-fold. During that period, he received $11,020 in dividends, or a yearly average of $580 for an annual return of 13 percent.

Notes

1. $10.75 was the price paid by Unigesco Inc. and Empire Company Ltd. on June 20, 1988 in a takeover bid to acquire 8,535,000 Provigo common shares on the floor of the Montreal and Toronto Exchanges.

APPENDIX V

MEMBERS OF THE BOARD OF DIRECTORS AND ITS COMMITTEES FROM 1969 TO 1989

Members of the Board of Directors and its committees
from 1969 to 1989

Early 1969 — Before the merger
COUVRETTE & PROVOST

CARRIÈRE, Gérard
COUVRETTE, Bernard
COUVRETTE, Jacques
DLOUHY, Dominik
GODON, André
JACKMAN, Henry N.R.
LEROUX, Lionel
MELANÇON, Jacques
PROVOST, Ernest
PROVOST, René
PROVOST, Roland
VAILLANCOURT, Paul

DENAULT

BÉLANGER, Marcel
DESRUISSEAUX, Paul Hon.
GENEST, Claude
JUTRAS, Jean
LAGASSÉ, Jacques
MARCOUX, Jean
PICHÉ, Gérard
ROY, Gaston
TURMEL, Antoine
VILIM, Georges C.

LAMONTAGNE

BARDOU, Paul
BERGERON, Pierre
DESCHÊNES, Yvon
GAGNON, Robert
HUDON, Guy L.
LABERGE, Pierre E.
LAMONTAGNE, Jean-Louis
OSTIGUY, Jean-Paul W.
ROBERT, Marcel
TREMBLAY, Guy
TREMBLAY, J.A.

1969–1970

July 1969 — After the merger

In accordance with the merger agreement between Couvrette & Provost, Denault and Lamontagne, the Board of Directors of the new Couvrette & Provost Ltd., which would become Provigo Inc. in 1970, consisted of 21 members. Each of the three constituent companies was represented by seven members:

BÉLANGER, Marcel (D)
BERGERON, Pierre (L)
COUVRETTE, Bernard (CP)
COUVRETTE, Jacques (CP)
DESRUISSEAUX, Hon. Paul (D)
DLOUHY, Dominik (CP)
GENEST, Claude (D)
JACKMAN, H.N.R. (CP)
LAGASSÉ, Jacques (D)
LAMONTAGNE, Jean-Louis[1] (L)
LAMONTAGNE, Robert (L)
OSTIGUY, J.P.W. (L)
PROVOST, Ernest (CP)
PROVOST, René[1] (CP)
PROVOST, Roland[1] (CP)
ROBERT, Marcel (L)
ROY, Gaston[1] (D)
TREMBLAY, Guy (L)
TREMBLAY, J.A.[1] (L)
TURMEL, Antoine[1] (D)
VILIM, Georges (D)

CARRIÈRE, Gérard - Secretary

1. Member of the Executive Committee
(D) Appointed by Denault
(L) Appointed by Lamontagne
(CP) Appointed by Couvrette & Provost

1970–71 and 1971–72

This board of directors remained in place throughout the 1969–1970 and 1970–1971 fiscal periods.
With the exception of Marcel Robert, C.A., who stepped down to join the senior civil service, there were no changes in 1971–1972.

1972–1973

At the May 1972 Annual Meeting, a bylaw was adopted to reduce the number of directors from 21 to 12.

The Board for 1972–1973 was made up of:

BÉLANGER, Marcel
COUVRETTE, Bernard
DESRUISSEAUX, Hon. Paul
GENEST, Claude
JACKMAN, H.N.R.
LAGASSÉ, Jacques
LAMONTAGNE, Jean-Louis[1]
PROVOST, René[1]
PROVOST, Roland[1]
ROY, Gaston[1]
TREMBLAY, J.A.[1]
TURMEL, Antoine[1]

CARRIÈRE, Gérard - Secretary

1. Member of the Executive Committee

Roland Provost retired in November 1972 and resigned from the Board of Directors. Subsequently, the Executive Committee consisted of five members.

1973–1974

With the exception of Claude E. Leduc, who was elected director to succeed Roland Provost, the 1973–1974 Board remained unchanged.

1974–1975

In May 1974, Bernard Couvrette and Paul Desruisseaux, who had reached the age limit for directors, retired, as did Claude E. Leduc, who had been appointed company secretary the previous year. A bylaw to reduce the number of directors from 12 to 9 was adopted at the May 1974 Annual Meeting.

The members of the Board in 1974-1975 were:

BÉLANGER, Marcel
GENEST, Claude
JACKMAN, H.N.R.
LAGASSÉ, Jacques
LAMONTAGNE, Jean-Louis[1]
PROVOST, René[1]
ROY, Gaston[1]
TREMBLAY, J.A.[1]
TURMEL, Antoine[1]

LEDUC, Claude E. - Secretary

1. Member of the Executive Committee

1975–1976

At the May 1975 Annual Meeting, the number of directors was raised to ten and the number of members of the Executive Committee to six.

These changes enabled Jean Boiteau (of the newly acquired JATO stores), who had been appointed Vice-President, Retail Operations, to accede to the Board of Directors and Executive Committee.

The 1975–1976 Board consisted of:

BÉLANGER, Marcel
BOITEAU, Jean[1]
GENEST, Claude
JACKMAN, H.N.R.
LAGASSÉ, Jacques
LAMONTAGNE, Jean-Louis[1]
PROVOST, René[1]
ROY, Gaston[1]
TREMBLAY, J.A.[1]
TURMEL, Antoine[1]

LEDUC, Claude E. - Secretary

1. Member of the Executive Committee

1976–1977

At the May 1976 Annual Meeting, the number of directors rose to eleven. Claude E. Leduc was elected once again but he stepped down in September of that year to make way for Pierre H. Lessard, who was appointed director and member of the Executive Committee. At the same time, Pierre H. Lessard became President and Chief Operating Officer. The Executive Committee comprised seven members.

On the Board for 1976–1977 were:

BÉLANGER, Marcel
BOITEAU, Jean[1]
GENEST, Claude
JACKMAN, H.N.R.
LAGASSÉ, Jacques
LAMONTAGNE, Jean-Louis[1]
LESSARD, Pierre H.[1]
PROVOST, René[1]
ROY, Gaston[1]
TREMBLAY, J.A.[1]
TURMEL, Antoine[1]

LEDUC, Claude E. - Secretary

1. Member of the Executive Committee

1977–1978

The 1977–1978 Board of Directors remained unchanged. That year Jacques Lagassé retired and Pierre Arbour, representative of the Caisse de dépôt et placement du Québec, was appointed to the Board.

1978–1979

J.-A. Tremblay reached the age limit and retired. At the May 1978 Annual Meeting, the number of directors was reduced to ten and members of the Executive Committee to six. Later in the year H.N.R. Jackman resigned and Guy St-Germain was appointed to the Board.

The 1978-1979 Board consisted of:

ARBOUR, Pierre[a]
BÉLANGER, Marcel
BOITEAU, Jean[1]
GENEST, Claude
LAMONTAGNE, Jean-Louis[1]
LESSARD, Pierre H.[1]
PROVOST, René[1]
ROY, Gaston[1]
ST-GERMAIN, Guy
TURMEL, Antoine[1]

LEDUC, Claude E. - Secretary

1. Member of the Executive Committee
a. Appointed by the Caisse de dépôt

1979–1980

All the members of the Board were re-elected in May 1979.

During the 1979–1980 period, Pierre Arbour and Guy St-Germain resigned. The first left his position with the Caisse de dépôt and the second was no longer eligible under the Bank Act. Guy St-Germain would recover his position the following year.

In May 1979, the Board formed an Audit Committee made up of outside directors. Its members were Marcel Bélanger (Chairman), Pierre Arbour, Guy St-Germain, and later Jean Boiteau, who had stepped down as Vice-President of the company in January 1980.

1980-1981

At the May 1980 Annual Meeting, the number of directors was raised to fifteen, which enabled the heads of subsidiaries to sit on the Board of Directors. Because of the acquisition of Loeb and Provigo's operations in Ontario, Western Canada and the United States, several new members joined the Board that year.

On the Board in 1980–1981 were:

BÉLANGER, Marcel[2]
BOITEAU, Jean
GENEST, Claude
GOLDEN, David A.[2]
GOSLOVICH, Carl R.
LAMONTAGNE, Jean-Louis[1]
LESSARD, Pierre H.[1]
MARIER, André[a]
PROVOST, René[1]
QUINN, Kenneth W.
ROBERTSON, Norman W.
ROY, Gaston[1]
ST-GERMAIN, Guy[2]
TURMEL, Antoine[1]
WARNOCK, Frank M.

LEDUC, Claude E. - Secretary

1. Member of the Executive Committee
2. Member of the Audit Committee
a. Appointed by the Caisse de dépôt

As of May 1980, proceedings would take place almost exclusively in English and notices of meetings, agendas and related documents, and minutes of meetings would be issued in both official languages.

1981–1982

At the May 1981 Annual Meeting, Claude Genest, who had reached the age limit, retired. The position would be filled by M. Brian Mulroney. During 1981–1982, Frank M. Warnock tendered his resignation as Director of Provigo Inc. and President and Chief Executive Officer of M. Loeb Limited.

The 1981–1982 Board consisted of:

BÉLANGER, Marcel[2]
BOITEAU, Jean
GOLDEN, David A.[2]
GOSLOVICH, Carl R.
LAMONTAGNE, Jean-Louis[1]
LESSARD, Pierre H.[1]
MARIER, André[a]
MULRONEY, M. Brian
PROVOST, René[1]
QUINN, Kenneth W.
ROBERTSON, Norman W.
ROY, Gaston[1]
ST-GERMAIN, Guy[2]
TURMEL, Antoine[1]

LEDUC, Claude E. - Secretary

1. Member of the Executive Committee
2. Member of the Audit Committee
a. Appointed by the Caisse de dépôt

1982–1983

Early in 1982, the Caisse de dépôt and the Sobeys concluded an agreement that would have a major impact on Provigo's history. In the wake of this alliance, both of these major shareholders demanded increased representation on the Board. As a result, the Caisse wound up with three representatives instead of one and the Sobeys obtained two seats.

At the May 25, 1982 Annual Meeting, a bylaw was adopted to increase the number of directors from 15 to 18.

The 1982–1983 slate of Board members reads as follows:

BÉLANGER, Marcel[2]
BOITEAU, Jean
FAUBERT, Jean[3,a]
GOLDEN, David A.[2]
GOSLOVICH, Carl R.
LAMONTAGNE, Jean-Louis[1]
LESSARD, Pierre H.[1,3]
MARIER, André[1,a]
MULRONEY, M. Brian[3]
NORMAND, Carmand[2,a]
PROVOST, René[1]
QUINN, Kenneth W.
ROBERTSON, Norman W.
ROY, Gaston
ST-GERMAIN, Guy[2,3]
SOBEY, David F.[b]
SOBEY, Donald R.[3,b]
TURMEL, Antoine[1,3]

LEDUC, Claude E. - Secretary

1. Member of the Executive Committee
2. Member of the Audit Committee
3. Member of the Human Resources Committee
a. Appointed by the Caisse de dépôt
b. Appointed by Sobeys Stores Limited

The Caisse now had a representative on the Executive Committee and one on the Audit Committee. In December 1982, a Human Resources Committee was set up, consisting of six members, four of whom were outside directors.

1983–1984

André Marier tendered his resignation. At the end of the fiscal period, Gaston Roy reached the age limit and retired. The position left vacant by André Marier was filled by Jacques Desmeules as representative of the Caisse and Gaston Roy was replaced by H. Paul Gobeil as Executive Vice-President of Provigo Inc., and President and Chief Executive Officer of Loeb Inc. A few weeks after the May 25, 1983 Annual Meeting, M. Brian Mulroney, who had entered the political arena, stepped down.

Thus, the members of Board for 1983–1984, numbered 17:

BÉLANGER, Marcel[2]
BOITEAU, Jean
DESMEULES, Jacques[1,a]
FAUBERT, Jean[3,a]
GOBEIL, H. Paul
GOLDEN, David A.[2]
GOSLOVICH, Carl R.
LAMONTAGNE, Jean-Louis[1]
LESSARD, Pierre H.[1,3]
NORMAND, Carmand[2,a]
PROVOST, René[1]
QUINN, Kenneth W.
ROBERTSON, Norman W.
ST-GERMAIN, Guy[2,3]
SOBEY, David F.[b]
SOBEY, Donald R.[3,b]
TURMEL, Antoine[1,3]

LEDUC, Claude E. - Secretary

1. Member of the Executive Committee
2. Member of the Audit Committee
3. Member of the Human Resources Committee
a. Appointed by the Caisse de dépôt
b. Appointed by Sobeys Stores Limited

1984-1985

As Jean Boiteau had not submitted his candidacy for another term, the number of directors was reduced to 16 at the May 28, 1984 Annual Meeting.

On the Board of Directors for 1984–1985 were:

BÉLANGER, Marcel[2]
DESMEULES, Jacques[1,a]
FAUBERT, Jean[3,a]
GOBEIL, H. Paul
GOLDEN, David A.[2]
GOSLOVICH, Carl R.
LAMONTAGNE, Jean-Louis[1]
LESSARD, Pierre H.[1,3]
NORMAND, Carmand[2,a]
PROVOST, René[1]
QUINN, Kenneth W.
ROBERTSON, Norman W.
ST-GERMAIN, Guy[2,3]
SOBEY, David F.[b]
SOBEY, Donald R.[3,b]
TURMEL, Antoine[1,3]

LEDUC, Claude E. - Secretary

1. Member of the Executive Committee
2. Member of the Audit Committee
3. Member of the Human Resources Committee

a. Appointed by the Caisse de dépôt
b. Appointed by Sobeys Stores Limited

1985–1986

May 1985 marked the end of Antoine Turmel's tenure as Chief Executive Officer. Early in the year, the principal shareholders had determined to find a successor to Antoine Turmel for the position of Chairman of the Board and Chief Executive Officer. The man they chose was Pierre Lortie.

At the May 27, 1985 Annual Meeting, 14 directors were elected, including Pierre Lortie and Bertin Nadeau.

After the Annual Meeting, Pierre Lortie was elected Chairman of the Board and Chief Executive Officer.

In September 1985, Pierre H. Lessard resigned from the position of President and Chief Operating Officer and retired from the Board and the committees. In December 1985, H. Paul Gobeil also resigned.

One of these seats would be filled. The other remained vacant. Jean-René Halde was appointed director.

During the year an Ethics Committee was established.

At the end of the 1985–1986, the Board was made up of:

BÉLANGER, Marcel[2,3]
DESMEULES, Jacques[1]
FAUBERT, Jean
GOLDEN, David A.[2]
HALDE, Jean-René
LAMONTAGNE, Jean-Louis[1]
LORTIE, Pierre[1,3]
NADEAU, Bertin F.[1,3]
NORMAND, Carmand[2,4]
PROVOST, René[1,4]
ST-GERMAIN, Guy[1,3]
SOBEY, David F.[1]
SOBEY, Donald R.[3]

LEDUC, Claude E. - Secretary

1. Member of the Executive Committee
2. Member of the Audit Committee
3. Member of the Human Resources Committee
4. Member of the Ethics Committee

Jacques Lesage, Vice-President, was also a member of the Ethics Committee.

1986–1987

At the end of 1985–1986, Jacques Desmeules tendered his resignation and Jean Faubert declined to renew his mandate.

At the May 26, 1986 Annual Meeting, a 15-member Board of Directors for 1986-1987 was elected.

BÉLANGER, Marcel[2,3]
GOLDEN, David A.[2]
GUILLEVIN-WOOD, Jeannine
HALDE, Jean-René[1]
LAMONTAGNE, Jean-Louis[1]
LORTIE, Pierre[1,3]
MARTIN, Louise
NADEAU, Bertin F.[1,3]
NORMAND, Carmand[2,4]
PROVOST, René[4]
REGAN, Gerald A.
ST-GERMAIN, Guy[1,3]
SOBEY, David F.[1]
SOBEY, Donald R.[3]
TURNER, William I.M. jr. C.M.

LEDUC, Claude E. - Secretary

1. Member of the Executive Committee
2. Member of the Audit Committee
3. Member of the Human Resources Committee
4. Member of the Ethics Committee

The Executive Committee, until then under the *de facto* chairmanship of the Chairman of the Board, would now be chaired by one of the members of the Executive Committee. Bertin F. Nadeau was elected Chairman of this committee.

1987–1988

At the end of 1986–1987, Jean-René Halde declined to renew his mandate. The May 29, 1987 Annual Meeting elected 16 directors for 1987–1988, as follows:

BÉLANGER, Marcel[2,3]
BIRKS, Jonathan H.
GOLDEN, David A.[2]
GUILLEVIN-WOOD, Jeannine
LAMONTAGNE, Jean-Louis[1]
LORTIE, Pierre[1,3]
MARTIN, Louise[5]
NADEAU, Bertin F.[1,3]
NORMAND, Carmand[2,4]
PROVOST, René[4,5]
REGAN, Gerald A.
ROY, Henri A.
ST-GERMAIN, Guy[1,3]
SOBEY, David F.[1]
SOBEY, Donald R.[3]
TURNER, William I.M. jr. C.M.[1]

LEDUC, Claude E. - Secretary

1. Member of the Executive Committee
2. Member of the Audit Committee
3. Member of the Human Resources Committee
4. Member of the Ethics Committee
5. Member of the Donations Committee

Jean-Claude Merizzi and Patrick Robert, two Provigo Inc. vice-presidents, were also part of the Ethics Committee.

During 1987, the Donations Committee became a committee of the Board of Directors. Its members also included Kathy Megyery, a Provigo Inc. executive, and Gérald A. Ponton, a Provigo Distribution Inc. officer.

1988–1989

On December 31, 1987, Marcel Bélanger left the position of director which he had occupied since the inception of Provigo in 1969. In May 1988, David A. Golden, who had joined Provigo in 1980 after the acquisition of Loeb, reached the age limit and retired.

At the May 25, 1988 Annual Meeting, the 15 men and women below were elected directors for 1988–1989.

BIRKS, Jonathan H.
DESPRÉS, Robert[2]
GUILLEVIN-WOOD, Jeannine[5]
LAMONTAGNE, Jean-Louis[1]
LORTIE, Pierre[1,3]
MARTIN, Louise[2,5]
NADEAU, Bertin F.[1,3]
NORMAND, Carmand[2,4]
PROVOST, René[2,4]
REGAN, Gerald A.[4]
ROY, Henri A.
ST-GERMAIN, Guy[1,3]
SOBEY, David F.[1]
SOBEY, Donald R.[3]
TURNER, William I.M. jr. C.M.[1]

LEDUC, Claude E. - Secretary

1. Member of the Executive Committee
2. Member of the Audit Committee
3. Member of the Human Resources Committee
4. Member of the Ethics Committee
5. Member of the Donations Committee

M. Yvon Marcoux, Senior Vice-President of Provigo Inc., joined the Donations Committee.

1989–1990

The Board of Directors remained the same with one exception. Louise Martin passed away in January 1989. Her position on the Board was taken by Richard Drouin, elected at the May 26, 1989 Annual Meeting.

APPENDIX VI

ORGANIZATION CHARTS OF THE PROVIGO GROUP OF COMPANIES

FROM 1979 TO 1988

Provigo Chart - 1970

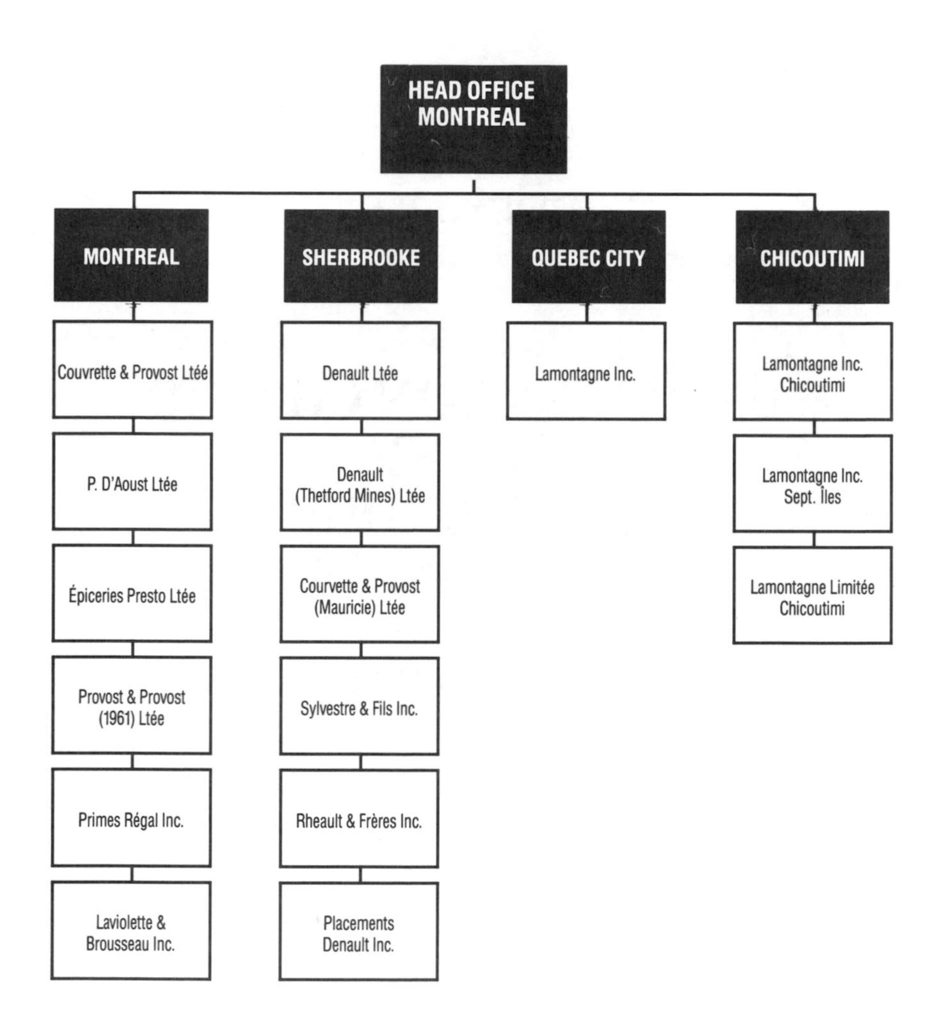

Provigo Group of Companies – 1972

PROVIGO inc.

RETAIL OPERATIONS

Traditional Supermarkets

Provigo (Saguenay) Ltée
16 supermarkets throughout the Saguenay/Lac Saint-Jean and North Shore regions.

Other Subsidiaries
5 supermarkets

Discount Food Stores

MARCHÉ D'ENTREPÔT AVA LTÉE
8 AVA warehouse markets in various Quebec regions.

WHOLESALE OPERATIONS

Grocery

Provigo (Montréal) Inc.
One regular wholesale grocery division and one distribution centre catering to the institutional trade serving the Montreal region.

Provigo (Québec) Inc.
3 wholesale grocery divisions in Quebec City, Chicoutimi and Sept-Îles.

Provigo (Sherbrooke) Inc.
5 wholesale grocery divisions in Sherbrooke, Trois-Rivières, Saint- Hyacinthe, Victoriaville and Thetford Mines.

Provigo (Ottawa) Inc.
Wholesale grocery division and produce operation serving the Ottawa region.

Produce

J.V. Halle Inc.
Produce wholesaler with operations concentrated in the Quebec City, Saguenay and Lac Saint-Jean regions.

Frozen Products

Beau Fruit Ltée
Frozen products distributor serving the Montreal region.

OTHER

Self-serve Operations

Presto - Cash & Carry Division
28 self-serve warehouses throughout the Provigo territory.

Real Estate and Investment

Les Placements Denault Inc.
Owner of facilities used by subsidiaries or affliated group members.

Provigo Group of Companies — 1978

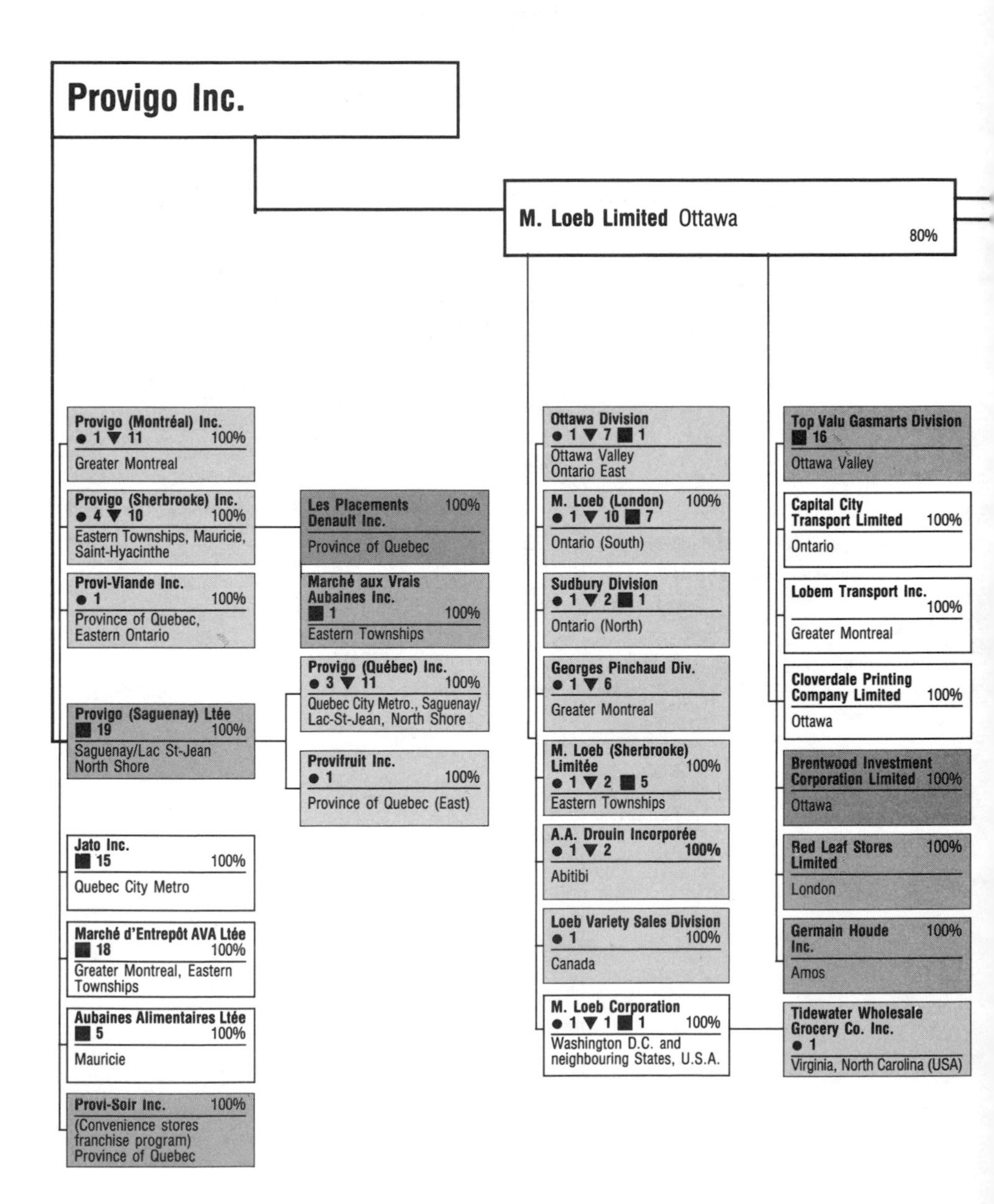

Wholesale Distribution
Retail Distribution
Real Estate Investment
Other
Distribution Centre
Cash-and carry Warehouse
Corporate Retail Store

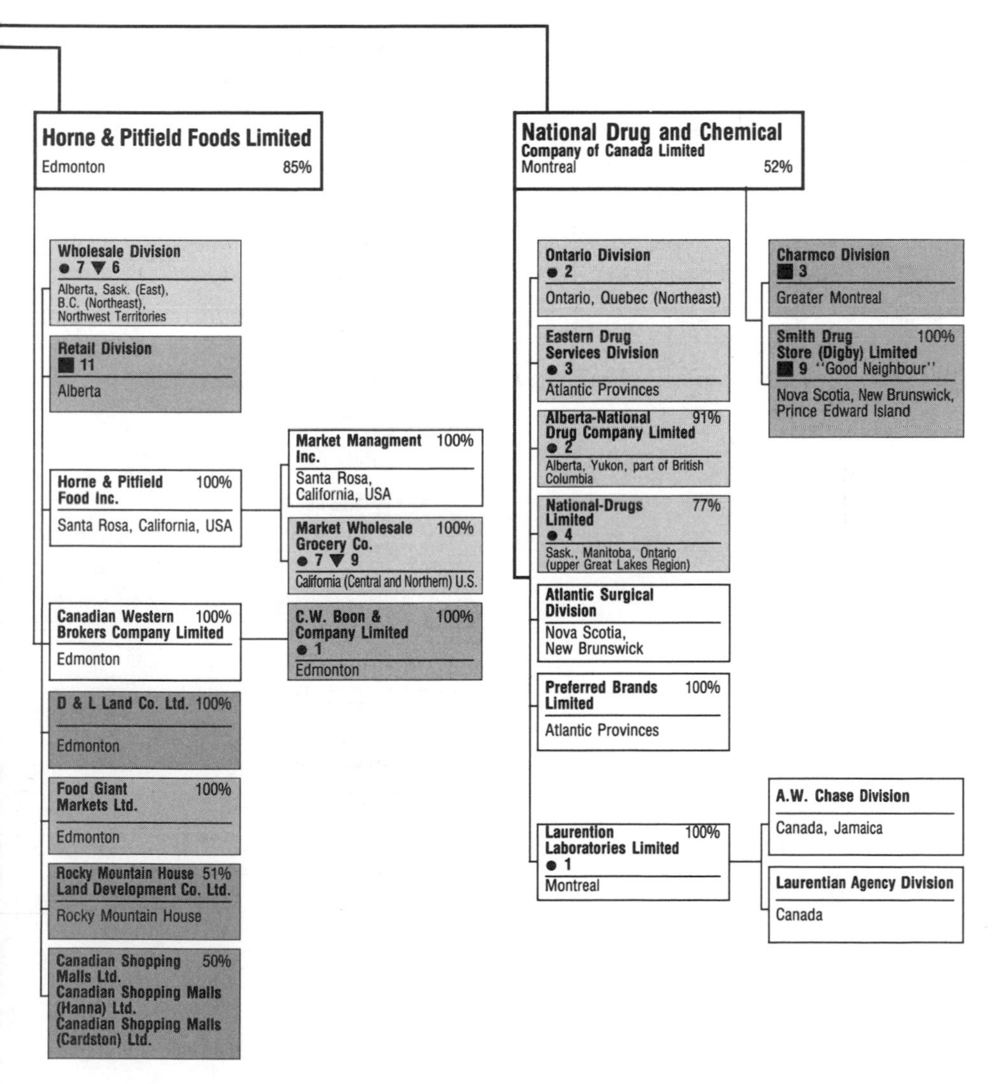
Horne & Pitfield Foods Limited
Edmonton 85%
Wholesale Division
● 7 ▼ 6
Alberta, Sask. (East), B.C. (Northeast), Northwest Territories
Retail Division
■ 11
Alberta
Horne & Pitfield Food Inc. 100%
Santa Rosa, California, USA
Market Managment Inc. 100%
Santa Rosa, California, USA
Market Wholesale Grocery Co. 100%
● 7 ▼ 9
California (Central and Northern) U.S.
Canadian Western Brokers Company Limited 100%
Edmonton
C.W. Boon & Company Limited 100%
● 1
Edmonton
D & L Land Co. Ltd. 100%
Edmonton
Food Giant Markets Ltd. 100%
Edmonton
Rocky Mountain House Land Development Co. Ltd. 51%
Rocky Mountain House
Canadian Shopping Malls Ltd. 50%
Canadian Shopping Malls (Hanna) Ltd.
Canadian Shopping Malls (Cardston) Ltd.
National Drug and Chemical Company of Canada Limited
Montreal 52%
Ontario Division
● 2
Ontario, Quebec (Northeast)
Eastern Drug Services Division
● 3
Atlantic Provinces
Alberta-National Drug Company Limited 91%
● 2
Alberta, Yukon, part of British Columbia
National-Drugs Limited 77%
● 4
Sask., Manitoba, Ontario (upper Great Lakes Region)
Atlantic Surgical Division
Nova Scotia, New Brunswick
Preferred Brands Limited 100%
Atlantic Provinces
Laurention Laboratories Limited 100%
● 1
Montreal
Charmco Division
■ 3
Greater Montreal
Smith Drug Store (Digby) Limited 100%
■ 9 "Good Neighbour"
Nova Scotia, New Brunswick, Prince Edward Island
A.W. Chase Division
Canada, Jamaica
Laurentian Agency Division
Canada

Provigo Group of Companies
1979 – Organization Chart

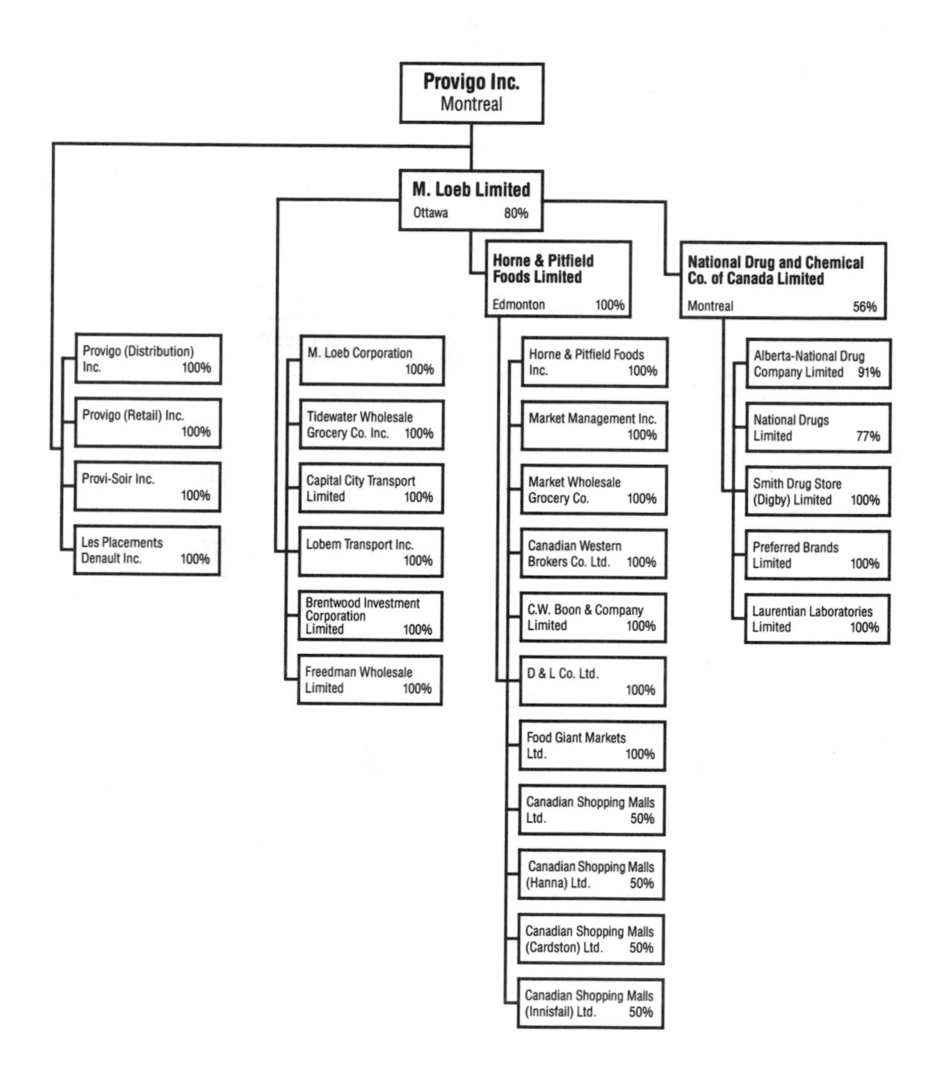

Provigo Group of Companies
1980 - Organization Chart

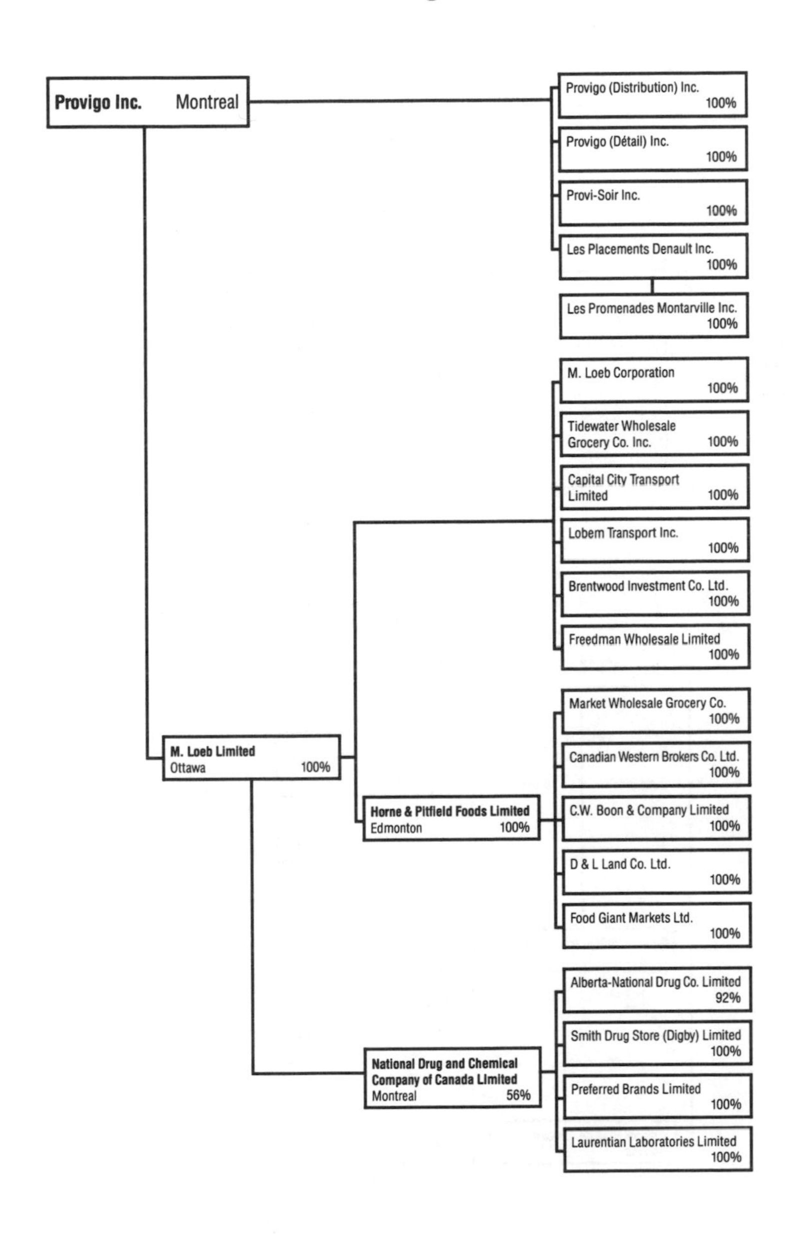

Provigo Group of Companies
1982 – Organization Chart

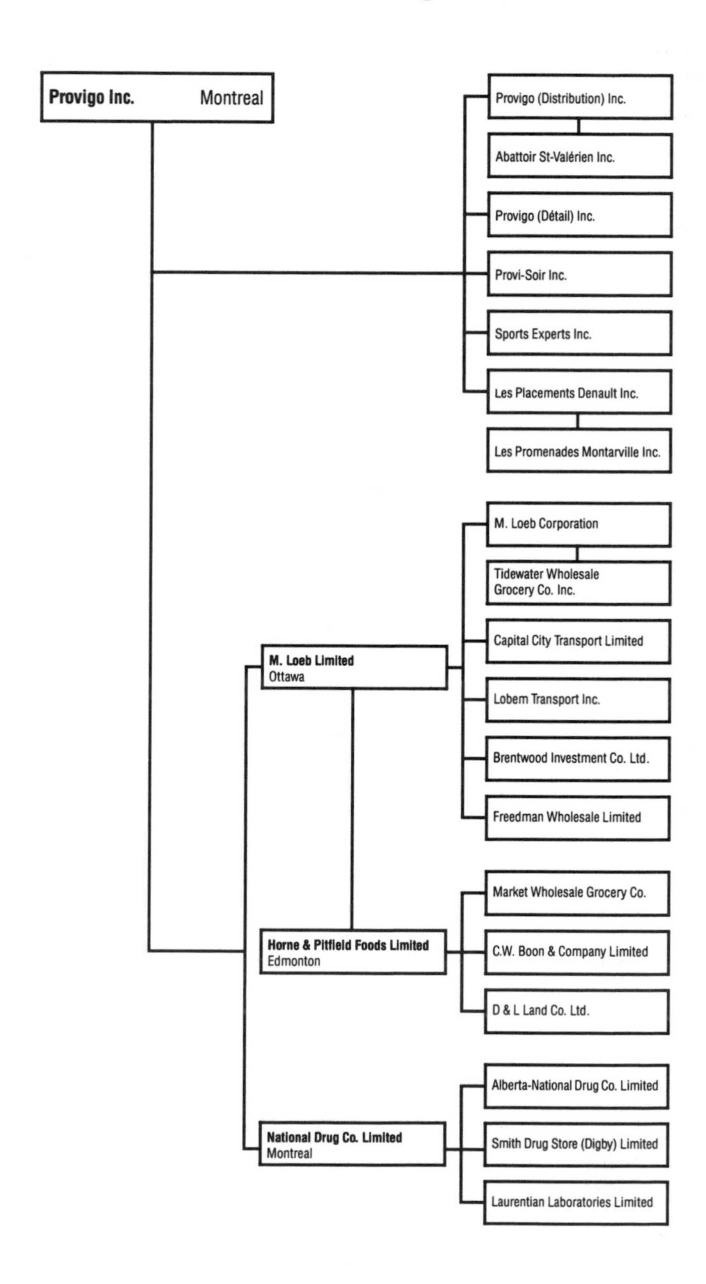

Provigo Group of Companies
1983 – Organization Chart

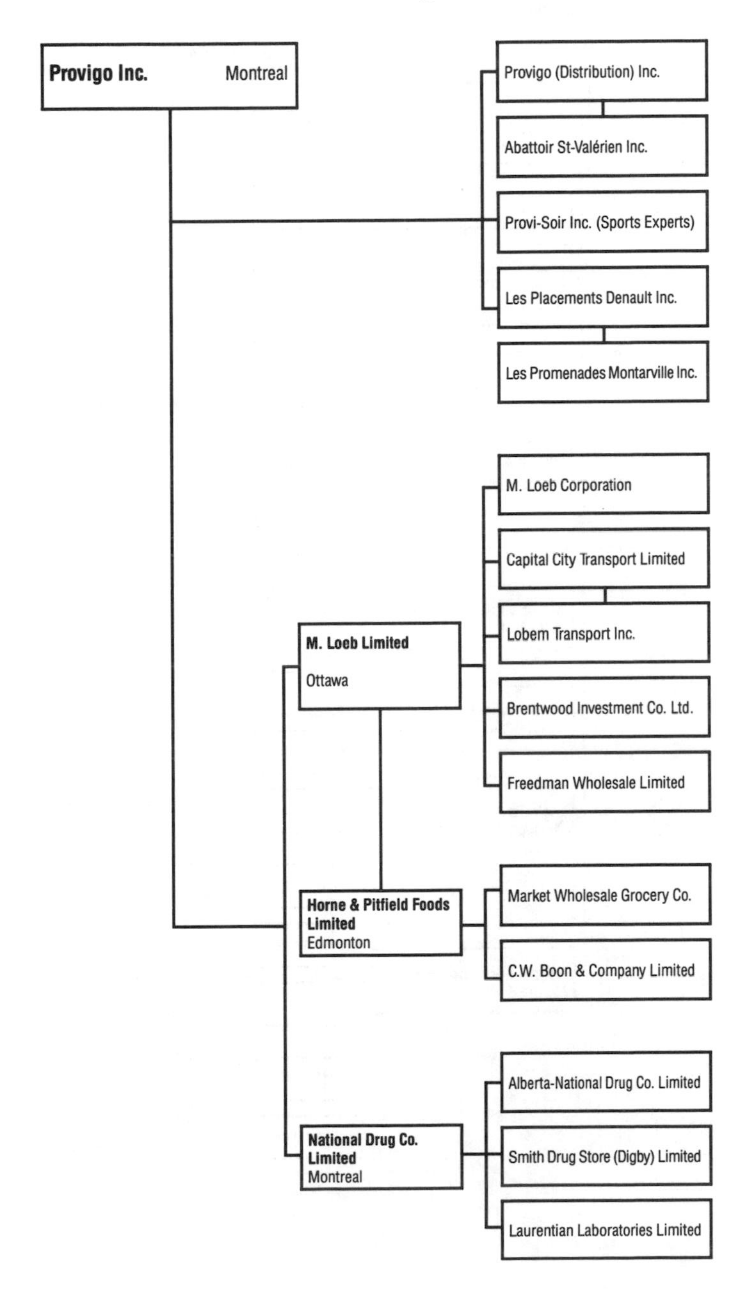

Provigo Group of Companies
1984 – Organization Chart

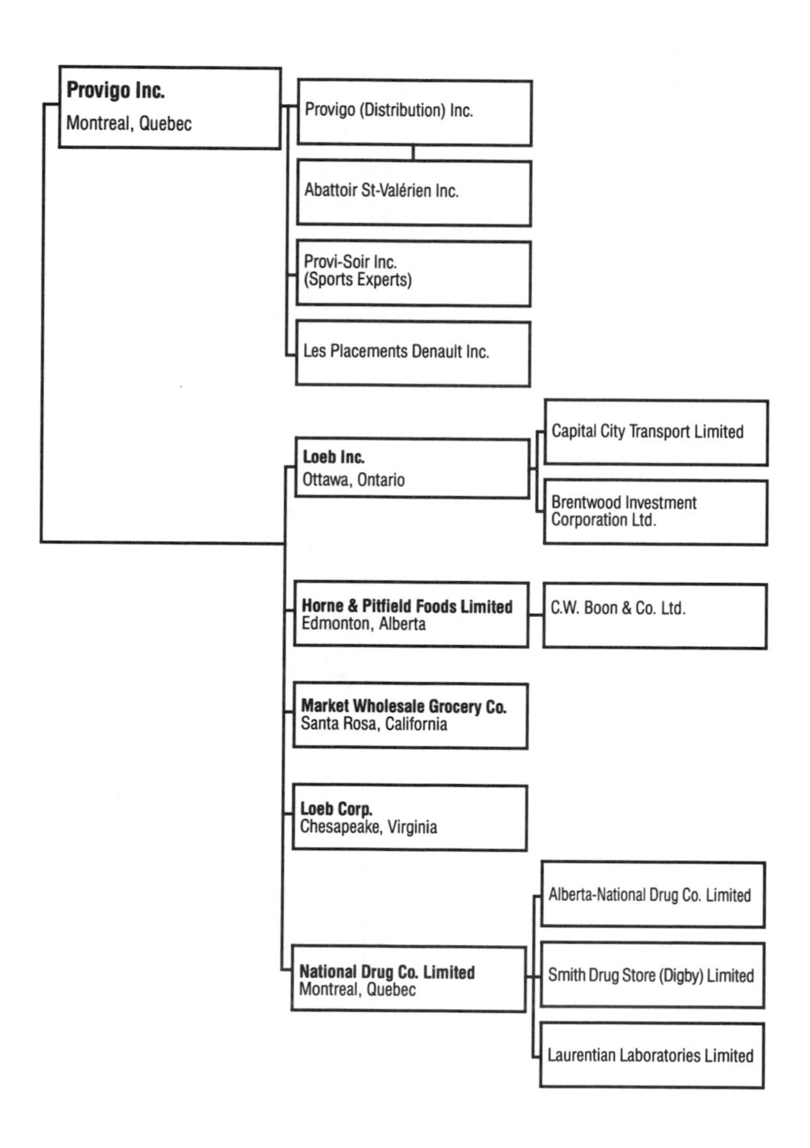

Provigo Group of Companies
1985 – Organization Chart

provigo

IGA

heritage

FOOD GIANT

Heritage FOOD MARTS

AXEP

Jovi

mayfair foods

Better Buy

provi-soir

RED ROOSTER

sports/experts

INTERSPORT

BRICO CENTRE

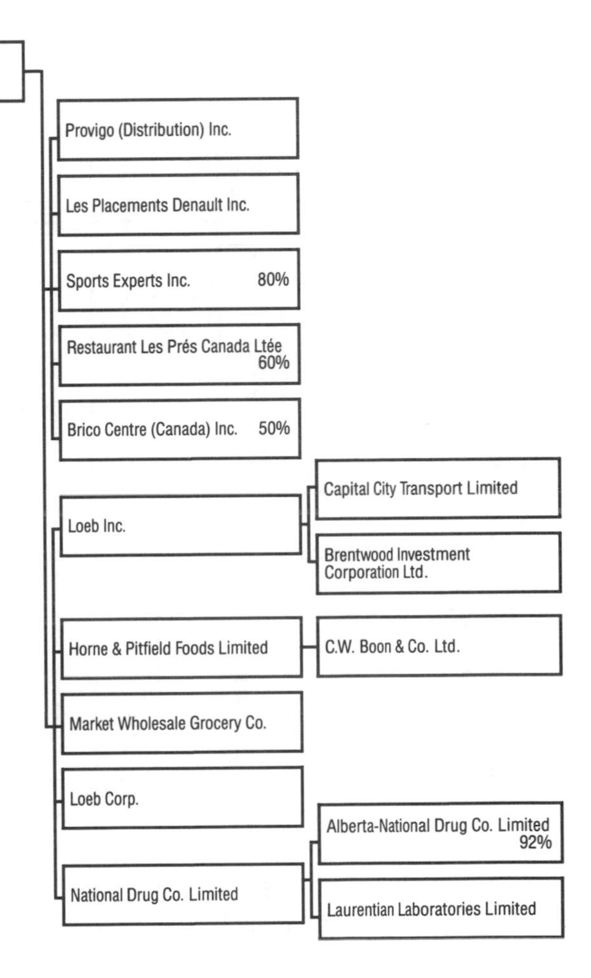

Companies grouped by sector of activities
following the 1986 ''Structure for the Future''
- PROVIGO INC. -

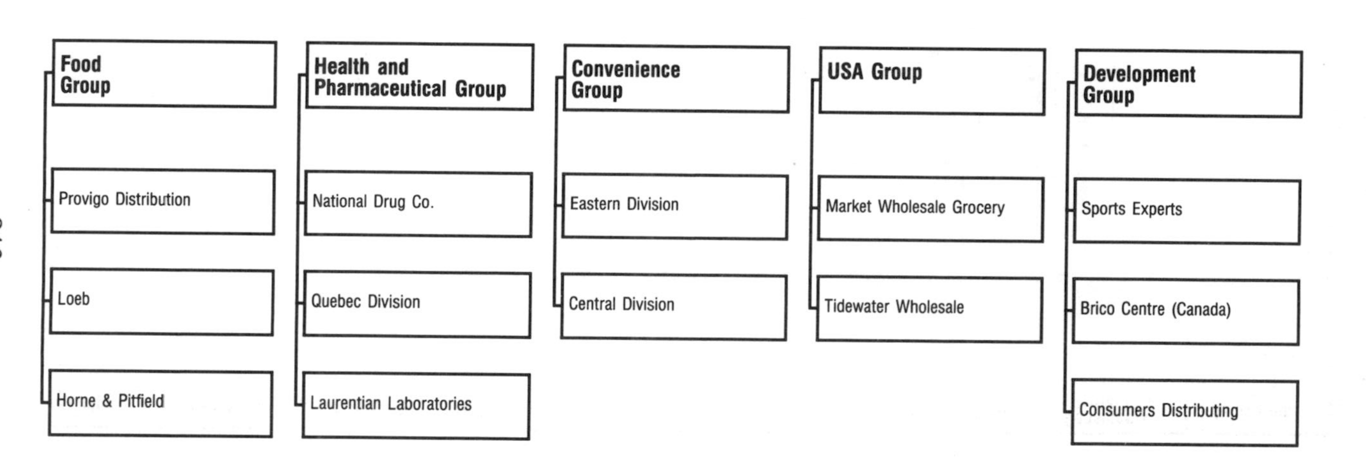

Provigo Networks - 1988

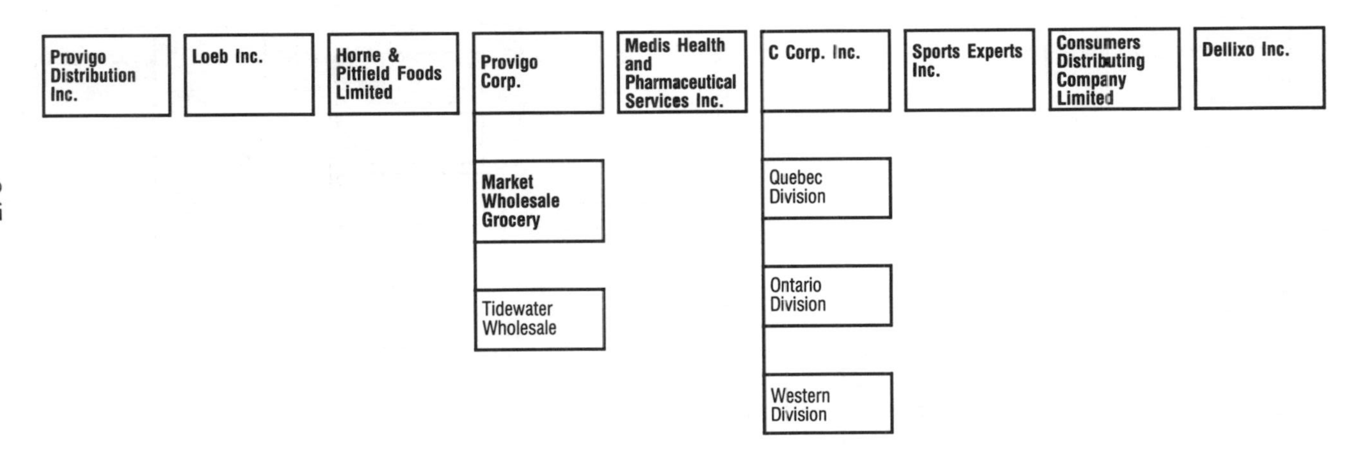

Development of Provigo from 1970 to 1988
Acquisitions and formation of companies

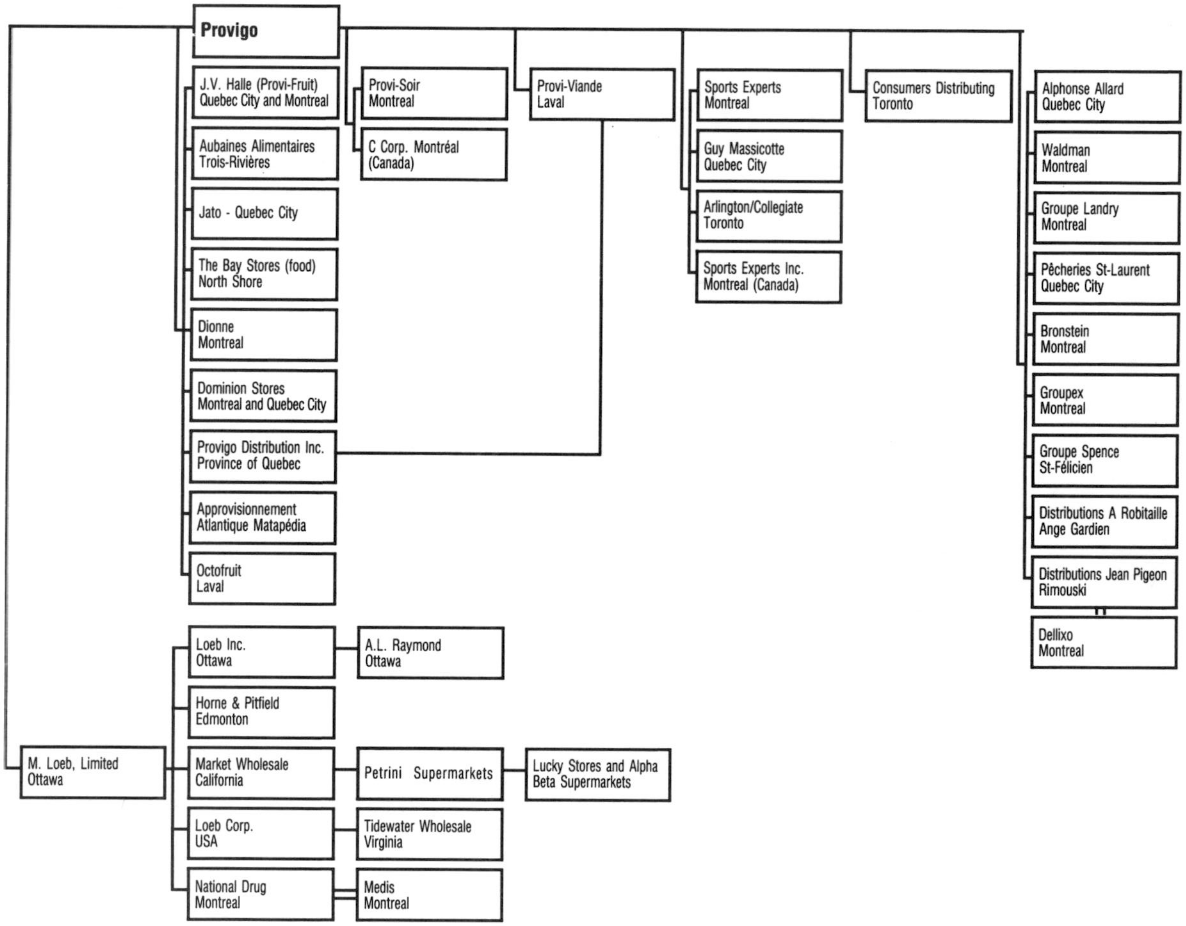

Provigo

J.V. Halle (Provi-Fruit)
Quebec City and Montreal

Aubaines Alimentaires
Trois-Rivières

Jato - Quebec City

The Bay Stores (food)
North Shore

Dionne
Montreal

Dominion Stores
Montreal and Quebec City

Provigo Distribution Inc.
Province of Quebec

Approvisionnement
Atlantique Matapédia

Octofruit
Laval

Provi-Soir
Montreal

C Corp. Montréal
(Canada)

Provi-Viande
Laval

Sports Experts
Montreal

Guy Massicotte
Quebec City

Arlington/Collegiate
Toronto

Sports Experts Inc.
Montreal (Canada)

Consumers Distributing
Toronto

Alphonse Allard
Quebec City

Waldman
Montreal

Groupe Landry
Montreal

Pêcheries St-Laurent
Quebec City

Bronstein
Montreal

Groupex
Montreal

Groupe Spence
St-Félicien

Distributions A Robitaille
Ange Gardien

Distributions Jean Pigeon
Rimouski

Dellixo
Montreal

M. Loeb, Limited
Ottawa

Loeb Inc.
Ottawa

A.L. Raymond
Ottawa

Horne & Pitfield
Edmonton

Market Wholesale
California

Petrini Supermarkets

Lucky Stores and Alpha
Beta Supermarkets

Loeb Corp.
USA

Tidewater Wholesale
Virginia

National Drug
Montreal

Medis
Montreal

EPILOGUE

EPILOGUE

Address by Antoine Turmel (Chairman of the Board of Provigo) to The Montreal Society of Financial Analysts on January 7, 1970 and to The Toronto Society of Financial Analysts on January 14, 1970

After briefly relating the events that led to the creation of Provigo in the summer of 1969, Antoine Turmel delivered an address that charted the future of Provigo not merely for the five or six years ahead but for the long term. The substance of this message has lost none of it relevance.

Written and delivered barely six months after the merger, the text of this speech, reproduced below, is of such quality and conveys such a clear-eyed vision of the future of Provigo that it cannot but convince the reader that Antoine Turmel and those who set out on this adventure with him were destined to succeed.

Philosophy

One of the key principles that has guided the reorganization is, in one word, flexibility. Changes take place so rapidly in our markets and the innovations are so drastic, that it is almost impossible to predict the form of the food distribution business ten or fifteen years hence. An organization that, for example, invests heavily in buildings or one that is concentrating its efforts exclusively in shopping centers, will certainly face serious growth problems in the future. Moreover, the new philosophy of the Minister of Consumer Affairs in Ottawa will be imposing new rules which the retailers, wholesalers and manufacturers will have to take into account. In short, flexibility appeared to us to be a key element for a new organization such as ours because it is impossible to predict what distribution patterns will be favoured by consumers in the future. We expect that new firms will make their appearance and that the more traditional organizations will lose some of their importance. It is to meet the new needs of a growing number of consumers that we are seeking the greatest possible flexibility in all our operations. It is essential that we be able to switch our operations from one type into another, whether it be from a traditional store to a warehouse store, a large supermarket or a convenience store, to wherever the needs and opportunities appear to be.

We accept as a basic premise that our role is in the retail food distribution business and that the ultimate aim of our organization is to serve the consumers by supplying food products. We do not want to define ourselves as being a voluntary chain where our exclusive role would consist of assembling merchandise from various manufacturers in a suitable form for distribution to retailers. Our role is to ensure that the public is supplied in whichever form it prefers, but with maximum efficiency. This puts us under an obligation that we accept and intend to fully discharge.

It would be unfortunate if we chose to put a ceiling on our growth by defining our aims as being in a specific area of food distribution. We want to keep all options open so that we can render the required service in the right place and at the right time. For example, I want to refer here to our new retail discount store in Sherbrooke, which has just recently opened for business, and which is aimed at a specific segment of the market requiring the supply of food products in relatively large quantities at the lowest possible prices. Our system of distribution in that region did not contain a structure which would have enabled us to serve that specific market. We took note of the untapped opportunity and developed our new vehicle so that we will be able to supply this market. After only several months of operations I can tell you that our experience exceeds our predictions.

Here is a striking example of how we can move from one type of operation to another when we sense that there is an unfilled market opportunity. It is therefore our basic philosophy that puts us in the business of general food distribution in preference to being, for example, a corporate chain, enabling us to invest in diverse food distribution facilities with ease.

This philosophy is quite fundamental to us and I think it clearly defines us as a business oriented towards the needs of the consumer rather than a business oriented towards its own operations. It is the same philosophy that has, in the past, guided Lamontagne, Couvrette & Provost and Denault and that has made the task of the integration much easier.

A third aspect of our philosophy, and surely the most important one, is the stress on efficiency of our management team. The merger has put at our disposal a group of specialists in merchandising, control, personnel, administration, marketing and in all other sectors. With the assistance of our consultants who have met with all people at the management level, we have established an organization where everyone's role is clearly defined. The integration of human resources is taking place gradually and should be completed within one year. We have no intention of weakening our separate units without strengthening the whole. We have every confidence that the experience of our people will help us in consolidating our positions. As the Americans say, 'It's the men up front that count.''

Objectives

I would like to repeat again my conviction that our basic role is to supply our clients at maximum efficiency and minimum cost. Our profit is the measure of our efficiency, the efficiency with which we identify the requirements and patterns of our markets and the efficiency of operations in satisfying these needs. Our directors are aware of the responsibility towards shareholders to achieve a reasonable return on equity. This is the main objective. Let me spell it out in more detail.

In the merger, the three companies were pooling their resources. The human capital is basic to the pursuit of the basic aim. We need marketing specialists to study market patterns. We need financial and control people for maximum profitability of our operations. We need research specialists to provide detailed information on which decisions by management and directors are based.

As a short term objective we are developing working units of people who are at a high point of advancement in our operation and who will help us in using the most modern management methods. We will be obtaining all available information on factors affecting the choice of sites for retail food stores in order to define the variables that bear most heavily on such a choice and we will be starting with our present operations. We will also be in a position to simulate the operations of new stores to help us determine expected costs, revenues, volume of sales, profits, etc. Only complex simulation models on our computer will enable us to develop this aspect. I have only mentioned one example to show you that we are fully aware of the new science of management and that we intend to fully benefit by it. We are creating a group of people in our Company whose job it will be to keep themselves informed and to study the experiences of other companies in or out of Canada, and to develop new patterns of operations so that we will achieve and stay at the pinnacle of progress. We already have such specialists amongst us and we intend to obtain the services of others as the need develops. The ability and competence of our personnel will thus help us in achieving our objective of providing the best possible distribution services.

In this we will be aided by the opportunity we have of reducing our costs of operation and increasing our volume of sales. Six years from now, we expect our volume to reach $400 million, both as a result of increasing the percentage of business obtained from our present customers and also by getting new customers or opening new company-owned stores. Our objective then is to increase our sales by about 12 percent per year, or by a total of $200 million during the next six years.

We also intend to reduce our operating costs and this we will achieve by a greater mechanization and automation of our operations — I do not but have to mention here increasing uses of the computer, but also the mechanization of materials handling and by continuous improvement of our management methods. We are perfectly well aware that a business on such a bigger format cannot in theory have the flexibility that we sought when this new organization was created through the merger. Being aware of this limitation, we will make sure that our management systems are continuously analysed in depth to give us rapid and precise information.

Another objective we will pursue, in terms of breaking out of our present territory, will be to expand our services to areas currently not covered by us, including an extension of operations to other provinces. We have given serious thought to opportunities afforded us by expanding beyond the borders of the Province of Quebec and we have concluded that sooner or later we must forget our present territorial limits and concentrate on market opportunities in other provinces. In other words, if we believe that Ontario, for example, is suitable for our type of operations and that we have an opportunity to operate in a section of the market that we may believe is not properly serviced, we will enter that market.

Another goal we have given ourselves is to reduce costs. It is self-evident that the integration of the Lamontagne and Denault warehouses in the Quebec City region and of Denault and Couvrette & Provost operations in the St. Maurice Valley region will allow us to operate there at a lower cost. In these areas there was a duplication of efforts, of personnel and of investment which we will be able to eliminate in very short order. The integration is already completed in the St. Maurice region and will soon be accomplished in the Quebec City area. Even in these cases I wish to repeat that it is not the intention to remove competent personnel but rather to provide opportunities for them to play a positive role. There will also be a reduction of costs at the level of Head Office personnel of the three organizations, since each company had its own computer system, its own merchandising and promotion group, personnel administration, etc. We will combine most of these services with the result that a single supervisory role will exist for each such department.

Together with everyone else, we are aware of the competitive battle which exists in our field and we know that the huge profits being made 7, 8 or 10 years ago are no longer possible, precisely because of the stability the food business has perhaps achieved. We therefore must be prudent while we are daring, pessimistic in our optimism, conservative in our agressiveness, in a word, be flexible to get the most out of our operations.

But I do not want to dwell any deeper on our philosophy or objectives, because a lecture in philosophy or planning does not assure the services we want to render nor does it bring the profits we want to distribute. Let us turn to the operations of our new organization and let me spend a few minutes on certain characteristics of these operations.

Operations

In this area, in order to preserve the basic principles I mentioned earlier, we have divided the operations of the Company in four divisions. These are Montreal, Quebec, Eastern Townships and St. Maurice Valley region, and the Saguenay-Lac St. Jean region. Each of these divisions will be operated more or less on an autonomous basis while following, of course, the basic policy of the Company. One of the basic criteria for operations of these divisions will be a full analysis of costs. Each division will operate within norms set by the Company and within profit objectives established for all different departments.

In addition to this geographical structure, the head office of the Company will operate an institutional division and will, in due course, include other specialized departments: mobile canteens, for example. Let us bear in mind that we have defined our Company as providing a food distribution service and that this does not necessarily limit us to retail distribution but opens to us all other services for which there is a demand.

To ensure a smooth functioning of these two operational structures, we will use groups of specialists who will be able to render assistance to the different divisions in order to help them obtain the maximum impact, both as far as market penetration is concerned as well as profitability and management efficiency. Such key personnel will be available in each regional unit but overall planning of operations, evaluation of results and control, will be in Montreal. Operations and decisions will thus be decentralized at the level of the various divisions; planning and control will be centralized at the head office. The executive committee has the task of establishing objectives, policies, strategy and systems of control.

To maintain our concept of flexibility, I must immediately point out that our long range objectives remain unchanged. It is only in the area of strategy that differences will exist at the operational level. At present, we operate company-owned stores and stores which belong to our partners, the voluntary members. What will be our mode of operation in the future? It may be that it will be entirely different from what it is now and if anyone could tell me what the food business will be like in six years from now, I would tell him which form of food distribution we will be favouring. Nonetheless, I can assure you that we have some basic ideas on this subject and that our flexibility, which so characterizes us, will help us in adapting new ideas without much delay.

People will still be eating six years hence, that is one thing which is quite certain. Where will they eat? This is where the difficulty lies, in predicting the relative importance of the different food distribution techniques. For example, we think patronage of restaurants will increase, that the consumption of frozen foods will grow and that greater stress will be laid on specialty stores serving specialized products such as dietary foods, pastries, delicatessen and others. But before we get into such diverse areas, we will first consolidate our existing position in the market in which we are already active.

Again, in response to our desire for flexibility, we intend to reduce to a minimum long term investment in land and buildings, be it through direct ownership or long term leases. We believe it is undesirable in these days of rapid technological changes and evolving social values to commit oneself on a long term basis in buildings which may not be efficient and suitable only ten years from now. Wherever possible, we will prefer to sign short or medium term leases. Our present operations cover those of corporate stores, voluntary groups, the Cash & Carry business, discount operations and large supermarkets. In some of these areas we will expand our operations and we are preparing for others. Certain basic trends, however, must be observed. For example, wages and salaries as a percentage of total revenues have increased from 9 percent to 14 percent, or by about 50 percent, during the last five years. Such trends must obviously be borne in mind in the planning of our future operations.

We are presently trying to find a new corporate name which would encompass all the operations of Couvrette & Provost Ltée, a new "Family name", as the Americans would call it. We intend that this name help create an image of efficiency and ability to serve consumers by supplying their needs in ways they wish to be served. We are proceeding with the creation of private labels that we will own and that will meet our standard of high quality at the lowest possible price. Our products and our outlets will thus be identified with the new "Family Name", which in due course will replace that of Couvrette & Provost Ltée.

All the electronic equipment used for analyses, planning and control purposes will be centralized in Montreal. We have embarked on the development of programmes to simplify these operations and to achieve substantial savings. A program recently developed for our warehouses, for example, allows a growth in sales of $3 to $4 million in some of our warehouses without increasing warehouse space. We have also developed a program of automatic space selection in which we feed the computer a number and the space required for a product; later, in the receiving department, the computer selects automatically the spot where the product is to be stored in the warehouse. One day we are hoping to have complete control of a retail operation through the means of a computer. The cost of operations, the cost of merchandise, the margin of profit, the level of inventory, the need for and the profitability of shelf space will all be under consideration. This will allow us to follow the operations of all the retail outlets and to discover at the very beginning weaknesses or deficiencies at the retail store level.

Finally, our premium stamp Company will, in our view, experience substantial expansion during the next few years. It is obvious that premium stamps represent a system of publicity which appeals to a certain group of consumers and that they thus have a specific purpose. Premium stamps are one of the promotional means at our disposal to help us ensure the loyalty of the consumer. Between premium stamps and advertising, we feel that such loyalty is better achieved through the use of premium stamps.

Numerous experiments are currently under way in the U.S. and we think that our premium stamp Company can not only serve our own needs but also those of others, as a means of promotion.

Permit me to close this part by saying that whatever type of operation we are in and whatever type of promotion we are using, it has to generate the same profit.

Financial Projections

Our sales are currently at a level slightly in excess of an annual volume of $200 million and we intend to achieve sales of $400 million by the end of the next six years. By comparison, the projected doubling of sales in the next six years compares with an increase in sales of about three and a half times in the last six years. Should you wish it, I will be pleased to explain in more detail why we think the expected increase during the next six years is realistic and will be achieved by following established plans.

The margin of net profit after tax will be about $0.90 per $100 of sales after the first year of combined operations of the three companies. Within six years, our objective is $1.10 after tax. With a volume of $400 million, $1.10 after tax would leave us a net profit of $4,400.000. This works out to about $1.20 per share, compared to $0.47 pro forma in fiscal 1969. This represents a projected cumulative growth rate in profits of 18 percent per year. Again, comparing this to the last six years, the profit in that period more than tripled. Our future projections are based on a detailed and serious analysis and I will again be pleased to discuss it in more detail with those of you who are interested. Our goal concerning our capital structure is to allow only the smallest dilution. In the case of acquisitions or other developments, we expect that these will be financed mainly through internally generated profits, or through loans. This implies that we will be keeping appropriate reserves and that our borrowing capacity is not fully exploited.

Finally, I would like to take a few minutes to tell you why we think the food distribution business affords an interesting vehicle for investment. First of all, the demand is there. The whole world will continue to eat and as I said before, the trick is to determine where people will be eating and what they will be eating. That is our business. Secondly, the food business is not a cyclical one and is characterized by growth stability. In the food business we do not experience the same ups and downs known by other sectors of the economy and we are less exposed to the danger of recession or rapid inflation.

Thirdly, it is almost impossible to lose money on inventory. This is not the case in other fields, where the turnover may only be two or three times a year. In the steel business, for example, even if order books do not live up to expectations, numerous expenses continue to be incurred — specialized personnel cannot be laid off, warehousing costs continue and so on. Such a situation is unknown in the food business. Inventory losses are unknown, there is no obsolescence, no seasonal products, no fashions, etc. Moreover, from the time the voluntary groups began to exercise closer supervision over the independent grocers, look at the decrease in the bankruptcies. According to a D.B.S. bulletin entitled "Commercial Failures", the number of bankruptcies in Quebec of food wholesalers and retailers has shown a consistent decline, from 175 in 1955 to 119 in 1968, with the exception of 1958 when a peak of 182 bankruptcies was reached.

Another feature that has made its mark during the last few years in our business is that it is becoming more and more a cash business. You will note that this trend is in direct contrast to many other sectors in our economy. In our Company, customers pay cash, thus reducing the danger of losses in accounts receivable.

A good deal of stability in accounts receivable and in the value of inventory, a minimum of fixed assets, minimal exposure to economic cycles, a permanent and unquestionable consumer demand and improved management techniques -- those are the elements that make food marketing rewarding for the investor.

REFERENCES

SOURCES OF INFORMATION

References — Sources of Information

1. *Interviews*

ARBOUR, Pierre
BEAULIEU, Claude
BÉLANGER, Marcel
BOITEAU, Jean
BUSSIÈRES, Yvan
CONSTANTINEAU, Richard
COUVRETTE, Bernard
DESCHÊNES, Yvon
DLOUHY, Dominik
DUFOUR, Claude
GOBEIL, H. Paul
JUTRAS, Jean
KIPP, William
LAMONTAGNE, Jean-Louis
LEDUC, Claude
LESAGE, Jacques
LESSARD, Guy
LESSARD, Pierre H.
LORTIE, Pierre
MERCIER, Jacques
MERIZZI, Jean-Claude
NADEAU, Bertin
ODELL, Gordon J.
OUELLET, Roland
PARIS, Michel
PERRAULT, Claude
PROVOST, Ernest
PROVOST, René
PROVOST, Roland
ROY, Gaston
ROY, Henri
SOBEY, Donald R.
TREMBLAY, Gérard
TREMBLAY, J.-A.

2. *Meetings*

CAMPEAU, Jean
CAZAVANT, Marcel
GOSLOVICH, Carl
SICOTTE, André
QUINN, Kenneth
TURMEL, Antoine

3. *Additional documentation*

A D A
AGROPUR
BEAULIEU, Claude
BEAULIEU, France
BÉLANGER, Madeleine
BIRON, PAUL
BOILY, Jean-Guy
BOITEAU, Jean
BUSSIÈRES, Yvan
CHARETTE, Gérard
COMTOIS, Sylvie
COUVRETTE, Bernard
DESCHÊNES, Yvon
DESROCHERS, J.-Claude
DUFOUR, Claude
DUFRESNE, Yves
FRIESEN, David R.
GAGNÉ, Pierre
GAGNÉ, Reynald
GIRARD, Marlène
JUNEAU, Élise
JUTRAS, Jean
KELLY, Erika
KILGOUR, Barbara M.
KIPP, William
LAMONTAGNE, Jean-Louis
LARUE, Michel
LARUELLE, Christiane
LÉGER, Pierre-Paul
LESAGE, Jacques
LESSARD, Guy
LESSARD, Pierre H.
L'HÉRAULT, Debbie
LOEB Family Memorabilia
MARTYNSKI, John
MASSÉ, Édouard
MEGYERY, Kathy
MERCIER, Jacques
MERIZZI, Jean-Claude
MIRON, Gérard
MULTIMARQUES
MURRAY, Bernard
ODELL, Gordon J.
OUELLET, Roland
OUIMET, Jacques
PELLAND, Wellie
PERRAULT, Claude
PONTON, Gérald A.
PROVOST, René
PROVOST, Roland
QUINN, Kenneth W.
ROBERT, Patrick
ROY, Henri
SAUVAGEAU, Fernand
SICOTTE, André
TEIXEIRA, Alfred
TREMBLAY, J.-A.
TREMBLAY, Gérard
TURMEL, Antoine

4. *Annual Reports*

Caisse de dépôt et placement	1976 to 1988
Couvrette & Provost ltée	1961 to 1970
Denault limitée	1961 to 1969
Distribution aux Consommateurs	1984 to 1987
Lamontagne limitée	1961 to 1969
M. Loeb, Limited	1956 to 1978
National Drug and Chemical Company of Canada Limited	1937 to 1980
Provigo Inc.	1971 to 1989
Sobeys	1980 to 1988
Unigesco Inc.	1986 to 1988

5. *Notices of meetings* for annual general and special meetings of the shareholders of Couvrette & Provost ltée and of Provigo Inc. from 1969 to 1989, and primarily information contained in the circulars enclosed with these notices.

6. *Prospectuses* for issues of shares and bonds of:

Couvrette & Provost ltée	1961 to 1969;
Denault limitée	1961 to 1969;
Lamontagne limitée	1961 to 1969;
Provigo Inc.	1970 to 1988;
M. Loeb, Limited	1959 to 1966;
Provigo Inc. Annual Notice	1985 to 1988.

7. *Material related to takeover bids*

   Couvrette & Provost ltée to the shareholders of Denault limitée and Lamontagne limitée — May 23, 1969.

   Provigo Inc. to the shareholders of M. Loeb, Limited — July 15, 1977.

M. Loeb, Limited to its minority shareholders — May 18, 1979.
Provigo Inc. (Loeb) to the shareholders of National Drug — January 30, 1981.
Provigo Inc. to the shareholders of Consumers Distributing Company Limited — October 9, 1987.
Unigesco Inc. and **Empire Company Limited** to the shareholders of Provigo — June 3, 1988.

8. *Addresses, talks and messages of*

Pierre Lortie

Sept./Dec. 1985	A structure for the future
December 1986	Peering at the future: direction for sustainable growth
December 1987	Building a winning organization
From 1985 to 1988	Messages to the shareholders, talks and addresses in Quebec, Canada and abroad.

Antoine Turmel

January 1970	Address to The Montreal and Toronto Societies of Financial Analysts.
April 1975	Address to The Montreal and Toronto Societies of Financial Analysts.
June 1984	Address to The Montreal and Toronto Societies of Financial Analysts.
From 1969 to 1985	Messages to the shareholders, talks and addresses.

Pierre H. Lessard

1971	''Mergers and acquisitions'', co-author
From 1976 to 1985	Messages to the shareholders, talks and addresses.
June 1984	Address to The Montreal and Toronto Societies of Financial Analysts.

9. *Financial Press*

Research on the principal landmarks in the Provigo history: 1969 merger; acquisition of Loeb and the arrival of the Sobeys on the Provigo scene in 1977; acquisition of the Dominion stores in 1980–1981; alliance between the Caisse de dépôt et placement and the Sobeys in 1982; succession of Antoine Turmel in 1985; nomination of Pierre Lortie in 1985; and the emergence of Unigesco in 1986.

This research was carried out by Alida Gualtieri in such publications as *Le Devoir, La Presse, The Gazette, The Globe and Mail, Report on Business, Les Affaires* and *Finance.*

10. *Periodicals*

Canadian Business

November 1985:	"The Sobey boys meet the man from Provigo"
August 1986:	"The successors"

Executive

September 1980:	"Turmel of Provigo"

L'Actualité

September 1985:	"Le mariage Provigo-Lortie : la naissance d'une multinationale"
October 1987:	"La nouvelle star de la finance" (Bertin Nadeau)

Québec Business (published by *The Gazette*)

January 19, 1988:	"Le Grand Dieu gris" (Pierre Lortie)

Reader's Digest

January 1987:	"The Grocery Kings From Stellarton"

Commerce Magazine — Man of the Month

April 1951:	Bernard Couvrette
July 1963:	Jean-Louis Lamontagne
November 1963:	Antoine Turmel
September 1968:	René Provost
May 1981:	Pierre H. Lessard
April 1982:	Pierre Lortie

11.*Other Publications*

Chronologie des épiciers en gros et détaillants au Québec, by Gérard Bélair, economist and administration consultant, Association des épiciers en gros de la province de Québec, 1982.

"Les groupes volontaires au Québec", series of six articles by Gérard Bélair published in *Alimentation au Québec*, 1986.

Les grands événements du monde alimentaire des 25 dernières années, special report in *Alimentation au Québec*, 1986.

Frank Sobey — The Man and the Empire, by Harry Bruce, Macmillan of Canada, 1985.

La Caisse de dépôt et placement du Québec (its mission, impact and performance), a collaborative effort under the direction of Claude E. Forget, C.D. Howe Institute.

12.Miscellaneous Sources

Documents presented to the Provigo Inc. Board of Directors regarding the purchase of companies or other matters

Press releases

Annual information forms

Studies by financial analysts published by various securities firms

Data from the files of the Financial Post Corporation Service

Financial Post 500

The 500 largest companies in Quebec — *Les Affaires*

The 500 largest companies in Canada — *Commerce Magazine*

Canadian Grocer

Statistics Canada

INDEX